Car Suspension at Work

Car Suspension at Work

Theory & Practice of Steering, Handling & Roadholding

Jeffrey Daniels

MRP

MOTOR RACING PUBLICATIONS LTD
Unit 6, The Pilton Estate, 46 Pitlake, Croydon CR0 3RY, England

First published 1988 as *Handling and Roadholding*, this revised and expanded
edition published 1998.

British Library Cataloguing in Publication Data
Daniels, J. (Jeffrey)
  Car suspension at work : theory and practice of steering,
  handling and road holding, – 2nd ed.
  1. Automobiles – Springs and suspension
  I. Title
  629. 2'43

ISBN 1-899870-31-8

Printed in Great Britain by The Amadeus Press Ltd
Huddersfield, West Yorkshire

Contents

Dynamic geometry lesson: few other vehicles reveal the workings of their suspension linkage as clearly as this Mercedes-Benz F300 Life-Jet Research Car, a three-wheeler which leans inwards, motorcycle-style, when cornering. Note, among other things, the large change in the angle of the spring-damper units.

Preface

When setting the scene for the first edition of this book, I said it was rather a shock to realize that after graduating as an aeronautical engineer, I had actually spent the last 23 years working with motor cars. Well, now it is 33 years, and I have decided it is time to take stock of what has happened in chassis technology in the last decade and to examine its influence on the contents of that original edition.

On reflection, I have decided that the main chapters were so 'fundamental' that they should not be disturbed. Although we could have updated the example cars and inserted new figures for the wider tyres which are so much in fashion, it would not have changed the basic message. The rules of good chassis design remain the same. Knowledge has advanced a little, and the tools available to the engineer have certainly become more powerful, in fact almost beyond recognition. To illustrate this point, let me say that the original edition of this book was written on a first-generation IBM PC with two floppy drives and 640Kb of RAM; this revision has come from a machine with a 300MHz Intel Pentium II processor, 64Mb of RAM, an 8.4Gb hard disc and a 24-speed CD-ROM, an Iomega backup drive and an Internet connection.

My point is that the computing tools available to the chassis engineer and the tyre designer have improved in exactly the same way, if not more so. And they have been used to the full: the young men who are today's full-time consumer-magazine road-testers sometimes complain that there is no longer any such thing as a bad car, whose faults would enable them to wax lyrical. Well, that may be a problem for them, but it is good news for the average car buyer. It may frustrate the enthusiast, though, that the chassis limits of many modern cars are so high that you have to grit your teeth and resist severe forces in order to investigate and exploit them. Physically, those young men have to work much harder than I did in the 1970s.

I said in 1988 that the book was an attempt to draw a picture of chassis design knowledge as it has evolved, and to produce a book for the knowledgeable layman. I hope it remains so. As previously, it contains no mathematics beyond GCSE level, and it is certainly not a step-by-step guide on how to turn your road car into a racer – a process, incidentally, which even in real terms would now cost you many times as much as it did then.

The most fundamental changes have been to the first and last chapters, both of which are much larger than before. The first brings development up to date; the last looks further into the future, though whether with any more success than last time remains to be seen.

Even more than in 1988, I look back on so many names and faces who have helped me towards some understanding of what makes a good chassis. I still owe my debt to Colin

Sharply focussing attention on the importance of chassis engineering, the story of the Mercedes-Benz A-class illustrates very clearly that vehicle stability and handling are still not subjects to be taken for granted, despite the increasingly sophisticated techniques available to the designer. The changes made after the launch of this radical new front-driven small car in order to rectify shortcomings revealed in a Scandinavian 'moose test' (a simulated lane-change manoeuvre similar to the one being negotiated here) are discussed in Chapter 12.

Campbell and Donald Bastow, whose earlier books I devoured before setting their lessons alongside my own experience. Among many others, if they will forgive me, I remember especially valuable sessions with a few special people: Bob Knight and later Jim Randle at Jaguar; my one-time *Autocar* colleague John Miles, who went to Lotus; Magnus Roland at Saab; Nobuhiko Kawamoto at Honda; Richard Parry-Jones at Ford. All had the gift not only of explaining clearly, but of making me think for myself.

So where are we now? There may no longer be any bad cars, but as you may see in Chapter 12, there is still the occasional hiccup. People still need to understand and apply the fundamentals, and may need to do so even more in the future, if the temptation increases to let the electronics take the strain while cheapening the basic engineering. I hope it doesn't; but the 21st century may yet allow me a third edition in which to take stock.

Jeffrey Daniels
London SW20
February 1998

Chapter one

Introduction

I wrote the original edition of this book around a decade ago. Reading through it at this remove, I find that the cars have changed, but the fundamentals have not. Now, as then, as my opening line observed, a lot of people 'know' about car chassis design, though they may be hard put to define exactly what constitutes the chassis. They also 'know' about handling, though their conversation quickly reveals a confusion between handling, steering and roadholding. In both cases their confusion is understandable.

Eighty years ago there was no problem on either count. Nobody appreciated the difference between handling, steering and roadholding, inextricably linked though the three have always been. As for the chassis, that was the girder-like frame, two long side-members joined by crossmembers and some form of bracing, to which everything else on the car was attached. The body sat on top, the engine and driveline were located between the side-members, and the wheels were suspended below. The most forward-thinking of engineers, Budd in the USA, and Lancia and Citroen in Europe, had already devised ways to get rid of the chassis and attach all the mechanical parts directly to a stressed box forming the cabin and its extensions. By degrees, 'chassis' came to mean the suspension – the means of locating, springing and damping the wheels plus its attachment points and the structure between them. Today, therefore,

the chassis consists of the 'platform' – another of today's vehicle engineering in-words – plus the suspension linkages, springs, dampers, steering and braking systems. All of these things can affect the way a car handles, steers and holds the road. Even the stiffness of the platform itself, and the way it deforms under load, can affect stability and handling.

Having tried to define the chassis in modern terms, I should straight away tackle that other thorny question: the difference between handling, steering and road-holding. Laymen use the three terms indiscriminately, yet to the engineer and the professional road-tester they are three different things, no matter how much they may interact.

'Steering' is the connection between the driver and the car. Good steering enables the driver to transmit his wishes to the front wheels, quickly, precisely and accurately, and to receive messages in return. The 'feel' of good steering, through which a driver is conscious of how close he is to the limit of front wheel adhesion, is an important part of the quality of any car which is enjoyable to drive. Many enthusiasts think that light steering can never provide sufficient feel, and point to the way in which the steering of many 1970s and 1980s American cars (and of some European models built for export to the USA) managed to keep their drivers very much in the dark in terms of what was

1:1. To what extent the roadholding of a particular car – the available grip on the road surface – can be exploited, and what happens when the limits of that grip are approached and exceeded, is determined in very large measure by the handling. The exuberant test driver of this Toyota Starlet, pushing beyond its inherent understeer to hang the tail out, needs informative and responsive steering to help him keep it all under control.

happening in the front tyre contact patches. More recently, others – notably Ford's Richard Parry-Jones – have argued that there is nothing wrong with light steering so long as the 'signal-to-noise ratio' (the 'noise' being the friction and inertia effects which partly mask the steering feedback 'signal') is sufficiently high.

'Handling' and 'roadholding' are different aspects of the connection between the car and the road. Roadholding is simple and straightforward. The longer a car grips the surface as it is cornered progressively harder, the better its roadholding. In fact, the definition of roadholding is almost literal: it is the grip of the tyres on the road surface. It may seem simple in essence, but in practice, as we shall see, the grip of a tyre depends on many factors. In any case, we need to bear in mind two fundamental considerations. First, no tyre can grip the road unless it is firmly in contact with it. Second, there is no point in having good roadholding at one end of the car if it is poor at the other.

The definition of handling is much more subtle. Basically, a car has good handling if it does what you expect it to do, quickly rather than slowly, willingly rather than unwillingly, predictably rather than revealing nasty surprises. Handling specialists carefully distinguish between 'steady state' behaviour, in other words when cornering at a constant speed, and 'transient' behaviour, when entering and leaving a corner or adjusting the cornering line. Not surprisingly, most problems arise in transient situations, because that is where the car's behaviour is at its most complicated, and most difficult to analyze (and that is just the vehicle; engineers have also to examine the interaction of vehicle and driver behaviour, and drivers are much less predictable).

Understeer and oversteer, those two over-used words in saloon bars where motoring enthusiasts congregate, are essentially steady-state conditions – although oversteer can get out of hand if it is allowed to persist – but the real interest has transferred to transient phenomena. One of the handling buzz-phrases of the last few years is 'turn-

2

in', which is the transient behaviour of the car in the vital moments between travelling straight ahead and cornering. Turn-in can be slow, crisp or abrupt. Engineers with sheets of printout from on-board test instruments can put numbers on the build-up of cornering force with steering angle and time, and explain why one car is 'slow' and another is 'abrupt'. But the quality of turn-in is as heavily dependent on tyre characteristics and rear suspension design as it is on the steering itself.

While we are here, it is worth also thinking about 'stability', which is one aspect of handling. Stability is a good thing up to a point: we all like cars which continue in a straight line for a couple of seconds while we retune the radio. Too much stability, on the other hand, is a bad thing, which leads to sluggish turn-in and generally poor steering response. People talk about high-quality cars as having good stability and yet crisp and eager cornering behaviour, as though the two things were

incompatible. They aren't; it is a question of how you achieve the stability in the first place. If you do it by dialling a lot of castor trail into the steering, you will end up with a stodgy lump of a car – but more of that later (in Chapter 6, to be precise).

How do steering, roadholding and handling interact? Steering quality is fundamental. Poor steering may spoil good handling because it stops you sending sufficiently precise messages to the front wheels: in other words, the car is never properly aware of what you want it to do, and you can hardly blame it for not responding correctly. It may still have good handling, but it will be wasted. There were such cars, certainly up to the 1950s, when a couple of inches of slop at the steering wheel rim and far too much friction in the linkage were all too common, but they are few and far between today.

Roadholding and handling are complementary. A car with poor handling may have good roadholding, but you will

1:2. The way a car behaves during the transition from straight ahead to cornering, the 'turn-in' phase, will greatly influence the driver's perception of its handling. The quality of turn-in is determined by many factors, including tyre and steering characteristics and the design of rear as well as front suspension.

1:3. Twin-Cam Escort in a full-blooded power slide illustrates that, given enough space, a car with more power and handling than roadholding can be very entertaining, at the expense of very rapid tyre wear. Good handling offsets the limited capabilities of this rear-drive car's live-axle rear suspension – at least in the hands of a capable driver.

never be able to exploit it (unless you have the experience, intelligence and speed of response to make allowance for the handling). At the other extreme, a car with good handling but poor roadholding, such as some of the early high-powered saloons on narrow cross-ply tyres, can at least exploit to the limit all the grip it has, and can be great fun to drive as a result, especially if someone else is paying for the tyres.

1:4. Even on mass-produced front-drive cars, relatively sophisticated independent rear suspension layouts like this Honda CRX assembly are increasingly common. Their multi-link geometry permits very accurate control of wheel movements without unwanted camber and alignment changes.

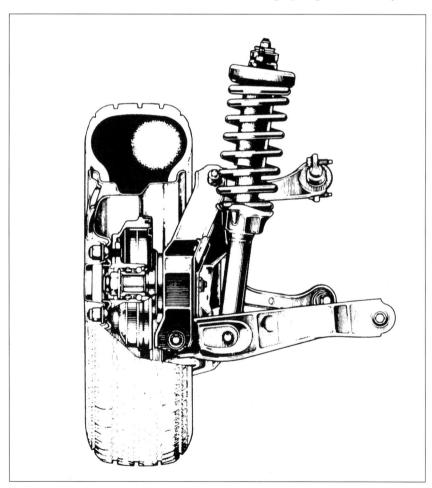

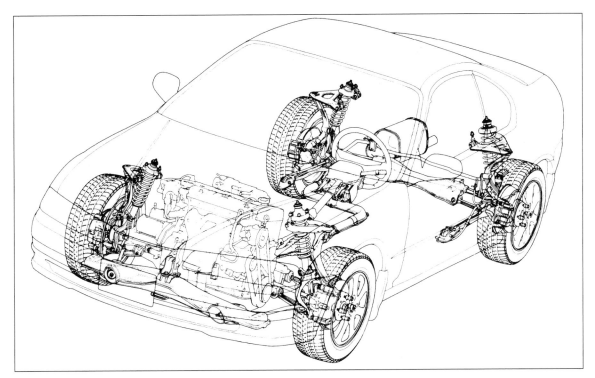

1:5. The front-drive layout, exemplified by this Honda Prelude, is now firmly established as the preferred design for small and medium-size saloon cars and is increasingly chosen for new larger models too. Advantages including compact drive-train, inherent stability and speed of manufacture have been compounded by suspension developments which have overcome most of the potential drawbacks.

Handling and roadholding are most closely related when the cause of poor handling is poor roadholding at one end (usually the back end) of a car.

Moves to uniformity

Even in the time of this book's first edition, there were enough 'maverick' car designs around to provide starting points for arguments about chassis design and the relative merits of different suspension layouts. But the world has changed since then. Where chassis design is concerned, there is a great deal more standardization. In 1988, it was still possible to point to cars which managed to achieve excellent handling despite having rigid rear axles rather than independent rear suspension. Today, the likes of the Alfa Romeo 33, the Saab 9000 and the Volvo 740 have all gone, or very nearly so. The 'live' axle survives only in off-road vehicles, where it is retained – if it is – for its constant ground clearance, and despite its adverse effect on steering

and ride comfort. Except for these special purposes, the number of rear suspension layouts is becoming almost as limited as those at the front. No engineer setting down the specification for a new car today would consider anything but independent rear suspension – unless, like so many of his contemporaries, he is swayed by the efficiency and low cost of the torsion beam layout for a front-driven model. In the same way, nobody today looks at anything but rack-and-pinion steering, and the handful of cars which used to achieve good results with worm-and-roller systems have disappeared. And the chances are that most drivers under 30 years of age will never have driven on cross-ply tyres ...

In effect, many of the technical discussions which raged through the 1980s have gone quiet. The evidence on one side or the other has become overwhelming, the technical developments too convincing. To take one example, the discussion as to the relative merits of axle beams versus

5

1:6. There is more than one way of designing a much admired small sports car. The success of the mid-engined layout in racing cars led some road car designers to follow suit, as in the case of the Fiat X1/9 and the much later Toyota MR2.

independent suspension is dead, at least for road-going cars. The last 10 years have seen the suspension engineers, aided by ever more powerful computers, overcoming the former drawbacks of independent layouts – most notably, their errant behaviour (in the form of embarrassing camber angle or wheel alignment change) at one or both ends of wheel travel. Today, provided the engineer is allowed to spend enough money, he (or she!) can make a multi-link independent layout do more or less exactly what he wants it to do, and ways have been discovered of 'tweaking' even the simpler independent layouts, the MacPherson strut and the

double-wishbone, to avoid most of their former pitfalls without having to restrict wheel travel too much.

Today's arguments
The big arguments today rage around something even more fundamental: the relative merits of front, rear and four-wheel drive, and to some extent also (among sports car enthusiasts) on the rival claims of the front-engine and mid-engine layouts. There is both less discussion, and less understanding than there should be, about tyres.

You might well say that the first of those

1:7. Other designers proved that front-engined, front-driven cars could also be nice to drive, as in the case of the Alfa Sprint and the Honda CRX. Whatever the advantages of the mid-engined layout from the handling point-of-view, there is no question that the front-drive cars are better 'packaged', with far more interior and useful luggage space.

arguments has been just as firmly settled. Rear-drive is now confined to a handful of cars at the prestige end of the market. The borderline beyond which the advantages of front-drive (compact driveline, 'natural' stability and inherently safe behaviour in slippery and icy conditions) no longer outweighs its potential problems (uneven weight distribution, excessive understeer, complex steering arrangements, heavy front tyre wear) has been pushed ever further outwards or upwards. In 1988, you could still argue over the relative merits of the rear-driven Ford Sierra and the front-driven Vauxhall Cavalier. Now the Sierra has given way to the Mondeo, and the cheapest rear-driven new car you can buy in the UK is a BMW 3-series Compact. BMW, Mercedes and Jaguar – along with their would-be rival E-segment models from Ford and General Motors – have all remained faithful to rear-drive (except, obviously, for Mercedes with the A-class) partly because they build some of the heaviest and most powerful cars in production, but also because their regular customers still somehow regard rear-drive

1:8. While many enthusiasts argued through the early 1980s that a good modern sports car must have a mid-engined layout, Mazda's MX-5 breathed new life into the sports car concept with a very conventional, almost old-fashioned front-engine, rear-drive chassis which clearly had all the qualities so many buyers were seeking: good looks, a good engine, reasonable refinement and practical luggage space, the last two especially difficult to achieve when the engine is immediately behind the cockpit.

1:9. Despite (or perhaps because of) the position established by the Mazda MX-5, the MGF emerged as a compact mid-engined two-seater. Its handling has been generously and deservedly praised, and mid-engined drawbacks have been minimized by the compactness of the Rover K-series engine, and by some careful and expensive sound insulation. Even so, would you rather go long-distance touring in this car or in the Mazda?

1:10. Jaguar had no doubts about the optimum chassis layout for the XK8, as the 'F-type' project eventually emerged. Although the company had earlier developed and run a mid-engined prototype, the XJ13, it had no illusions about the drawbacks of the layout for a production model and remained faithful to a front-mounted engine and rear-wheel drive.

as a 'prestige' thing. The fundamental differences between the layouts are discussed in more detail in later chapters, but I cannot resist pointing out the way in which BMW and Mercedes (and latterly their Japanese imitators) have resorted to equipping their most powerful cars with hundreds of pounds' worth of electronic 'stability enhancement systems' to make them behave as safely and controllably on skidpan surfaces as front-driven cars do of their own accord.

As for four-wheel drive, there are fewer purely road-going models available now than there were 10 years ago. Audi, and therefore also Volkswagen, persist, as does Subaru, but some other companies who once felt they could not hold their technical heads high without a token 4WD in the range have long since cooled off. They have done so largely because of the efficiency and cost-effectiveness of traction control systems. A TCS may not give you the same ability to accelerate on sheet ice, but it works well in most circumstances while also

costing less, weighing less, creating no noise or vibration problems, and (assuming a front-drive starting point) leaving boot space and fuel capacity unimpaired. As for handling, back-to-back tests have suggested time and again that the practical effect of 4WD is to make car control on slippery surfaces much easier right up to the moment when the roadholding runs out. It does not create any significant margin in ultimate cornering power compared with a skillfully driven 2WD version of the same model; rather it makes it easier to approach and stay close to the limit.

As for the mid-engine debate, in 1988 I observed that the well but superficially informed 'know' that mid-engined cars have the most agile handling because they have the least polar moment of inertia, even if they would have a job defining polar moment. I pointed out even at the time how upsetting it was that years after Fiat launched the X1/9 to convert the world to the mid-engined ideal for small, affordable sports cars, Honda should offer its front-

1:11. One of the less desirable trends of recent years has been the adoption of wider tyres on the sporting versions of production cars. Stylists love them, and so do people who don't appreciate that increasing tyre width doesn't 'put more rubber on the road' unless inflation pressures are lowered. What they certainly do is make the contact patch shorter but wider, reducing steering feel and self-centring. The chassis engineer can tune a potentially over-tyred car like this concept model to overcome the ill effects, but those who buy even wider wheels and tyres in the aftermarket may not be so lucky.

driven CRX in the same class, the front-driven Alfa Romeo Sprint should remain one of the most admired small sports coupes, Porsche should fail to offer a single current mid-engined model, and Britain's successful small volume sports car specialists ignore (with the solitary exception of the Lotus Esprit) the mid-engined layout altogether. Since then, the picture has been mixed, to say the least. Toyota launched the mid-engined MR2, but failed to set the world on fire with it. Mazda enjoyed arguably more success with the front-engined, rear-driven MX5. Today's Alfa Romeo Spider and Fiat Barchetta are both front-driven as well as front-engined, but the MGF and the Renault Sport Spider are mid-engined. Honda still makes a front-driven CRX, but its technically phenomenal NSX is mid-engined. Porsche now offers a mid-engined model in the Boxster, but the Aston Martin DB7 and the Jaguar XK8 are front-engined, as is Ferrari's 550 Maranello. And Britain's (still) successful small-volume sports car specialists, with the exception of

Lotus, still place their faith in front-mounted engines. This debate, clearly, is far from over . . . see later chapters!

Tyres: is wider really better?

Then there is the whole question of tyres. In recent years, a great many cars, and almost all cars with sporting aspirations, have been fitted with wheels and tyres which were wider than the chassis engineer would have chosen, if left to himself. The inevitable first step towards creating a sporting derivative of a modest standard hatchback is to remove the standard wheels and tyres and replace them with something wider, while also changing the wheels from steel to aluminium alloy. Once upon a time, this might have involved a switch from 155-13 tyres to a 175/70-13 size: and as pointed out in Chapter 5, there could be very good reasons for doing so. But 175/70-13 is probably close to the optimum tyre of a C-segment hatchback. That is a good reason for fitting that size as standard even to the 'base' versions; the trouble is, it creates pressure to move the high-performance derivatives onto something rather ridiculous. There are 'hot' C-segment models today running 205/50-15 tyres, and that is what the factory fits; there is no shortage of purveyors of expensive wheels and tyres selling even wider units in the aftermarket. It is all to little or no technical purpose.

I find that I only hinted at the problems in Chapter 5 all those years ago, before the trend had become established, when I said that wider tyres reduce self-aligning torque, and therefore natural stability and steering feel. I should have added that without proper engineering, they can also do dreadful things to stress levels in the wheel hubs. What actually happens is that beyond the optimum tyre size, the contact patch becomes shorter and wider. The total contact patch area is, more or less, the weight of the car divided by the tyre pressure, so there is no more 'rubber on the road', and the roadholding is not significantly improved, unless you actually run at much lower pressures – and the other technical drawbacks still apply. This idiotic state of affairs has arisen for two reasons, which sadly tend to feed off each other. In the eyes of most car designers, wide, 'chunky' tyres produce a purposeful, sporting look. And in the eyes of young high-performance enthusiasts, wider tyres mean better roadholding (and a purposeful, sporting look). The enthusiasts are merely ill-informed: the designers are blinkered at best, cynical at worst. Yes, full-race touring cars run extremely wide tyres, but they run them at remarkably low pressures, on purpose-designed suspensions, to cope with power outputs and cornering forces well beyond those of any driveable road-going version of the same car.

The reasons for choices

Having hopefully established a number of basic definitions and outlined some of the questions most often asked by interested and enthusiastic drivers, we need to look at why so many car designers apparently reject optimum solutions when it comes to chassis design and road behaviour.

The first excuse which springs to the defensive mind is that passenger car designers are far too concerned with pennypinching to adopt the most superior principles and fit the best of everything. Perhaps fortunately, it is no longer quite so easy to decide exactly what is 'the best of everything'. A decade ago, you could point a finger at any company not using (for example) rack-and-pinion steering and all-independent (preferably F1-type double-wishbone) suspension, and accuse them of being so concerned to squeeze production costs to the bare minimum as to be prepared to turn out cars which didn't behave as well as they might. But, as I pointed out in that first edition, was it really sensible to accuse Alfa Romeo, BMW, Mercedes, Saab or Volvo of being prepared to compromise handling, ride or stability for the sake of cost? Of course not. There were other factors at work, and there still are.

Put yourself in the place of an engineer given charge of designing a new passenger car. Needless to say, you are not free to lay out your car purely on the basis of optimum chassis design. You will be working to an outline specification carefully prepared by top management. This document, which the French graphically but untranslatably call the *cahier des charges*, will call for a certain size of car, this much cabin space, this much luggage room, this big a fuel tank. It will set performance and economy targets. It may set a target weight, though in effect the performance and economy targets do that anyway. It will certainly specify a target production cost.

Naturally, you as the vehicle designer want the best-behaving chassis design you can achieve, but other needs inevitably take priority. Unless your management has decided the market needs a two-seat sports car, your design must have a cabin big enough to accommodate four or five people in comfort. Except in a sports car, the cabin is the whole point of the vehicle so far as the user is concerned. But from the point of view of chassis design, any cabin is a nuisance: it is a clear volume which must be left more or less intact. It is no good hoping owner-drivers – let alone road-testers – will ignore the fact that the pedals are forced into a

1:12. After decades in which cars were built ever closer to the ground, designers are sitting people more upright again, as in the much admired Renault Mégane Scénic. From the chassis engineer's point of view, this leads to a higher centre of gravity – an obvious drawback – but it also enables a car with a given amount of interior space to be shorter, stiffer in torsion and lighter – the last two being distinct advantages. And in practical terms, sitting the driver higher tends to improve ability to 'read the road' and judge cornering lines correctly, which can be worth a whole dose of chassis engineering.

narrow and offset cluster by the front wheelarch. Nor will passengers forgive a back seat which has been made narrow and uncomfortable because it has been squeezed between the rear suspension mountings. On the contrary: the wheelarches and the suspension mountings must be spread around the cabin, and if that leads to chassis design compromises, they must be accepted.

The art of packaging

The design art called 'packaging' exercises a subtle effect on chassis engineering. However you look at it, seating people in two rows of two takes up a certain amount of space. Within limits, you can make the space shorter by making it taller, by sitting the people on upright dining-chairs rather than deck-chairs, as it were. The pressure on car designers to seat people as low and reclined as practicable is strong. It reduces the car's frontal area and thus its aerodynamic drag, it lowers the centre of gravity and so lessens the tendency to fall over in mid-corner, and it makes the stylist's job much easier.

From the chassis engineer's point of view

also, long, low cars are a much easier proposition. The reduction of overturning moment is obviously important to him, but also, as we shall see, cars with longer wheelbases (that is, with a greater distance between their front and rear axles) tend to ride better and to be more stable and more predictable, if less immediately agile in their handling, all other things being equal. On the other hand, short, high-built cars have their own advantages. They can be made lighter and stiffer. They are easier to get in and out of. The driver has a better view. This was mainly theory until Giugiaro shaped the Fiat Uno, but the trend is now well-established, not only in hatchbacks like the Uno's successor, the Punto, but most of all in 'mini-MPV' designs like the Renault Mégane Scénic.

The extent to which this trend can be carried is naturally limited: there is little point in making an ordinary road-going car more than about five feet high in any circumstances, because beyond that people will have to climb up into the vehicle rather than just stepping into it (an off-road vehicle with a large ground clearance is another

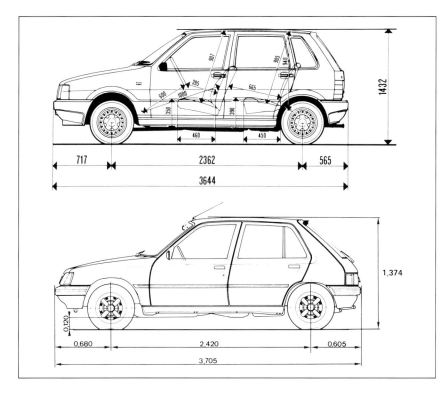

1:13. Seemingly small differences in the dimensions of a modern small car can be of considerable significance. The Fiat Uno (top) is only about 2 inches taller than its rival the Peugeot 205, but that is enough to allow it to provide the interior space required of a car in its class on a wheelbase over 2 inches shorter, with a concomitant saving in weight. It is in the context of such subtle design 'packaging', a delicate balancing of often contradictory factors, that the chassis engineer has to exercise his skill.

matter). Obviously, this argument works in favour of larger cars – they can be kept lower relative to their length and width, which not only makes them look better, but also increases their resistance to overturning. For practical purposes, there appears also to be a minimum wheelbase just as there is a maximum height. Anything with a wheelbase of less than around 80 inches, that of the Mini itself, in fact, cannot be considered a proper four-seater. Indeed, even 80 inches is too small in today's terms since the Mini was indeed a minimum four-seater when it appeared some 40 years ago, and people have become bigger since (and their standards of acceptable comfort have risen). It is interesting, for example, to find that all the modern Japanese 'microcars' have a wheelbase of 90 inches or more – it was 83 inches 10 years ago. The average European B-segment 'supermini' now has a 96-inch wheelbase.

Small changes in dimension can be significant to the chassis engineer. Length of wheelbase is one of his main working parameters: wheel track is another, with the extra complication that it need not be the same front and rear. Indeed, making the front and rear tracks different is one of the many chassis-tuning weapons available to the engineer at the design stage. In an overall sense, the wider you make the track, the more you are able to resist body roll and the overturning moment created by the inevitable fact that the car's centre of gravity is above the road surface. On the other hand, there is obviously a limit to how wide you can make the track without making the car less manoeuvrable.

Just as, within limits, there is a practical maximum height and minimum wheelbase, so there is a minimum car width, which in turn implies a minimum track. Few modern cars other than those Japanese 'micros' have an overall width of less than 60 inches because in anything less there is too little cabin interior width for two adults to sit comfortably side by side.

The chassis designer of a typical supermini, therefore, knows he will be constrained to work within tight limits, or more precisely, in a minimal space around the walls of a certain size of cabin. It is hardly surprising that he discards double

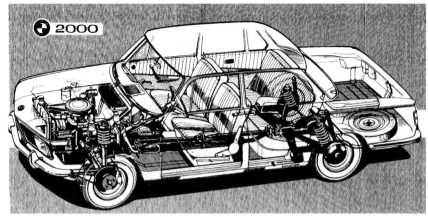

1:14. Through many years, BMW remained faithful to the same basic chassis layout of MacPherson struts at the front, semi-trailing arms at the rear. Comparison of a very early BMW 2000 chassis (top) with a much later 3-series reveals some of the detail changes that were made in the quest for better ride comfort, reduced road noise and more secure handling. Note especially the rearward-angled front struts of the later car and the offset spring axis, together with the repositioned rear springs.

wishbones (for the most part) in favour of suspension layouts which can be wrapped neatly round the corners of the cabin-box to take up the minimum of space. The man designing a larger car is in a different position. He can allocate more space to the cabin, but he need not be extravagant. A couple more inches of elbow and knee room, by comparison with the supermini's minimum acceptable four-seat cabin, can make a car seem positively spacious. The rest of the extra space can be given over to other purposes. Some of it will be needed for the inevitably bigger engine and transmission, some of it will undoubtedly be devoted to extra luggage space, and some will (or should) be given over to better chassis design.

It does not always happen. Cars far larger than the typical supermini somehow contrive to have cabins which are no more roomy, yet have apparently inferior chassis design as well. Should we put this down to incompetence on the part of the chassis engineer? Not very often. If he has failed in any sense, it is through failing to resist sufficiently the demands of his fellow designers and product-planners. The stylist, the production engineer and others conspire to make the chassis man's life difficult. Demands for an even bigger boot, or a bigger fuel tank, may encroach on the space he needs for a decent rear suspension. His ideally situated suspension mounting points may be squeezed inwards by styling changes, outwards by a need for more space in the engine bay, and in any direction by the structures expert seeking yet more weight-saving, or the production man who sees a method of making a body section from five welded components instead of six.

What is more, the chassis engineer has

1:15. Although BMW has moved to more complex but better behaved rear suspension arrangements for most of its current models, the 3-series Compact and Z3 sports car retain the semi-trailing layout to which the company was faithful for so long. In the Compact, it saves not only cost, but luggage space in the truncated back end; and Z3 drivers presumably appreciate the slightly more 'lively' cornering behaviour which results in extreme situations.

more to think about than steering, handling and roadholding. His design specification insists the occupants must be carried 'in comfort'. Now, his interpretation of comfort will certainly depend on the target price of his car – supermini passengers do not expect to enjoy Jaguar or Mercedes standards – but the onus is still upon the designer to achieve the smoothest and quietest possible ride within the stated cost limitations. This too will inevitably affect the choice of chassis layout. Suspension systems which promise the best handling and grip may have serious drawbacks when it comes to feeding shocks and noise into the cabin. Wheelarch dimensions will always be limited by other considerations, and so also the size of the wheels themselves (the larger the wheel diameter, the better the ride over poor surfaces, which is why some vintage cars are more comfortable than you might expect) and the vertical suspension travel,

which is one of the keys to ride comfort.

There are yet other considerations. For the sake of fuel economy and performance, a modern car must be as aerodynamic and as light as possible. A good aerodynamic shape not only adds a further dimension to the wishes of the stylist: it may not be at all in accord with the chassis engineer's wish to use a particular type of suspension. Double wishbones all round are fine for the Formula 1 designer who can hang them out in the breeze, but they pose major problems for anyone trying to design a saloon car with efficient use of internal space, minimum frontal area and a drag coefficient of 0.3 or less. Then again, a suspension layout which feeds its loads into the bodyshell (that is, the cabin walls, floor, roof and bulkheads) more efficiently, so as to permit a saving in structure weight, may command attention even though another system might promise better handling and roadholding.

The question of cost – and of experience

Other questions, less purely of engineering, will play their part. Cost, of course, is a vital consideration. Racing cars are designed to win regardless of cost, but production passenger cars are designed to cost what customers can afford or, to take the more cynical view, to meet or beat competitors on price. Exotic solutions are usually ruled out for this reason alone. Even where the designer can make a good financial case for breaking new ground in chassis design he may hold back for other reasons. No engineer lightly throws away a layout which has served him well in previous designs. It is not simply a matter of the factory knowing how to make it, and the dealers how to service it: with a familiar design the engineer himself knows exactly how fine he can cut his margins, and he knows its weakest points well enough to contain them with further detailed development. It is the old argument between evolution and revolution, and it explains why so many new cars resemble their predecessors in general layout. Consider, for example, that every new BMW design from 1963 to 1986 had MacPherson-strut front suspension and independent semi-trailing arms at the rear; the layout changed subtly through the years, but it takes an expert eye to appreciate the differences at a glance (*fig 1:14*). To this day, at least as I write, essentially the same layout is retained for the 3-series Compact and the Z3 sports car, although the larger BMW saloons have long since moved to a true multi-link arrangement for the rear suspension.

We have already seen that the actual size of the car makes a great difference to the way an engineer sets about planning the chassis. Small four-seat cars represent the most difficult design challenge because four people weigh the same, and take up as much room, whether they are sitting in a small car or a big one. It follows that four people represent a much smaller proportion of the weight and size of a large luxury car than they do of a supermini. Thus in the large luxury car, the designer ought to be free to a much greater extent to dispose his mechanical components, and his chassis, in the most advantageous way. In practice, it doesn't quite work out like that, which only goes to show how complex a subject chassis engineering has become. But to begin with, let us understand why almost all of today's smaller cars have front-wheel drive.

Later on, I devote a whole chapter to the detail considerations of chassis engineering as applied to front-wheel drive, but why does the designer accept the obvious difficulty of driving and steering the same wheels to begin with? Because, quite simply, a four-seat car can be made smaller and lighter if the front wheels are driven. It means all the main mechanical parts of the car can be assembled into a single compact mass, behind which there trails the four-seat cabin with its aft end supported on the two rear wheels. The cabin structure is lighter and simpler because there is no need for a propeller-shaft tunnel and no necessity to absorb the stresses set up between a front 'engine room' and driven rear wheels. It should also be easier to insulate the cabin against mechanical noise because it is all coming from one direction, forward of the front bulkhead.

There used to be arguments against front-wheel drive on the grounds of cost and ease of servicing, but never of weight or size. From the day Alec Issigonis' Mini was launched, the designers of rear-driven small cars were on the defensive. The only way they could deliver a similar combination of cabin space and performance was to build them into a larger, heavier car and hope for a cost advantage that would enable them to match the Mini on price. Ford and General Motors (Vauxhall/Opel) argued that way for many years, but today, the Fiesta, Escort, Corsa, Astra and Cavalier are all front-driven. A great deal of surprise was expressed in 1982 when the Cortina-replacement Sierra turned out not to be, but in 1992, the Sierra-replacement Mondeo abandoned rear-drive once and for all, so far as cars in this class were concerned.

The arguments for making a supermini front-driven are now so strong that nobody would consider designing one any other way.

The bigger the car becomes, however, the less clear-cut the decision. As the mechanical components become bigger, the front-drive mass becomes less compact and much heavier. As installed power (or rather, torque) increases, so the problems of transmitting it through the front wheels become more severe, for reasons we shall look into more closely later on. In other words, the designer is driven to consider more closely the alternative layout with the engine in front and a propeller-shaft running aft to drive the rear wheels; or, of course, the more complicated and expensive strategy of taking the drive to all four wheels.

As I pointed out earlier, the boundary beyond which front-wheel drive no longer presents significant advantages has edged steadily upwards. In Europe, Audi, Fiat Auto, PSA Peugeot-Citroen, Renault, Rover, Saab and Volvo (a relatively recent convert) all make front-driven models with engines of 2-litre or more capacity and considerable torque output. So do all of the American 'big three'. Yet there remains that handful of 'prestige' manufacturers faithful to rear-drive . . .

An easier task in some ways – maybe

All this begs a question: is the choice of basic car layout part of chassis engineering? It certainly is, in any real sense, because the choice of front, rear or four-wheel drive immediately presents the chassis engineer with a completely different task. While it is not necessarily true, whatever the prejudices of some 'experts', that front-driven cars are more stable but rear-driven cars handle better, it is a fact that the natural nose-heaviness of the front-drive design inclines it towards good stability at the expense of making hard work of cornering. The task of the chassis engineer is to overcome the inherent problems of whatever layout he is presented with, and ensure that the car behaves well by all reasonable criteria. He has a large number of techniques at his disposal to help him achieve this aim, and we shall look at them in detail.

If the point needs underlining, consider what might be called the 'missing chapter' in this book. Had I been writing 35 years ago, I would have had to devote some space to the rear-engine, rear-drive layout. I would have been able to point to examples from Fiat, Hillman, NSU, Porsche, Renault, Simca, Skoda and, of course, Volkswagen. Today, only Porsche remains, and that in highly specialized form and for equally specialized reasons of history and marketing. It is still just possibly a moot point whether you could design a more compact small car by tucking the engine and transmission beneath and aft of the

1:16. The transverse-engined, front-driven Ford Mondeo emerged in 1992 as the successor to the Sierra, which had been the last mass-produced, medium-sized, rear-driven European car. Partly no doubt because the Mondeo turned out to have a highly capable chassis, nobody complained at the passing of the rear-drive layout, which is now confined to larger and much more expensive 'prestige' models. There was a proposal to create a rear-driven Mondeo for circuit racing purposes only, but even here the advantages turned out to be largely illusory, especially in relation to the cost.

1:17. The original Volkswagen Beetle was rear-engined and rear-driven. But the car became a legend on the back of its build quality and reliability, not its chassis engineering. When Volkswagen decided to create the New Beetle, it had no hesitation in adapting the front-driven Golf platform to provide the foundation for the evocative 'retro' look of the body.

back seat, but that is no longer the point. The argument against rear-engined cars is almost purely one of chassis engineering. The basic layout is so deficient in inherent stability and handling that the poor chassis engineer has to employ drastic methods to render them acceptable. Volkswagen may have resurrected the Beetle, but under the skin the new model is a front-driven Golf.

In one sense, therefore, the chassis designer has won a battle in recent decades. He is no longer expected to massage the drawbacks of a rear-engined layout and still endow a car with sanitary handling: he can confine his main interests to front-driven cars and front-engined, rear-driven cars, with the occasional excursion, if he works for the right company, into mid-engined, rear-driven cars. But if his task has been simplified to that extent, it has become much more complicated in others.

So many of motoring's recent technical developments have a direct bearing on chassis engineering. The interest in four-wheel drive might not be as strong as it was 10 years ago – if you discount the greater number of off-road models – but the very availability of the option opens up all kinds of problems and possibilities. There have been developments in tyres, more subtle perhaps than the 1940s revolution which gave us the radial to replace the cross-ply, but highly significant in terms of what the chassis man can take advantage of or what

he must allow for. There has been a surge of knowledge and technique in the art of filtering road thumps and noise before they can be transmitted from the suspension to the body structure, an art built around the magic but sometimes confusing word 'compliance'. Limited-slip differentials, once the preserve of competition cars, are now found in all manner of road-going models above a certain price level. New steering systems have been introduced, including the concept of rear-wheel steering, which effectively rewrites many of the laws and assumptions governing car handling behaviour. Perhaps above all, levels of performance have grown to the point where road-going cars can experience acceleration forces that 10 or 15 years ago belonged to the world of competition; yet the customer still expects his vehicle to respond like a road car, not a competition car.

We shall look at the effect of some of these developments in the appropriate chapters of this book. Others still remain more in the world of the future. We shall not ignore them, but we shall confine our study to a final, crystal-gazing chapter which will try to plot the likely course of chassis design thinking, if not of the actual hardware, up to the end of the century. There is, however, plenty to occupy the mind, even in the present state of chassis engineering, without pondering immediately upon the future.

Chapter two

Basic principles

When it comes to chassis engineering, knowledgeable car buyers tend to fall into two categories. As I implied in my opening chapter, there are those who are confident in their own knowledge though it may consist, upon examination, more of prejudice than anything else. There are also those who think quite deeply about the engine and transmission of any car they buy, yet take the suspension design on trust. Whether or not a car buyer appreciates the difference between independent and non-independent suspension, or jumps to the conclusion that independent suspension must of necessity be better than a pair of wheels joined by an axle, too few take an interest in why one designer should choose MacPherson strut suspension while another uses double wishbones, for instance. Does the choice make any difference to the way the car handles? It does, of course – but how? And if one system gives better handling than another, why does everyone not use it?

In the previous chapter, I tried to define handling, steering and roadholding and to show that they could be discussed separately. We now need to look more specifically at which aspects of chassic design affect each of those basic qualities.

It is no simple matter. One might assume for instance that roadholding was simply a matter of how large the tyres are – of 'rubber on the road' in the language of the go-faster magazines. Yet the grip of a tyre depends in large part on the load it is asked to carry as well as on the size of its 'footprint'. It also depends on the tyre being kept more or less upright – and the wider the tyre, the more nearly upright it needs to be kept if it is to work properly. Furthermore, as I have already pointed out, no tyre can grip unless it is in contact with the road surface. If it is lifted or bounced clear, it will provide no grip at all. Thus good roadholding is not simply a matter of tyre choice, but of suspension design in its widest sense.

Steering is a slightly simpler proposition, yet it too poses problems which are frequently unappreciated. It is surely simple enough to design a linkage which will take the motion of the steering wheel to the front wheels? Yes and no. The designer of the linkage needs to allow for the fact that the front wheels move up and down in arcs defined by the front suspension, and that these movements can have awkward effects on the faithfulness with which the front wheels follow each movement of the steering wheel. Then again, the front wheels (and indeed the rear ones) effectively become large gyroscopes which store a fair amount of energy if the car is travelling fast, and most people are aware from infant spinning-top exercises, if not from O-level physics or mathematics, that gyroscopes perform odd tricks when you move them about one axis. If the car is front or four-wheel driven, the steering must also make some allowance for the effect of drive torque. Finally, it is often the case that the rear suspension feeds in its own steering effect.

It is, however, in the area of handling that

2:1. The Ford Model T shows many features typical of early front suspension systems. The front axle is a rigid beam with brackets for the kingpins at each end, while the suspension medium is a single transverse leaf spring. The designer's task was greatly simplified by the absence of separate dampers (the only damping effect came from inter-leaf friction within the spring) and of front wheel brakes. The narrow tyres were mercifully unable to generate enough sideforce to overstress the kingpin brackets or the wheel hubs themselves.

the full panoply of chassis design techniques comes into its own. This is really the starting point for any serious consideration of chassis engineering. Even as we start, though, we need to acknowledge the designer's equal need to provide an acceptable level of ride comfort. This is because the most fundamental design choice of all is that of springs and spring rate; and this is the point in the design at which handling and ride first become inextricably linked.

Good control of vertical wheel movement is essential for acceptable handling and road-holding, and for a decent ride. One does not necessarily trade one for the other. When he is looking at ride, the engineer is concerned primarily with ensuring that the car body bounces, pitches and rolls as little as possible (in engineering terms, these are three separate though related tasks) and that whatever movement takes place, does so at an acceptable *frequency* – an aspect we consider in more detail later.

The chassis designer will strive for the best results in all four areas – steering, handling, roadholding and ride – but he will take the first three in that order of priorities. Without good steering, good handling is wasted; without good handling, good roadholding is wasted. And good roadholding depends both on the suspension design, and on how much has been spent on the wheels and tyres.

Suspension – springs and dampers

In Chapter 1, I tried to outline some of the conflicting pressures suffered by the engineer responsible for a new car's chassis, and suggested that in modern terms 'chassis' meant everything about the car which affects the way it steers and rides. It is necessary, however, to be more precise in some of our definitions. We must at least have a clear idea what we mean by the suspension system, because this lies at the heart of chassis design.

To begin with, what *is* a suspension system? It is the linkages which attach the wheels to the car body, plus the springs and dampers. Were there no springs and dampers, there would be no need for a linkage. Unfortunately, for simplicity, the need for springs was realized in the stagecoach era, long before the first motor car spluttered on to the road. The need for dampers, on the other hand, really only emerged in the 1920s. It follows, perhaps, that the need for springs is more fundamental than the need for dampers, although any modern car would give you an extremely uncomfortable time without benefit of both.

Incidentally, I use the word 'damper' for what is often mistakenly called the 'shock absorber'; the springs absorb the shock, while the dampers are there to stop the springs continuing to bounce up and down after they have absorbed it – to damp down the resulting motion, in fact. It is worth noting that while dampers bring the body which is bouncing on its springs more quickly to rest, they have very little effect on the spring frequency - the rate at which the body bounces up and down (or pitches nose and tail down, or rolls from side to side). The frequency is a function almost purely of the spring system.

Just how a spring works to absorb the shock of a bump in the road is something which can only be properly studied with the aid of mathematics. This is not the place to go into such studies: suffice it to say that the starting point is the simple harmonic motion of the spring, a familiar enough part of A-level mathematics or physics. Any spring has a 'rate' – expressed as the force needed to compress or extend it by a given unit length (thus pounds per inch, or kilogrammes per metre).

If a spring which supports a load is first compressed and then released, it will push its load upwards, then pull it down, then push it up again and so on. In other words, it will cause it to oscillate. Eventually the movement will die away (in the absence of a separate damper) because the actual material of the spring absorbs a certain amount of energy which it turns into heat. The important thing is that as

long as the up-and-down movement continues, it does so at a constant rate (the frequency, or number of complete oscillations per second) which is determined by just two things: the spring rate, and the size of the load. As it happens, these two factors oppose one another. The greater the load, the lower the frequency. The greater the spring rate (in other words, the stiffer the spring), the higher the frequency.

The frequency is important because it is what actually determines ride comfort. Even the earliest investigators - including Lanchester – realized there were certain frequencies of car body movement which were best avoided because they were reflected by the human body in various uncomfortable ways. A very slow oscillation, about one every 2 seconds, induces the familiar problems of nausea and 'seasickness'. At other, faster frequencies, various parts of the body begin to resonate – to vibrate continuously and out of control. Worse still, the faster the vibration, the less vertical acceleration the human body seems able to tolerate without feeling discomfort. 'Doctor Fred' Lanchester suggested (in 1907!) that one should aim for about 1.5 cycles per second and the range 1 to 1.5 cycles (or Hertz, in modern scientific terminology) has remained nearly enough the target for chassis engineers seriously interested in ride comfort. For a long time, though, actually achieving it in anything with a body weight less than that of a massively coachbuilt Rolls-Royce was another matter.

We should certainly take note, at this stage, of the fact that the frequency is independent of how far the wheel travels vertically – just as the period of a simple pendulum remains the same whether you lift the bob-weight high or simply push it slightly to one side. The only reason why some cars are fitted with very long wheel travel is to allow their very soft springs to work properly, even when they have been compressed by an additional load, or by very large bumps in the road surface. Such cars can prove extremely comfortable across country or on very poor roads. The penalties they have to pay are those of extreme roll angles when cornering hard, and the need to provide huge wheelarches to accommodate the wheel movement on full bump. Also, unless the designer is

2:2. Very low spring rates ('soft' springs) can provide an extremely comfortable ride even over large obstacles. The price is paid in the kind of cornering roll exhibited by this 2CV-derived Citroen Dyane. Note also the size of wheelarches required to accommodate the long vertical wheel travel.

prepared to risk 'grounding' problems, the car's centre of gravity has to be fairly high.

Sprung and unsprung weight

What is also fundamentally important in suspension design is that the spring is sandwiched between the car body and the wheel (plus any components which are attached to the wheel rather than the body). Since there is no spring (other than the tyre) between the wheel and the road, the wheel and its associated components, including any axle to which it is attached, is known as *unsprung weight* (or more strictly, mass). The body and everything it contains is the *sprung weight*.

In non-mathematical terms, if the wheel hits a bump and is jerked upwards, it compres-

ses the spring which in turn tries to make the body oscillate. Like any physical mass, the body would rather stay where it is than move, so it 'fights back' along the spring against the force trying to move it. The success of this fight-back depends on the force at the other end, which depends on two things: the size of the bump, and the weight of the wheel. In effect, the spring can be regarded as two separate springs, one for the body, the other for the wheel, on either side of a 'neutral point'. The heavier the wheel, the greater the length of the spring it will claim for itself and the closer to the centre of the spring the neutral point will be.

However, the shorter a spring, the stiffer it becomes: if you halve the length of a spring, there are only half as many coils to compress and it takes twice the effort to compress it through the same distance. Therefore, if a very heavy wheel and tyre 'claims' a large share of its spring, two things happen. First, the body's share of the spring becomes shorter and thus stiffer, causing the body to move at a higher frequency. Second, the wheel's share of the spring being relatively long, is also relatively soft and allows the wheel to move at a low frequency.

As it happens, this is exactly the opposite of what we want. We need to maintain a nice low body frequency of not more than 1.5 Hertz, and if the wheel is claiming a large share of the spring's effective length then we need an even longer, softer spring to achieve the desired result; but long, soft springs are a recipe for body roll and possible handling problems, so we would rather not do that. At the same time, we want the oscillation rate of the wheel and tyre to be as high as possible: the higher it is, the more time the tyre will spend pressed to the ground and the better will be the roadholding (taking the argument to its impossible extreme, if we could mount the wheel on an infinitely stiff spring with an infinitely high frequency, it would remain on the ground whatever happened).

A simplistic way of looking at it is to say that the lighter the wheel (the smaller the unsprung weight) relative to that of the body, the more easily the body can 'squash' any attempt on the part of the wheel to move it, and the more thoroughly the wheel in its turn can be squashed on to the ground. The effect cannot be complete, of course. There will still be wheel movement, and there will be some body movement for any given wheel movement, but the heavier the body in relation to the wheel, the less those movements will be.

Hence, in slightly more technical terms, one of the critical parameters for any chassis engineer is the ratio of the sprung to the unsprung weight. The greater it is, the better not only for ride comfort (because the body movement is less) but also for the roadholding, because the wheel remains in firm contact with the road surface for more of the time. Thus the chassis designer's ideal is an extremely heavy body running on extremely light wheels and tyres, attached to the body by an equally light linkage. Sadly, it is an ideal

that is never achieved. Most of the engineers in a modern car design team are trying their hardest to make the body light, not heavy, and the chassis man's desire for the lightest wheels and suspension linkage conflict with the need to provide wheels and tyres strong enough for their job, and a suspension stiff enough to locate them accurately.

The significance of low unsprung weight was not appreciated in the early years of motoring. On the contrary, there are records of pioneer cars being fitted with extra ballast weights strapped to their axles in the hope that these would help to hold the wheels down and so improve roadholding!

Such apparent ignorance may seem appalling in our enlightened times, but we must remember that the early motor cars were developed directly from the horse-drawn carriage, and nowhere more so than in their chassis engineering. Even when Panhard and Levassor rethought the shape of the motor car in the 1890s and came up with the front-engine, rear-drive layout which was to remain the standard for the next 60 years, their vehicle was fitted with multiple semi-elliptic leaf springs. This was the type of spring which eventually and disparagingly became known as the 'cart' spring and with good reason, for that is basically what it was.

Leaf springs – accidents of history?
We should not be too rude about the semi-elliptic spring even though the last popular European road car to use it (the Ford Capri) is being withdrawn from production even as I write. The fact is that, almost by accident, such springs had two qualities which enabled early car suspensions to be simple yet sufficiently effective to cope with the vehicle performance and the tyre grip of the day. The stiffness of the springs *across* their direction of movement was enough to locate early axles sideways and prevent them moving in unwanted directions, while the friction between the multiple leaves as the spring flexed up and down provided sufficient damping to provide tolerable ride quality.

The arguable drawback was that for, perhaps, 30 years, these fortunate qualities discouraged engineers from thinking over-actively about the fundamentals of wheel location and movement. Those who did apply their minds to the problem, including, of course, those two formidable Doctors Lanchester and Porsche, together with Vincenzo Lancia, quickly realized that the proper location of any wheel is more difficult than the layman might imagine, given the need for the wheel to be able to move vertically relative to the body so as to allow the spring to absorb bump-shocks.

It is easy enough to drive a nail through the centre of a toy wheel into the corner of a wooden box: the wheel is free to roll, yet (as long as the nail fits tightly enough) it is kept both upright and pointing straight ahead. The moment you place the wheel at the end of some kind of linkage containing a spring, it all becomes much more difficult. That was the worry, and the starting point, for the engineers who slowly developed motor car suspension away from its horse-cart beginnings.

Forgetting for a moment about the need to make the front wheels steer – which raises the complication to yet another level – the chassis designer looks at two tasks in isolation: first the need to keep each wheel (more or less) upright as the body rolls in cornering or bounces up and down on a rough surface, and second, the need to keep it pointing straight ahead. Unfortunately, systems which are good at doing one of these things are often bad at the second – and systems which are good at both often have other disadvantages (like taking up too much space inside the car and/or costing too much).

I implied, when discussing the pressures on chassis designers, that, like most engineers, they are influenced to avoid unexpected problems by retaining and developing the systems they know best. It is a rare chassis man who cannot look at a car suspension he designed two or three years ago without pointing to details he now knows how to improve.

Yet the fundamental changes do take place from time to time. Were it not so, we would still be riding about in those rear-driven cars with a 'live' rear axle and a 'dead' front axle, with multi-leaf springs providing both axle location, and damping by way of inter-leaf friction. We laugh at the idea now, but that kind of chassis was common enough in British cars until the mid-1930s and could still be found (though with separate and better dampers)

until the 1940s.

Chassis engineering milestones

The fundamental changes in chassis design, each leading to an improvement in the handling and roadholding of ordinary production cars, are surprisingly few, even if one takes the widest possible view. So many things in car design have their effect on the chassis. The switch from a chassis frame to a stressed-box body was important, for instance. A separate chassis was inevitably flexible unless it was made absurdly heavy and bulky, but unitary body construction meant far greater stiffness and a more trustworthy relationship between the various suspension attachment points. It was also important because the car designer was no longer constrained to attach his springs directly to the chassis side-members, to which the multi-leaf spring so readily fitted.

If the adoption of a much more nearly rigid body was one of the major changes which had a profound effect on chassis engineering, then changes in tyre technology were another. The first major tyre development of the 20th century threw the ride comfort aspect of chassis design into sharper focus. Today one needs a long memory, or a look back at contemporary motoring magazines, to realize that during the 1920s a ferocious argument raged about the merits of low-pressure 'balloon' tyres compared with the then-conventional high-pressure type. Those who favoured the high-pressure tyre pointed to lighter steering and superior puncture resistance (still a major consideration in the 1920s) but in the end, the low-pressure tyre won the day. It is easy enough to appreciate now that the real merit of the low-pressure tyre was not so much its superior ride, but its contribution to roadholding by putting more rubber on to the road surface. At the time, though, it was the search for ride comfort which seems to have been the deciding factor.

The ride advantage came about mainly because the low-pressure tyre formed a much more effective secondary spring between the wheel and the road surface, and this softened the total spring rate without interfering with the movement of the wheel itself relative to the body. The end result – which again depends on mathematical proof – is that the *frequency* of the disturbance resulting from passing over a bump was reduced, in other words the up-and-down movement of the body was slower.

We shall look at the part tyres play in modern chassis engineering in a later chapter, but no brief history of the subject would be complete without reference to the radial-ply revolution. The credit for the radial falls entirely to Michelin who launched the original X in the 1940s and waited about 10 years to see it accorded the honour and respect it was due. In at least two respects, the radial transformed car steering and handling, though not without penalty, at least in its early days. It needed to be turned through a much smaller angle to develop a given amount of cornering force, and it was much less sensitive to being run at a camber angle (that is, tilted away from the truly vertical). Without the radial, it is likely that other modern chassis developments, and especially independent rear suspension, would have taken longer to appear in production cars.

Damping is another chassis design area in which major advances first began to appear in the 1920s. The need for damping had been realized much earlier – Mors fitted friction dampers to some of his cars before 1900 – but the development of the separate, purpose-designed damper was slowed by the incidental advantage of the multi-leaf spring which, as we have seen, provided a measure of built-in damping because of the friction between the leaves. This was often deliberately increased, especially as cars became faster, by binding the leaves tightly together with strong wrapping such as whipcord.

Such a situation could not last for ever. Inter-leaf damping could hardly be relied upon from an engineering point of view because its strength could not be predicted. The car owner faced the headache of wondering whether to lubricate his springs, thus reducing the friction and suffering inferior ride and handling, or leave them dry for improved damping at the expense of greater wear and annoying creaks and groans. Besides, with the arrival of suspensions which used other types of spring without inherent damping, some kind of separate damper became essential rather than merely desirable.

From the early years of the century, work had been done on the two obvious types of damper system, using mechanical or fluid friction. The mechanical systems, of which the most familiar was the Hartford multi-disc type, depended on exactly the same friction effect as occurred between spring leaves. They suffered some of the same drawbacks, by far the most notable of which was the phenomenon known to modern chassis engineers as 'stiction': the need to apply a certain 'break-out' force to get the damper moving in the first place. All cars which depend on friction damping exhibit an underlying ride harshness caused by the initial friction effectively stiffening the springs before there is enough force to start the rubbing surfaces sliding past one another.

This drawback is much less evident in the hydraulic damper which generates its friction by forcing fluid through a series of small holes or orifices. This system also has the considerable advantage that the faster you try to force fluid through the holes, the greater the resistance to movement. Thus unlike the mechanical friction damper, the hydraulic type naturally damps rapid movement much more quickly than slow movement. By the mid-1920s this principle was being employed in the Houdaille damper, the first widely used hydraulic type in which a vane attached to the operating arm rotated in a chamber of fluid. Lever-arm type hydraulic dampers of various kinds remained in use into the 1980s, most notably in some BMC cars including the Minor, Marina/Ital and MG sports cars. By that time, however, the telescopic damper had long been the preferred type.

Like most of the better things in motoring life, the telescopic damper had been thought of around the turn of the century, but took a long time to grow into the familiar modern type. Its development was certainly encouraged, though, by the emergence of independent front suspension. When Lancia adopted sliding-pillar IFS for the Lambda, for instance, his own ingenious form of telescopic damper was an integral part of the system.

The mention of Lancia and his Lambda brings us directly to another major part of the chassis engineering story – the move away from rigid axles to independent suspension systems. The appeal of the rigid axle to the early chassis designer was simplicity and familiarity. It was a system which had the benefit of literally hundreds of years of practical experience, though in truth any visit to a good transport museum should convince anyone that decent vehicle suspension systems – proper axles properly sprung – were very much products of the 19th century. Horseless or not, the carriage of the 1890s was a far safer and more comfortable device than that of the 1820s.

The rigid axle has both advantages and drawbacks. Apart from simplicity, it is an excellent way of ensuring that the wheels at each end remain upright and (except when the front wheels are steered) parallel to one another. This is a virtue not to be lightly dis-

carded, which is why the axle still finds its place in today's chassis designs, albeit in very sophisticated form. However, the axle also suffers two snags. In the first place, it is heavy. We have already seen the importance of minimum unsprung weight, yet, when a pair of wheels is attached to an axle, the axle shaft, as well as the wheels, is unsprung. Second, the faithful connection of the two wheels means that whatever happens to the first wheel is to some extent transmitted to the other, and this leads to some daunting problems, especially at the front end of the car.

The root of the trouble is that, as I have already pointed out, a rotating wheel is also a gyroscope. Like any gyroscope, it precesses: that is, if you rotate it about an axis at an angle to its spindle, it will try to move off in a

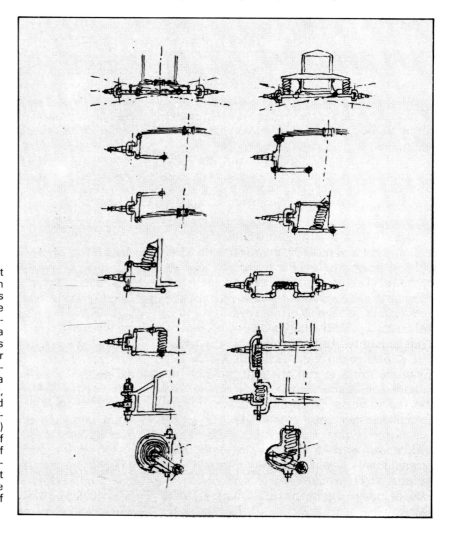

2:3. One of the most fascinating documents in the history of chassis design is this page from the notebook of Vincenzo Lancia's draughtsman, Battista Falchetto, showing no less than 14 possible layouts for independent front suspension. In the event Lancia chose the sliding pillar (left, first from bottom) and rejected both the swing-axle arrangements (top) and the various forms of double wishbone, some of which have ingenious inboard springs. Note that three of the layouts make use of a transverse leaf spring.

straight line in another direction (and, indeed, *vice versa*). Now, if you are bowling along in a car with a rigid front axle and one of the front wheels is pushed upwards by a bump, precession will also try to turn it. This force can be resisted by various means but the presence of the axle also means that when one wheel is lifted by a bump, the axle itself is tilted and so are both wheels. It is then all too easy to arrive in a situation where the combination of gyroscopic forces in the two wheels, plus the forces trying to resist unwanted steering movement, result in a 'resonance' – a vibration which, instead of being damped, actually increases as the turning wheels feed further energy into the system.

This phenomenon led to the dreaded wheel-wobble which increasingly afflicted cars with rigid front axles during the 1920s and 1930s. It has been analyzed mathematically by practical chassis engineers like Maurice Olley and Donald Bastow, who pointed out that the mechanics of the system made it easier to 'drive out' of wheel-wobble, once it had started, by accelerating rather than slowing down. The accuracy of this diagnosis will be vouched for by prewar Austin Seven drivers, among others!

There was a strong incentive, therefore, for designers to do away with the rigid front axle in favour of independent front suspension so as to break up the mechanical linkage which caused wheel-wobble. The search began for linkages which would keep wheels (more or less) upright and pointing in (more or less) the right direction whatever the motion of the car. There had been some extremely strange, but very early essays into independent front suspension on what seems to have been an empirical basis; the 1895 Knight, for example, used what amounted to twin spring bicycle forks. But it needed an engineer with a tidy but inventive mind to run through most of the obvious possibilities, which was exactly what Vincenzo Lancia did in 1921. His surviving sketchbook shows no less than 14 possible variations, including both swing-axles and double wishbones with a variety of springing arrangements, even including inboard coil springs which would seem very familiar to some of today's top racing car designers. However, Lancia, being a purist, opted for the sixth of his variations which was one of the three sliding-pillar arrangements he had sketched (in fairness, it should be added that Morgan had been using sliding-pillar geometry at the front end of its three-wheelers since before the First World War).

The sliding-pillar system appealed to Lancia because the pillar itself defined exactly the path along which the centre of the front wheel could travel. There was no question then of the wheel assuming awkward angles and having unanticipated effects on the steering. Against that, the system ensured that the front wheels rolled at the same angle as the body, which was not necessarily a good thing; also it called for a substantial cross-frame to which the pillars were attached, in order to collect all the suspension stresses and feed them into the body. Lancia felt he could live with this, but others sought systems which transferred the same stresses directly through the linkages locating the wheels. A flood of inventiveness through the 1930s gave rise to some peculiar systems long since discarded, and the designer's choice now rests essentially between two systems, double wishbones and the MacPherson strut, which we shall look at in more detail in later chapters. The significant point to make at this stage is that the move from a rigid front axle to independent front suspension was one of the major turning points in the overall development of chassis engineering.

While the advantages of independent front suspension were obvious, independent rear suspension took far longer to happen. This was not really because the advantages of adopting it were any less obvious, but rather because of the problems of taking the power to independently suspended wheels – bearing in mind that apart from a few maverick designs, the cars of the 1920s were universally rear-driven.

In fact, the argument in favour of independent rear suspension was a strong one. The extra unsprung mass added by a live rear axle, a massive tube with a hefty final-drive unit at its centre, was far more than that of any front axle, with a correspondingly adverse effect on ride comfort. It was simply that the difficulty of articulating the drive-shafts to follow the movements of independently suspended

2:4. The Renault 8 of the early 1960s was one of many rear-engined cars which used simple swing-axle rear suspension. The drive shafts themselves, hinged only at their inboard ends, carried the wheels which therefore had to assume the same camber angle as the shaft. The only other suspension members are the long radius-arms locating the wheels fore and aft. As a layout, the swing axle is simple, has low unsprung weight and a high roll centre. Unfortunately, it also leads to major handling problems in some circumstances. Note the crude check-straps intended to prevent the drive shafts drooping *too* far!

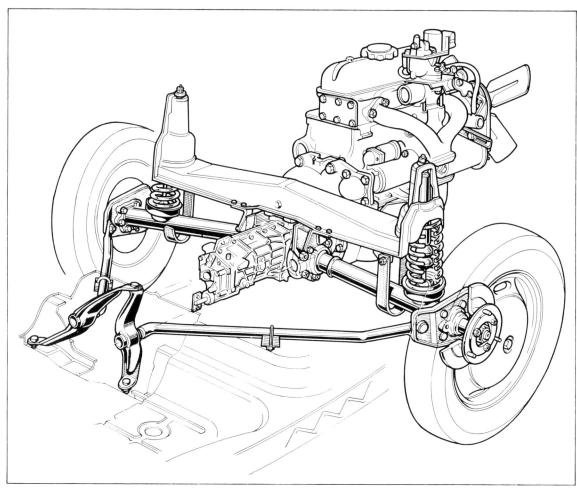

wheels looked so frightening. Nor was it simply a matter of carrying the drive round corners, so to speak. Most of the obvious linkages also involved changing the length of the drive-shafts at some point. Besides, designers could argue, the problem of wheel-wobble, which had so encouraged the adoption of independent front suspension, did not apply at the rear of the car.

This was something of a counsel of despair, and not all designers accepted it. Rumpler and then Porsche developed systems in which the drive-shafts were simply articulated immediately outboard of the final-drive housing, and carried directly to the rear wheels — the classic swing-axle layout. In this connection one uses the word 'classic' in the sense of pure, simple, but obsolete: it eventually became clear that the swing axle posed problems of its own so far as car handling was concerned. Other forms of independent rear suspension have since been developed which are more complicated, but less drastic in their effect on handling — especially in extreme situations.

In a sense, that is the short, short story of chassis engineering development. The universal adoption of independent front suspension; the widespread adoption of independent rear suspension, or (as we shall see) of ingenious nearly-independent equivalents; the arrival of independent damping systems; and the continuous developments in tyres have been the background stories to the entire picture. Many of the other developments which have taken place can be seen to fit into this general background. Front-wheel drive, for example, made no difference to the need for independent front suspension: it merely meant that designers *had* to overcome the problems of power transmission, for which they were compensated by a new-found freedom to develop independent rear suspension with relatively few problems. Developments like Citroen's hydropneumatic suspension merely (if that is the word) extend the principles of all-independent suspension and hydraulic damping, though with a new approach to springing — and the choice of springing medium is something we shall consider in detail in a later chapter.

If all this makes it seem that chassis design has become an essentially simple art, do not be misled. This is the fundamental point beyond which things become steadily more complicated. Thus far, we have done no more than define what a chassis and a suspension system are, and what we are trying to achieve when we design them. Considered in more detail, the choices and techniques available to the modern designer are as varied as they are powerful.

Chapter three

Definitions

A car's suspension system consists of four linkages, four springs and four dampers – one of each for the wheel at each corner of the vehicle. Even that is a simplification because, for example, there are ways in which two wheels may share a single spring, just as there are systems which use two springs or two dampers per wheel.

We have already looked, in the previous chapter, at the fundamental laws of spring operation and the reason why the chassis designer's choice of spring rate (or stiffness) is constrained by the need to achieve at least acceptable ride comfort. We now need to look in more detail at the other aspects of suspension design and especially at the question of linkages.

For many years it was assumed that the ideal suspension system was one which kept all four wheels of its car perfectly upright on the road surface and (steering apart) pointing perfectly fore and aft in all circumstances. In practice, no suspension system in current production achieves this, but in any case, designers are no longer by any means sure that it would be the ideal.

In practice, then, the wheels *are* allowed to tilt – to change their camber angle – and to diverge from the straight-ahead (to toe-in or toe-out); strictly speaking, they cannot be prevented from doing so with practical suspension systems. The different ways and different extents to which suspension systems allow wheels to move other than directly up and down is one of the main reasons why different cars handle in different ways. This ability to influence handling through accepting and exploiting the wheels' movements out of line is the main reason why the pure approach to suspension design is now well out of date. Instead, chassis engineers control the way in which the wheels move (the *geometry* of the suspension) as a convenient way of compensating for the other important influences on a car's behaviour, such as its static balance and its aerodynamic properties.

Like all mechanical designers, chassis engineers have developed standard names and definitions for the things that matter most to them – a kind of verbal shorthand to make discussions quicker and easier.

The starting place for this kind of exercise is the overall shape and mass of the car. The principal dimensions of interest to the chassis engineer, apart from the *wheelbase* (the fore-and-aft distance between the wheel centres) and the front and rear tracks (the side-to-side distance between the front and rear wheels, are the position of the car's centre of gravity and the height of its front and rear *roll centres*. He is also obviously concerned with the car's *static balance* – the way in which the weight is distributed among the tyres when the vehicle is at a standstill.

Forces through the centre of gravity

One of the things too little appreciated by any but chassis designers is that there is no direct relationship between the force (more strictly speaking, the moment) which makes a car's

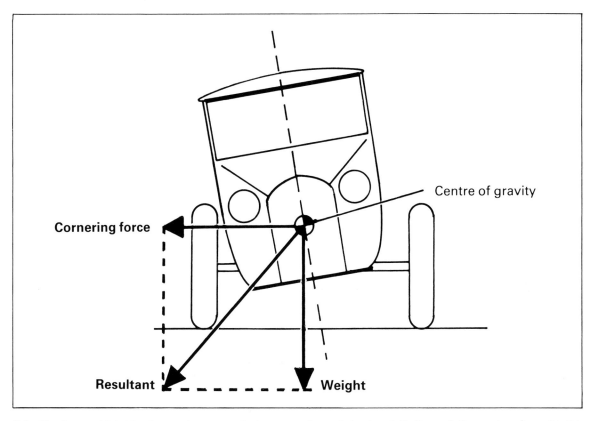

Centre of gravity

Cornering force

Resultant

Weight

3:1. The force which tries to overturn a car during cornering acts horizontally through the centre of gravity. It is opposed by the weight of the car which tries to keep it upright. When the resultant of these two forces meets the ground *outside* the wheel track, the car will begin to overturn.

Note: 1) Body roll moves centre of gravity outwards, increasing overturning risk. 2) Even 'upright' vintage cars, as here, can corner very hard without risk of overturning . . . but 3) Beware those independent suspension layouts which try to lift the body and move it outwards!

body roll, and that which tries to overturn it. The overturning moment is easiest to understand – since the centre of gravity is above the road surface, then whenever a car is cornering and its tyres are exerting a sideways force at ground level, the overturning moment is the sideways force multiplied by the height of the centre of gravity. Should this moment become large enough to exceed the one which opposes it (in simple terms, the weight of the car multiplied by half the wheel track) then the car will lift its inside wheels and, in the absence of very rapid corrective action by the driver, will flip over *(fig 3:1)*. Since the height of the centre of gravity is usually much less than half the wheel track, once the movement starts there is a tendency for the overturning moment to grow while the 'righting' moment shrinks.

The force which makes the body roll is less obvious than it may seem, and we shall discuss it in more detail a little later. It is important to appreciate that a car which rolls a great deal may actually be very difficult to overturn (like the Citroen 2CV) while one whose body rolls very little may actually be liable to overturn more readily.

In short, there is no direct link between body roll and the risk of overturning, although some factors, like a wide wheel track and a low centre of gravity, will tend to reduce both. It is also important to understand that both the overturning moment and the body rolling moment have an effect on handling. The overturning moment transfers weight from the inner to the outer wheels when the car is cornering *(fig 3:2)*; the body roll angle which results from the rolling moment deforms the

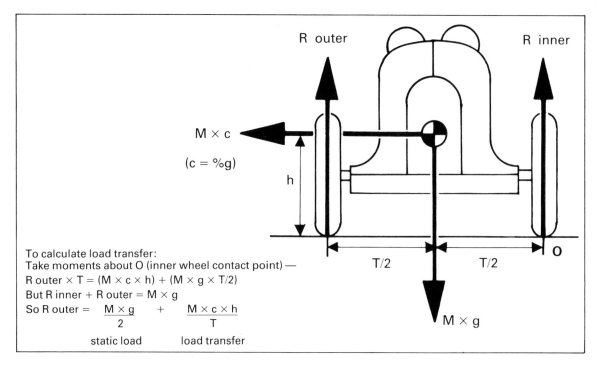

R outer
R inner

M × c

(c = %g)

h

To calculate load transfer:
Take moments about O (inner wheel contact point) —
R outer × T = (M × c × h) + (M × g × T/2)
But R inner + R outer = M × g
So R outer = $\dfrac{M \times g}{2}$ + $\dfrac{M \times c \times h}{T}$

static load   load transfer

T/2   T/2   O

M × g

3:2. The mathematics of load transfer in cornering. The overturning force acting horizontally through the centre of gravity also has the effect of transferring load from the inner to the outer wheels in the turn. In the extreme case, just before overturning takes place, the outer wheels are carrying all the car's weight while the inner wheels carry none.

suspension linkages and causes the wheels to move in a particular way.

It is as well to note at this stage that the simple concept of a centre of gravity through which the whole mass of the car can be considered to act is not always enough to explain a car's behaviour. When we start looking at *transient* car behaviour – what it does when it is turning into a corner, or straightening up again, or half-way through an S-bend – we actually need to split the mass into two 'centres of gravity' in line with the front and rear wheels, to form a dumb-bell as it were with the original centre of gravity somewhere along its length; but we can cross that bridge when we come to it.

To begin with, we usually assume for the sake of simplicity that the centre of gravity lies on the centre-line of the vehicle though we should note, for instance, that in the case of a small saloon car occupied only by a large driver, it certainly doesn't. Neglecting that complication for the time being, the position of the centre of gravity can be defined as so far aft along the wheelbase from the front 'axle'

(front axles being notable for their absence these days, the line between the front wheel centres must suffice) and so far above the ground. Chassis engineers usually consider the wheelbase as two sections, of lengths **a** and **b**, fore and aft of the centre of gravity, and assign a value **h** to its height from the ground.

Sticking for the moment with the simple centre of gravity, it is evident that when a car is cornering, a sideways force (giving rise to the overturning moment) is applied through it proportional to the rate at which the car is being turned. This force has to be opposed by sideways forces generated by the tyres. It is worth an early thought about the size of force involved. If you drive at 20mph round a roundabout of 100ft radius (which means over 60 yards across, so it is a fair-sized roundabout), the sideways force on a 1-ton car is almost exactly 600 pounds. This is for a *lateral acceleration*, created by the fact of the car's cornering, of 0.27g, which is commonly enough reached by the average driver. Note in passing that stepping up the speed to 30mph increases the lateral acceleration to 0.6g, which is some way beyond the inclination of the average driver, though well within the limits of any good modern car; the sideways force then becomes 1,350 pounds.

As we have already seen, as the car circles the roundabout it is subjected to an overturning moment and a body rolling moment; the latter compresses the springs on the outside of the corner and extends those on the inside. That is clear enough. What is less obvious is just how the body rolls. Ask someone who has never thought about it, and he may guess that it rolls about its centre-line at ground level, or more likely at axle level. He would be wrong, and this is where the idea of roll centre needs to be introduced.

Roll centres, roll axis

For any particular front or rear suspension arrangement, there is a roll centre about which the body will try to roll whenever a sideways (cornering) force is applied. It will normally lie on the centre-line of the car, but its height – which depends entirely on the geometry of the suspension linkages – can vary a great deal according to the actual suspension system fitted. It may be anything from slightly above the axle line, to well below ground level.

Thus any car has one roll centre at the front and another at the rear. They may be at the same height, though this is unlikely in practice. In any case, the line joining the front and rear roll centres is called the 'roll axis', entirely logically because it is the axis about which the body rolls during cornering.

It follows that the force which causes the body to roll depends on the distance of the centre of gravity from the roll axis. The less the distance, the smaller the rolling moment. Since the roll axis is usually somewhere above ground level where it passes beneath the centre of gravity, the rolling moment is usually substantially less than the overturning moment.

One thought which immediately occurs is that it would be nice to arrange for the roll axis to pass through the centre of gravity, when no body roll at all would occur. Sadly, this is not possible in most circumstances. Practical centres of gravity are too high and practical roll axes too low to allow it. Even if that were

not the case, close examination of the idea shows that while you would gain zero roll, you would hit other drawbacks including possibly violent reaction to a single wheel passing over a bump. The lowest and fastest racing cars come close to the 'ideal', but the family car's chassis engineer is actually not against a modicum of roll because it gives him another weapon in his armoury with which to tune the chassis.

This comes about because by suitable choice of front and rear suspension systems, he can make the roll axis slope nose-down or tail-down. To appreciate the subsequent effect, we need to return to the idea of splitting the centre of gravity into a fore-and-aft dumb-bell, as already described. In a typical modern saloon car, the front and rear weights are likely to be at about the same height, even if they are of notably different size, as they certainly will be in a front-driven car. Thus if, for instance, the roll axis slopes nose-down, then the height of the front weight above the roll axis will be greater and the front end of the car will try to roll through a greater angle than the rear *(fig 3:3)*. Since the body obviously cannot roll through a greater angle at one end than the other (neglecting a tiny though inevitable degree of body twisting) then the balance must be maintained by the springs which are resisting the roll.

If the front roll centre is lower than the rear so that the roll axis slopes nose-down, the front springs find themselves opposing a much larger roll moment. However, because the body must roll through the same angle all the way along its roll axis, the outer and inner rear springs find themselves compressed and extended just as much, exerting the same anti-roll forces on the body and the same opposing forces on their respective wheels. What has happened, because the roll axis was inclined nose-down, is that the rear springs have been forced to apply more effort than the weight at their end of the car required them to. This is turn has caused more weight to be transferred from the inner to the outer tyre, with a consequent effect on the car's handling. In effect the body shell has been used as a torsion beam to transfer some of the roll-resisting load from front to rear. As we shall see, this kind of forced weight transfer causes *under-*

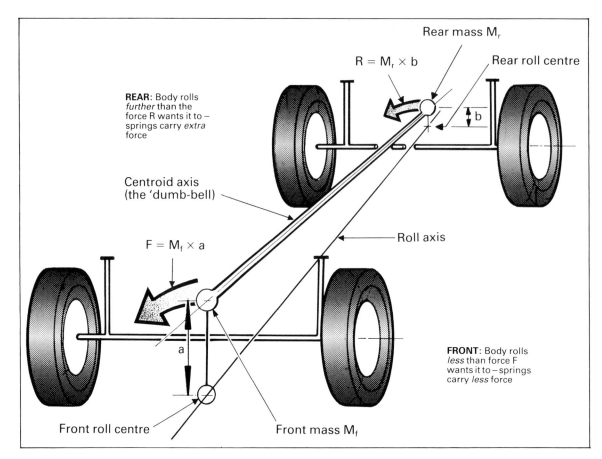

REAR: Body rolls *further* than the force R wants it to – springs carry *extra* force

Rear mass M_r

$R = M_r \times b$

Rear roll centre

b

Centroid axis (the 'dumb-bell')

$F = M_f \times a$

Roll axis

a

FRONT: Body rolls *less* than force F wants it to – springs carry *less* force

Front roll centre

Front mass M_f

3:3. Where a car's roll axis slopes down towards the nose, a greater force will be trying to roll the body at the front than at the back. Since the body can only roll through one angle — neglecting any tiny degree of twisting that takes place — balance is achieved by transferring force from front to rear.

 ∗ Greater rolling force at front — *thus*
 ∗ Body wants to roll more at front — *but*
 ∗ Body can only roll at one angle (unless it twists) — *so*
 ∗ 'Average' roll angle means less at front, more at back — *and*
 ∗ This means more inner-to-outer load transfer at back — *thus*
 ∗ Back tyres run larger slip angles — *so*
 ∗ Understeer is *reduced*.

steer when it happens at the front end and *oversteer* when it happens at the rear. Thus, inclining the roll axis nose-down reduces understeer, and *vice versa*. Exactly what we mean by understeer and oversteer is a problem we shall tackle a little later.

It is very important, when looking at the way body roll is tied up with car handling, to remember it is the body alone, or more strictly the sprung mass, which rolls. The wheels and tyres may lean over at various angles, but they do this because of the way they are attached to the body, not because they are directly influenced by the rolling force. On the

other hand, the tyres are loaded, vertically, by the spring loads caused by the rolling action of the body as well as by the car's weight.

There is a further complication before we look at the way the body resists roll and why that comfort trade-off occurs. I said that the roll axis was the axis about which the body rolled, but it would be more strictly accurate to say it is the axis about which it *starts* to roll when entering a corner. This is because with some suspension layouts, the position of the roll centre can change drastically once the suspension geometry has been altered by the action of the body rolling. This again is some-

34

thing to be looked at more closely in the next chapter; it is enough to point out for now that the effect can form a serious objection to some otherwise admirable-looking suspension systems. The last thing the chassis designer enjoys is anything which changes all his basic calculations in mid-corner.

Resisting the roll

As we all know, any normal car body rolls away from the direction of cornering, though some cars roll much more than others. In the simplest terms, the roll angle is determined by the size of the cornering force (the body mass times the lateral acceleration), the height of the centre of gravity above the roll axis, and the *roll stiffness* of the car.

The roll stiffness, which opposes the roll moment, is created by the springs and, in most modern cars, by additional *anti-roll bars*. As

we have seen, during cornering the outer springs are compressed, while the inner ones are extended; together they create a moment which tries to pull the body upright. The size of the roll stiffness obviously depends on the stiffness of the springs themselves, and their distance from the centre-line of the car *(fig 3:4)*. We can now begin to see why some cars roll less than others. The stiffer the springs, and the more widely spaced they are, the less the roll angle will be – but this has little to do with the overturning moment.

It would not be true to say that it has nothing to do with the overturning moment because as the body rolls, it carries the centre of gravity with it to some extent. In any car which rolls significantly, the centre of gravity will be carried outwards which will reduce the 'righting' moment and make overturning rather easier; the centre of gravity may also

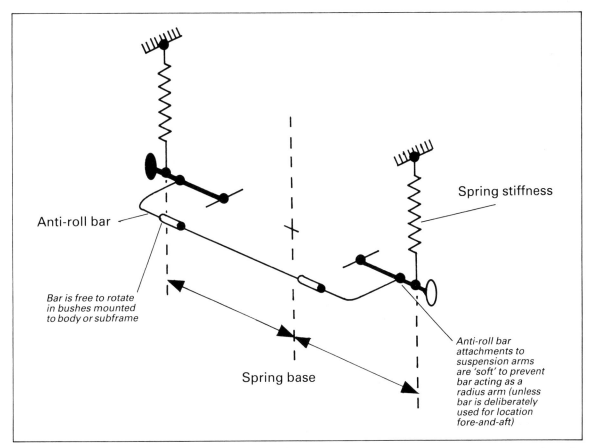

Anti-roll bar

Bar is free to rotate in bushes mounted to body or subframe

Spring base

Spring stiffness

Anti-roll bar attachments to suspension arms are 'soft' to prevent bar acting as a radius arm (unless bar is deliberately used for location fore-and-aft)

3:4. The roll stiffness of any car depends not only on the stiffness of the wheel springs and their distance from the car's centre line (the spring base), but also on the additional effect of anti-roll bars, if fitted, which oppose roll without influencing the wheel spring rate.

rise and actually increase the overturning moment. In any case it is clear that quite apart from considerations of passenger comfort, body roll should be discouraged in so far as it can be without upsetting the ride or handling.

The stiffer the springs, and the further they are away from the car's centre-line, the greater the roll stiffness will be. There are obvious limits to how widely spread the springs may be, with the result that greater spring stiffness is the engineer's first weapon when it comes to making his car stiffer in roll. There is a snag, however. The stiffer the springs, the higher the ride frequency will be: if they are made very stiff, the frequency will be much higher than our ideal 1.5 cycles per second and the ride will become 'joggly' and harsh.

The alternative solution is the anti-roll bar. This is a spring so arranged as to resist body roll while not affecting the basic spring rate of the suspension. It takes the form of a torsion bar which runs between the two sides of the front or rear suspension. When both wheels move up or down together, as over a bump or hollow, the ends of the anti-roll bar also move together without resisting the movement. When the body rolls, however, one end of the anti-roll bar moves up and the other moves down. Now the bar is twisted, and opposes the body's rolling movement.

Anti-roll bars have become increasingly common on modern cars. Their main advantage is that they enable the designer to choose softer springs for the suspension for a more comfortable straight-line ride, without allowing the body to roll so much. They have one other advantage, but also drawbacks. The second advantage is that, as we shall see, a car's handling can be adjusted by fitting an anti-roll bar to one end of the car only, or by fitting bars of different stiffness front and rear. This is another useful weapon in the designer's armoury of techniques with which to adjust the handling, along with his ability to incline the roll axis.

An anti-roll bar has two disadvantages. The first is that in resisting body roll, it tries instead to roll the suspension to which it is attached. Since the suspension cannot roll except by lifting one wheel off the ground, the practical effect is that the anti-roll bar lifts some of the load off the tyre on the inside of the corner and transfers it to the outer tyre which is, of course, already the more heavily loaded. This can have serious implications for both handling and traction in some circumstances, and we shall look at these when we consider the whole question of tyres later in the book.

The second disadvantage is a more subtle one. When a wheel at one end of an anti-roll bar runs over a bump, the bar's reaction is to create roll rather than resisting it: all it knows is that its wheels are not level, but ought to be. The result can be a rather unpleasant sideways jerking motion felt worst at head level. For this reason, there is a practical limit to the stiffness of an anti-roll bar which can be used. Few chassis designers seek to increase their roll stiffness by more than about 50% through their use.

Roll damping

Just as the car needs vertical damping for a good ride, so its rolling movement into and out of corners needs to be damped. The four suspension dampers fulfil this function quite naturally, since the rolling action of the body compresses the outer ones and extends those on the inside of the bend. However, dampers which are chosen for the best results in a straight line are not necessarily best suited to damping the roll movement. To some extent (within his space limitations) the chassis engineer can tune his roll damping by fitting the dampers at the right distance from the car's centre-line: from the point of view of the straight-line ride, this distance is less critical.

Roll damping need not be the same at both ends of the car, and it is therefore yet another of the engineer's techniques for adjusting car handling, though its effect is more subtle and complicated. While the anti-roll bars have an effect whenever the body is rolled to an angle, as it is whenever the car is cornering, roll damping is effective only in the transient condition when the body is actually rolling to or from that angle - in other words, when the car is turning into the corner or straightening up from it. It will obviously have an effect on the way a car feels during these critical phases if the rolling motion of one end of the car is less powerfully damped than the other.

It has to be said, though, that there are

plenty of modern cars in which the roll damping seems to be deficient, leading to the feeling that the car 'rolls first and corners afterwards'. It is, for example, one of the less endearing features of the big, hydropneumatically suspended Citroens, in which the designer's scope for adjusting spring and damper rates in roll as well as vertically is limited by the fact that the springs and dampers are one and the same component. Despite this drawback, no chassis engineer has yet gone to the trouble and expense (in a production car) of fitting a horizontal damper specifically to control roll movement without affecting the vertical damping effect – the damping equivalent of the anti-roll bar, in fact.

Pitch movements

A car body can move in three senses relative to its wheels. It can move up and down at any time; it rolls in cornering; and it can *pitch*, nose or tail-down. A pitch movement may occur because a bump has lifted one end or other of the car, or it may be that strong acceleration tries to make the tail dip, or that hard braking causes nose-dive. Pitch movements are important because they have a great influence on overall ride comfort; many of the world's weaker-stomached car passengers insist that large pitch movements are the most upsetting of all. Physiologists may argue whether it is the movement or the actual acceleration or braking force which is truly responsible, but in recent years car designers have taken an increasing interest in suspension layouts which reduce such pitch movements. I can only suggest from many years' personal experience of brake testing that cars which nose-dive heavily under braking appear to be more upsetting than those which remain on a more even keel!

There is a danger, if sufficient care is not taken in suspension design and particularly the choice of spring rates, that the pitching movement caused by bumps can be severe and uncomfortable. This will happen if the front and rear spring rates are badly matched, and it means the designer suffers yet another constraint on his freedom of choice.

The car's *pitch rate* depends on its *moment of inertia*, its wheelbase and its spring rates. The picture is more complicated than that for simple vertical motion because we have to look at the effect of both the front and rear springs – it is not just their rate that matters, but their rate multiplied by their distance from the centre of gravity. That in turn means the simple centre of gravity needs to give way to the dumb-bell picture we discussed earlier.

The dumb-bell represents the moment of inertia. The heavier the two weights, or the further apart they are, the greater the moment of inertia will be and the greater the force needed to rotate the car at a given rate. Note that we need to look at two moments of inertia, one in which the dumb-bell rotates about the axis across the car and through the centre of gravity, and the other about a vertical axis. The former determines pitching behaviour, while the latter, the *polar moment of inertia*, is that famous factor which is supposed to have so much to do with handling.

Where pitching is concerned, the ideal situation is to have a pitch rate which is the same as the car's vertical suspension frequency so that there is no chance of the two rates getting in and out of phase to generate large and uncomfortable movements. It can be shown mathematically that this situation is achieved for a particular ratio of the moment of inertia to the product (**a** times **b**) of the two sections of wheelbase fore and aft of the centre of gravity. In practice this ideal is not quite achieved though most modern cars come close to it. Problems arise where the moment of inertia is too small, when pitching movements on poor surfaces can be severe.

As it happens, there is usually little difference between the pitching moment of inertia and the polar moment. This means that cars with a low polar moment – that is, with as much weight as possible concentrated close to the centre of the car, as in most mid-engined sports models – can be uncomfortable on poorly surfaced roads unless their wheelbase is kept short to restore the proper ratio. It is also interesting that most modern cars are much closer to the ideal ratio than the typical prewar design, partly because designers are now aware of the problem, but also because of the way car design has evolved towards shorter wheelbases and more front and rear overhang. Getting the wheels as close as possible to the corners of the car may appear best for sta-

37

3:5. One of the many problems facing the chassis designer is that of nosedive under braking and tail squat under acceleration. In powerful cars, like the rallying Opel Manta 400 shown here, the squat effect can be very strong. In a rear-driven car like this it actually helps traction, but the situation is very different when the car is front-driven; and in both cases the unloading of the front wheels can lead to lighter steering or even a loss of front-end grip.

bility and handling, but the man whose job is to make it ride comfortably would not necessarily agree with you.

We shall look at the actual design techniques involved in resisting pitch movements due to braking and acceleration in the next chapter, but since this is the place for definitions, we need to bear in mind that *anti-dive* is mainly the function of the front suspension, while *anti-squat* geometry, if employed, is built into the rear suspension.

Compliance and noise isolation

If the modern chassis engineer was concerned only with achieving good handling in a car with spring rates that give the right kind of ride frequency, he would be a relatively happy man. Sadly, he has other worries.

When engines, transmissions and exhaust systems were noisy and harsh, few people realized how much noise and vibration was being fed into the body by the suspension. Then designs improved and the techniques of

mounting the main mechanical components became better, while at the same time wheels became smaller and tyres wider; the result was that in many cars, road noise became the loudest single source and the chassis engineer found himself under pressure to cure it.

Most of the road noise and vibration could be filtered out by mounting the suspension on large, soft rubber blocks, but that approach needs great caution. In cutting off the noise path, it is all too easy to allow the suspension so much 'flop' that its movements are no longer accurately controlled and the car's handling and stability suffer in consequence. Of course, suspension members *are* mounted to the body on rubber bushes wherever practicable but other, more subtle techniques have also to be employed.

There are various things the body designer can do to isolate the cabin from noise but this is not a book about body design. From the point of view of the chassis engineer, the starting point is the way in which noise and vibration are generated within the suspension.

In our simple, ideal world of suspension spring behaviour, we think about the wheel being pushed upwards by a bump, and falling again on its far side with both the body and the wheel vibrating according to their relative masses, the spring rate and the damping. In practice, things are more complicated. For a start, any real-world bump (or the far side of any real-world pothole) tries to push the wheel back as well as up. The springs, however, are there to cope with vertical, not horizontal shocks. At least, that used to be the case. Nowadays, chassis designers increasingly seek ways in which the wheels are effectively sprung against horizontal forces. Fortunately, on any normal road surface, these are far less than the vertical ones and the spring effect can be very stiff without causing discomfort. It should, however, be noted that for any given bump, a small wheel will react more sharply than a large one, vertically and horizontally, which is one reason why small cars with 10in or 12in wheels appear to ride less comfortably than larger-wheeled equivalents.

The problem for the chassis engineer in trying to provide a measure of horizontal springing is that it implies the need for horizontal wheel movement or *compliance*. The trick is to allow this in a way which will not affect the stability and handling of the car, and without

interacting with the vertical movement to cause other problems. Thus, within the last decade, designers have started looking at suspension arrangements much harder in plan view, so to speak, as well as in cross-section. Suspension designers have always asked themselves what happens to the camber angle as the body rolls and the wheels go up and down; now they have also to look at the way toe-in varies as the wheels move backwards and forwards. The penalty for trying to prevent such wheel movement is noise and harshness.

Allied to this problem, and the question of compliance, is another. Going back to our simple, ideal world of suspension behaviour, there is just one spring rate and two masses, the wheel and the body, to worry about. In reality there are several springs of different rates: the spring proper, the tyre, any rubber mounting bushes, and those parts of the suspension linkage which are not extremely rigid. The shock of the wheel hitting a bump sets the whole system vibrating like a nest of tuning forks. The designer's task is to ensure that each of the many possible vibration rates is outside the frequency range which can cause annoyance, directly physical or through noise. It should not, in theory, be a difficult task, especially in these days of computers, but in practice it takes up a good deal of development time.

39

Chapter four

Fundamental choices

As we have seen, the chassis engineer like most of his colleagues in the car design team, has to compromise all along the line. He would like to use soft, low-rate springs for the most comfortable ride, but if he chooses spring rate for the sake of ride alone he may end up with a car that seems to corner on its door handles. He would like to use a long wheel travel, but if he goes to extremes he will increase the possible roll angles still further. Besides, his colleague the body designer will only allow so much room for the wheelarches, so wheel travel towards full bump is restricted whatever happens.

The chassis man would also like to use a suspension system which makes the handling as safe and predictable as possible, but again he has to compromise. His ideal suspension system from the handling point of view may add too much to the unsprung weight for good ride comfort, or take up too much room within the body shell, or feed stresses into the body at awkward places, or simply cost too much. So the chassis engineer works through the practical choices available to him and chooses on the basis of their contribution to his compromise.

The first choice which confronts the engineer is whether to use independent suspension or an axle. There is really no choice at the front of the car: independent front suspension is universal, except on some four-wheel drive, off-road vehicles (like the Range Rover) where a rigid front axle has the advantage of keeping the front differential well clear of the

ground when the front springs are compressed. Otherwise, the choice is a different one: what kind of independent front suspension to use?

At the rear of the car, it is another matter. Here, the virtue of the axle in keeping its wheels parallel and more or less upright at all times has a definite appeal, the more so because this happy situation is difficult to achieve with any kind of independent suspension. If the car is rear-wheel driven, the axle has the further advantage of simplifying the drive arrangements. There is the further advantage that with any kind of axle, the roll centre is quite high, at or about the centre point of the axle, and it remains in the same place all the time; the designer is spared the anxieties of the 'roll centre migration' we mentioned in the previous chapter. These advantages have to be weighed against the axle's disadvantage, especially if it is a live axle including the final-drive unit, of giving a very high unsprung weight which can upset the ride.

If the car is front-driven, the designer can use a dead axle, in other words a simple tube joining the wheel hubs. The tube should be light enough to keep the unsprung weight well down, leaving the engineering advantages without the major disadvantage. This is why some front-driven cars with good reputations for handling, like the classic little Lancia Fulvia, the Alfa Romeo Alfasud/Sprint/33 and all the Saabs, use a dead rear axle in preference to independent rear suspension. The tube does not have to be straight, of course – it can be bent round the fuel tank or below the boot floor, as long as it is stiff enough.

There are, however, plenty of front-driven cars, as well as rear-driven ones, that use independent rear suspension. Their designers have looked at the options and decided that while the dead rear axle has the merit of simplicity, they can still save unsprung weight – and precious boot space as well – by adopting some form of independent suspension.

The axle, live or dead, may appear to make life simple for the chassis engineer, but in practice its location needs great care. It may keep its wheels parallel, but keeping them pointed exactly fore and aft is much more difficult.

Front suspension
Two or three decades ago, there were several possible choices of front suspension layout; now there are only two – double wishbones

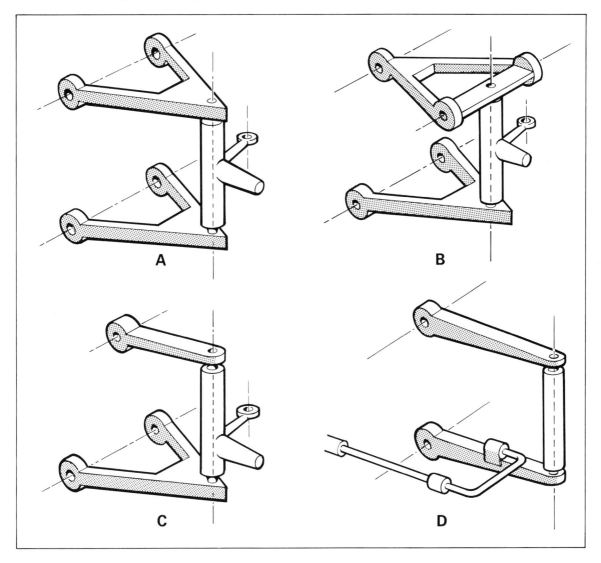

4:1. Double-wishbone suspension can take several forms. The classic arrangement which gives the system its name (A) has two links with their forked ends attached to the car; a subtle variation (B) reverses one of the links to give more positive hub location. Money, space and weight can be saved by turning one link into a simple transverse member and making the other do all the fore and aft location work (C), and even this may be simplified by leaving fore and aft location to a separate radius rod or the trailing ends of an anti-roll bar (D).

and the MacPherson strut. The twin trailing links of the Volkswagen Beetle have been discarded, likewise the single leading arm of the Citroen 2CV and the swing-axle of the Hillman Imp. For the front end of the car, the choice is simple – or is it?

If one of the two systems had a genuine advantage over the other, there would be no choice at all. In fact each one has its firm supporters and always, it seems, for the best of reasons. Some design teams, notably Ford's, have in recent history swung between one and the other – MacPherson struts on the earliest Cortinas, double wishbones from the Cortina Mk3 onwards, then back to MacPherson for the Sierra, for instance. We obviously need to look very carefully at these two competing systems, bearing in mind that they are both candidates for rear suspension use also.

Double wishbones

The 'classic' independent suspension is the double wishbone. The wheel hub carrier is attached to the structure by means of two forked transverse arms, which are free to rotate in the vertical plane.

The name 'wishbone' can be misleading. The classic picture *(fig 4:1)* is indeed of two arms resembling wishbones, their forked ends attached to the body structure and their single ends jointed to the hub carrier. Thus, while allowing the wheel to move up and down, they prevent it moving (in other words they *locate* it) fore and aft by taking up any twisting stress between the mountings of the forked ends. However, there are installations in which one of the wishbones is actually reversed so that its forked end carries one of the hub carrier joints - usually the upper one. This makes for a very strong, solid hub carrier design where stresses are expected to be high.

Designers long ago realized, especially if they were looking for ways to save money, that adequate fore-and-aft location can be achieved with just one proper wishbone, the other being a simple swinging arm. In such cases the wishbone is usually the lower member of the two. More economical still, if you are looking for ways to save money on a small car, the job of fore-and-aft location can be left to the trailing ends of the anti-roll bar, so that both the 'wishbones' can be simple swinging links.

Confining ourselves for the moment to the classic wishbone arrangement, we find that the position of the roll centre is determined by the angles which the two wishbones make with the horizontal. If we extend them until they meet, the line from their meeting point to the ground beneath the wheel crosses the car's centre-line at the roll centre. Because the designer is free, within certain practical limits, to choose the angles of his wishbones, he can set the resulting roll centre at whatever height he wishes.

The important proviso here is 'within certain practical limits'. Wishful thinking suggests that if we can choose the roll centre height, we can set it very high so that the centre of gravity lies beneath it and the car will roll into, rather than away from, the corner – banking in the 'correct' sense, as with a motorcycle or an aircraft.

In *fig 4:2* I have drawn three double-wishbone suspensions with roll centres at ground level, some way off the ground (level with the wheel end of the lower wishbone) and very high – certainly high enough to drop the centre of gravity beneath it. I have used the same-length wishbones in each case, that at the top being shorter than the bottom one – which is typical modern practice. In *fig 4:3* I have drawn the same suspensions rolled through 10 degrees – a very large roll angle by modern standards, but some exaggeration makes things clearer.

The suspension with the ground-level roll centre has kept its wheels not far from upright, which is actually what the tyre man wants to see (as we shall discover). The higher roll centre arrangement has rolled the wheel on the outside of the turn to a much larger positive camber (top outwards) angle; to be fair, for a given cornering force this suspension should not roll so much because the centre of gravity is closer to the roll centre. There is nothing here the suspension and tyre designers cannot live with.

Then there is the ultra-high roll centre. In this case we *have* to make the proviso that the roll is actually into, not away from, the corner (which is the whole purpose of the exercise). What we find is first, that the top wishbone is fighting the wheel rim for the same space

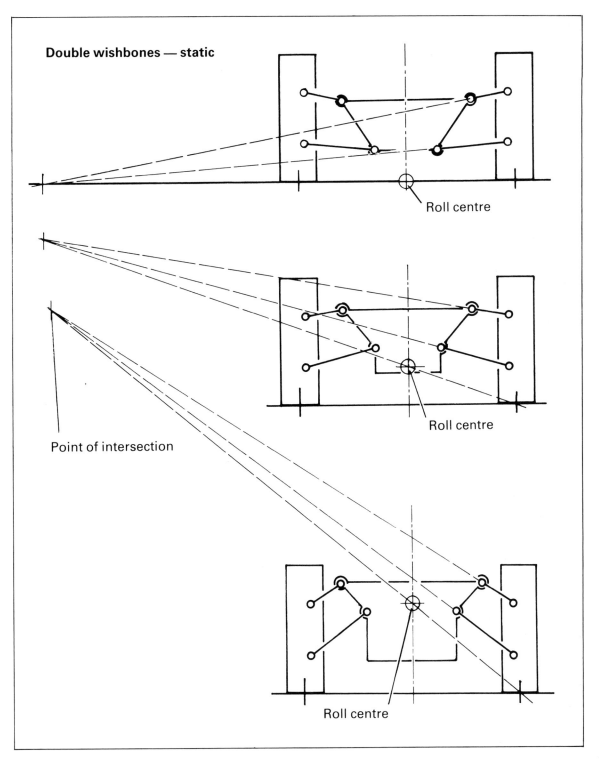

Double wishbones — static

Roll centre

Point of intersection

Roll centre

Roll centre

4:2. Double-wishbone suspension geometry. The height of the roll centre is determined by the angles of the upper and lower links: in the examples shown the roll centre is positioned at ground level (top), above ground at the height of the wheel end of the lower wishbone (centre) and high enough to be above the centre of gravity (bottom). In the last case, of course, the car rolls into the turn, motorcycle fashion, rather than away from it.

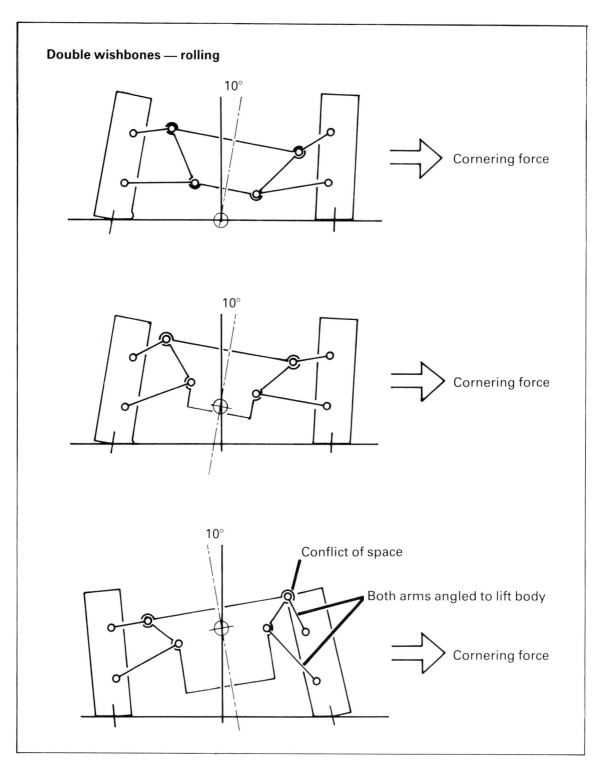

Double wishbones — rolling

10°

Cornering force

10°

Cornering force

10°

Conflict of space

Both arms angled to lift body

Cornering force

4:3. Double-wishbone suspension systems, with the same geometry as the examples in the preceding drawing, rolled through 10 degrees. The higher roll centre arrangement (centre) rolls the wheel on the outside of the turn to a greater positive camber angle than the ground-level roll centre layout. The ultra-high roll centre (bottom) produces several problems including a severe jacking effect and a conflict of space between wishbone and tyre.

Double wishbones — body rising in rebound (no roll)

Ground-level roll centre:
a) Almost no track change
b) Wishbone inclination not severe — no serious jack-up force
c) No risk of wheel/body conflict

Roll centre above ground:
a) Small amount of track narrowing
b) More severe wishbone inclination — possible jack-up force
c) Possible risk of wheel/body conflict

Roll centre very high:
a) Severe track narrowing
b) Severe wishbone inclination — serious risk of jacking/tipping
c) Severe wheel/body conflict

4:4. The same three double-wishbone layouts with no cornering force but with the suspension links drooped as the body rises in rebound: wishbone inclination, with the attendant risks of jacking and tipping, increases with the higher roll centres, as does the narrowing of the track, and the ultra-high roll centre arrangement again results in the conflict of wheel, suspension and body components trying to occupy the same space.

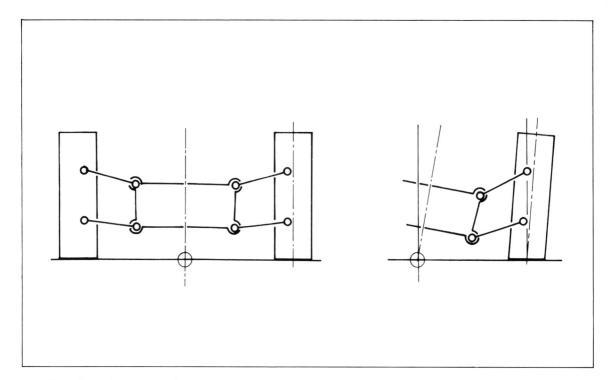

4:5. The effect of equal-length wishbones is to ensure that both wheels have positive camber when cornering, which reduces roadholding. Ideally, the heavily loaded outer wheel needs to be kept as near vertical as possible.

because the wishbones, which started off very 'droopy' anyway, have almost folded themselves against the side of the car. Second and even more frightening, although we may have the reassuring feeling of banking into the corner, the opposing sideways forces acting on the centre of gravity and the tyres are very close to tipping the whole car on its side; the steeply inclined wishbones are tending to 'jack up' the vehicle, a drawback also found in swing-axle suspension, as readers old enough to remember the Triumph Herald and the VW Beetle will surely recall. The tendency is much less strong when the roll centre is merely high, and when it is at ground level the wishbone inclination actually tries to jack the body down, if anything. The sad but inevitable conclusion is that designing a double-wishbone suspension for an ultra-high roll centre is a non-starter.

The suspicious reader might at this stage suspect I had pulled a fast one by opting for a long lower wishbone and a short upper one. In *fig 4:5*, therefore, I have drawn an arrangement with everything as before, but with equal-length wishbones (the length actually being the average of the former upper and lower ones). When this system is rolled through our standard 10 degrees it is clear that both wheels are rolled in the same direction as the body when cornering. This is not good news for the roadholding.

In *fig 4:6* I have played by the same rules, but switched the wishbones so that the upper one is long and the lower one is short. When this arrangement is rolled through 10 degrees the result looks very similar: note, too, that the long-upper-wishbone layout is much less convenient for the body designer trying to fit things in and around a sensible engine compartment. It is possible by juggling with wishbone angles to make the outside wheel adopt negative camber as the car rolls. At first sight, this may look like good news for the grip, since common sense suggests it must be better for the tyre to 'push into' the corner in this way. In fact the car tyre specialist would not agree. He would rather the tyre remained as upright as possible. It is worth remembering that modern car tyres are a very different shape from motorcycle tyres. Also before enthusing too much, you should consider

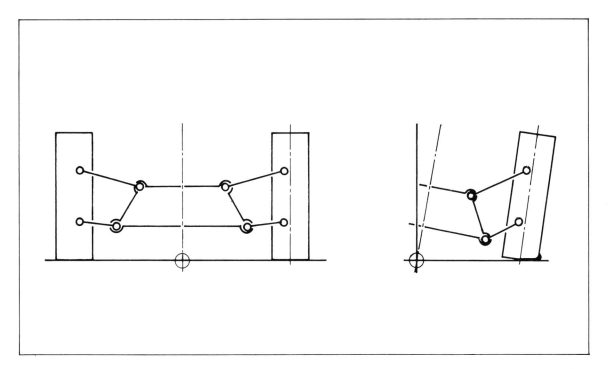

4:6. The third possible double-wishbone arrangement is that in which the upper link is longer than the lower. This does little to reduce the unfavourable camber change for the heavily loaded outer tyre and there are a number of practical disadvantages which cause chassis designers to favour the layout with a shorter upper link.

another point: how much room will you need in the top of your wheelarch for that negatively cambered outside tyre?

For all these reasons, the modern saloon car designer usually opts for a double-wishbone arrangement with a short upper link and a roll centre somewhere between ground level and the engine sump. Or, of course, he chooses the MacPherson strut; but before we move on to that, we should consider what happens to the double wishbone roll centre once the car has rolled. As we pointed out in Chapter 3, the roll centre can migrate as the suspension deforms, and this can cause problems. With double wishbones, in fact, the centre moves sideways towards the centre of the corner and it also tends to rise, which causes no serious problem.

One interesting modern double-wishbone front suspension is that used in the Honda Accord, introduced in 1985. This uses a hub carrier with a very long upward extension, taking the upper mounting point well above the top of the wheel. There must be a penalty in unsprung weight and production cost, but against that the extremely wide vertical spread of the attachment points probably per-

mits a lighter structure because they more easily resist drive and braking torques. A second interesting point in the Accord is that the upper wishbone hinge line is not parallel with the car's centre line, but is angled. This causes the top attachment point to move inwards as the wheel moves up or down, giving a mild tendency towards negative camber to offset the basic positive-camber geometry. The wheel thus remains more nearly upright more of the time.

The MacPherson strut

The MacPherson strut is the upstart newcomer to the suspension business, its first use on production cars being in Fords from the 1950s. However, it has proved outstandingly successful for a number of reasons.

The MacPherson arrangement is for the wheel hub carrier to be rigidly clamped to a near-vertical strut which, in practice, always consists of (or contains) the telescopic damper. Most often, though not always, the coil spring is wound round the strut, making the unit very compact and easily exchanged for service purposes. The lower end of the strut has to be

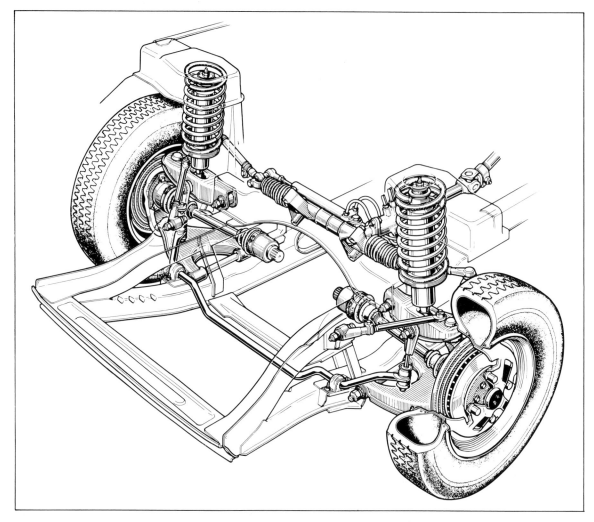

4:7. The Renault 30 provided an example of a front-driven car with double-wishbone front suspension. Note that while the lower wishbones are wide-based, the upper member has been simplified to a single transverse link. Because of the need to leave space between the wishbones for the drive shafts, the coil spring/damper assemblies act on the upper links, which makes the whole arrangement less compact. The anti-roll bar is carefully mounted to the upper suspension members, using flexible attachments so that it cannot feed in forces other than the vertical ones essential to its role.

located both across and along the car, by a single wishbone or a transverse link and the trailing end of the anti-roll bar. It is worth noting that the Chapman strut, named after Colin Chapman, shares its geometry with the MacPherson but differs, strictly speaking, in using the drive-shaft as the transverse link plus a trailing radius arm for fore-and-aft location. Chapman first used this arrangement for the rear suspension of the Lotus 12 Formula 2 racer, then for the original Lotus Elite, with great success.

Apart from its compactness, the MacPher-

son strut appeals to car designers for two reasons. First, it guarantees small changes in camber angle – these cannot exceed the angle through which the strut itself swings about its top mounting. Second, it is structurally efficient. Its three mounting points can be widely separated, especially if the anti-roll bar option is taken, and fed into the structure at convenient strongpoints. This contrasts with double wishbones whose loads are usually more concentrated and fed into side rails low in the engine compartment. It is probably fair to say the MacPherson strut has extra appeal for the

48

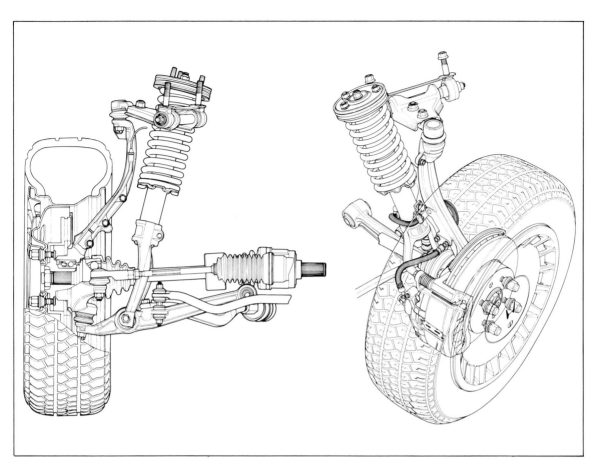

4:8. The Honda Prelude double-wishbone front suspension of the mid-1980s makes an interesting contrast with the Renault 30 of the previous decade. Here the lower 'wishbone' is formed by a transverse link and a trailing link, while the lower end of the spring/damper assembly is forked to allow the drive-shaft to pass through. A long, sweeping upward extension of the wheel hub carrier assembly is located by the small upper wishbone. Note that this upper wishbone is cunningly angled to provide a further desired input to the wheel's movement in camber. The components of the same design as utilized on the Rover 800 are shown assembled for display (left) with a second example of the long, curved hub carrier lying in the foreground.

designer when weight saving is critically important.

The MacPherson arrangement does have one drawback. Its initial roll centre is found first by discovering the point where a line through the strut's upper pivot point, at right angles to the strut itself, meets the line of the lower link. The roll centre then lies on the centre-line of the car on the line drawn from the intersection point to the centre of the tyre

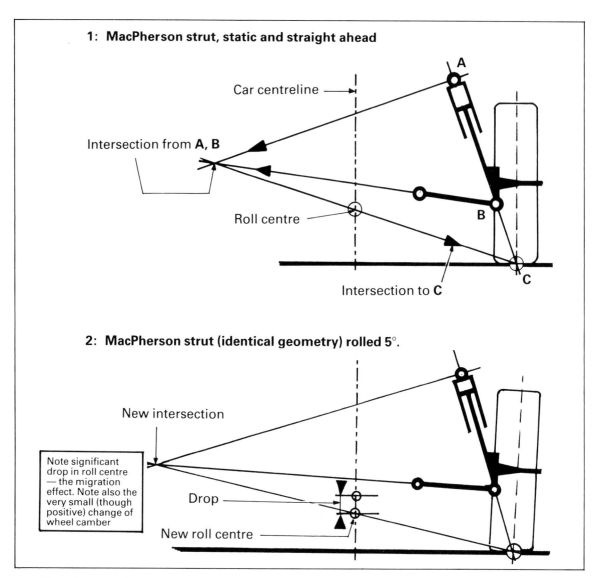

1: MacPherson strut, static and straight ahead

Car centreline →

Intersection from **A, B**

Roll centre

Intersection to **C**

A

B

C

2: MacPherson strut (identical geometry) rolled 5°.

New intersection

Note significant drop in roll centre — the migration effect. Note also the very small (though positive) change of wheel camber

Drop

New roll centre

4:9. The roll centre of the MacPherson strut suspension system is found by drawing a line from the strut's upper mounting, at right angles to the strut, to meet the line of the lower transverse link or wishbone: a line from this intersection to the tyre contact patch passes through the roll centre on the car's centreline. Note that the roll centre height can easily be adjusted by changing the angle of the lower link; also that one of the main drawbacks of the MacPherson layout is that the roll centre moves smartly downwards as the car rolls.

contact patch *(fig 4:9)*. This geometry means the height of the roll centre is quite easily adjusted by changing the angle of the lower link: making it drop towards the lower end of the strut means a high roll centre, angling it upwards makes for a low centre. This is no bad thing, in fact the ease of adjustment is another of the MacPherson's appealing points. Unfortunately, the geometry makes it almost inevitable that when the car rolls, the roll centre falls and also moves away from the outward,

heavily loaded tyre. This increases the effect of the rolling force so that in effect, the further you roll, the further you tend to roll. This certainly explains the popularity of anti-roll bars in conjunction with MacPherson-strut suspensions.

Anti-dive and squat arrangements

As we saw in Chapter 3, it is increasingly common to arrange the front and rear suspensions to resist the tendency of cars to nose-dive

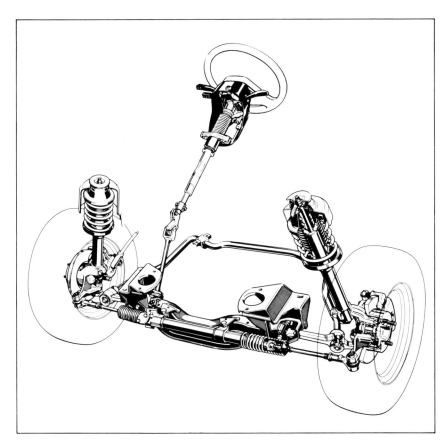

4:10. The Ford Sierra front suspension is typical of a MacPherson strut layout in which drive shafts are not involved. Fore/aft and sideways wheel location is achieved by means of a 'wishbone' consisting of a single transverse link plus the swept-forward ends of the anti-roll bar, which runs beneath the engine compartment well aft of the front axle line. The loads from each wheel are thus fed into the body through three widely separated, and fairly convenient, points.

under braking, or squat when accelerating. This is done by angling the wishbones (one or both in a double-wishbone system; the lower wishbone locating a MacPherson strut) nose-down rather than parallel to the ground. When this is done, the braking or accelerating force acts not only horizontally, to slow or speed the car, but also vertically. Under braking, the reaction of the angled wishbone tries to lift the nose, so cancelling out (or at least reducing) the nosedive. Similar arrangements at the rear tend to lift the tail in opposition to acceleration-squat.

It is important, however, not to overdo the effect, especially at the front. If the wishbone hinge lines are not horizontal, the wheel hub carrier attachments will move slightly backwards and forwards as well as vertically. The movements will not be large, but they could be enough to affect the steering in some circumstances. This apart, front suspensions with very large amounts of anti-dive are very difficult to endow with enough compliance and can react extremely sharply to bumps. Once again, the message is one of compromise.

Rear suspensions

At the beginning of the 1950s it was rare to find a British car whose rear suspension consisted of anything but a live axle carried on multi-leaf cart springs. Before we go on to look at independent rear suspensions, we should consider the non-independent type. As I mentioned earlier, the erstwhile conventional live axle/leaf spring finally died, so far as European passenger cars were concerned, with the Ford Capri, though light commercial vehicles are another matter. There was a phase, lasting a decade or so, when the manufacturers of rear-driven cars retained live axles, but sought to locate them by more sophisticated means, using multiple links and coil springs. That approach, too, has now virtually ceased with the notable exception of the bigger Volvos and (as I write) of the Capri's lingering rival the Opel Manta. Otherwise we have reached the stage where small cars are front-driven and big cars, by virtue of their market status, justify independent rear suspension. There remain, as I have pointed out, several front-driven cars which have quite deliberately retained a dead rear axle.

One of the problems with a live rear axle is that provision must be made to accept the drive torque which is being passed through it. The inexorable law of Newton tells us that just as the car turns the wheels, so the wheels try to turn the car – or at least the live axle. It has to be stopped. As it happens, leaf springs did this more or less automatically since they could wind themselves into a kind of sideways S-shape. They could in fact resist the torque while still transmitting the drive force through the front shackle to the rest of the car (it should be increasingly obvious to the reader that the leaf spring had – and has – more going for it than the derisive 'cart-springers' of the 1960s properly appreciated).

The only unfortunate result of this spring wind-up effect was that it could be unleashed if the wheel was lifted clear of the road by body torque reaction, as might happen in (for instance) a rapid standing start. Axle-tramp would then ensue, the springs alternately winding up and relaxing as the unfortunate wheel bounced up and down. The continued shock-loading could be enough to break the final-drive unit. A cunning leaf-spring 'tweak' – one applied to the Capri – was to mount the axle forward of centre on each spring. This greatly reduced the severity of the effect. An alternative was to append one or two anti-tramp trailing arms to the axle to discourage it from rotating under the torque effect. These arms had to be of suitable length (some of them were, in fact, far too short) to avoid spoiling the geometry.

When the designer wanted to retain a live axle but do away with leaf springs, he had to find some other way of doing two things. First he had to absorb the drive torque; second he had to locate the axle sideways, that other job so usefully done by the despised cart spring. To absorb the torque, he could use a combination of upper and lower trailing arms, or a simple pair of trailing arms plus a 'torque tube' attached to the nose of the final drive unit and mounted to the car body further forward. Sideways location could be achieved by angling two of the four trailing arms (usually the upper pair) inwards, either keeping them separate – as in the Hillman Avenger and

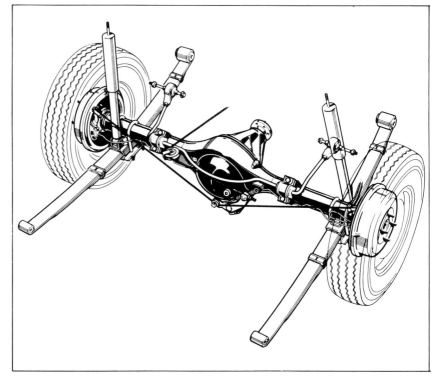

4:11. The rear suspension of the Ford Capri was the last example on a European passenger car of the once widely used combination of a live axle carried on multi-leaf springs. Its simplicity conceals a couple of subtleties, the mounting of the axle forward of the centre point of each spring and the staggering of the damper lower mountings, one forward of the axle and the other aft, both aimed at reducing the tendency to axle tramp which was one of the system's inherent weaknesses.

4:12. Without leaf springs, the job of controlling the live axle has to be taken over by suspension links. In this example, from the Ford Cortina Mk3, the combination of four trailing arms absorbs the drive torque while the angling of the upper arms enables them to provide lateral location as well.

4:13. Saab's 9000 uses a 'dead' axle at the rear, located by trailing arms and Panhard rod. The positioning of the Panhard rod relative to the axle is crucial to the car's stability. Side forces on the rear wheels are reacted in such a way as to provide an automatic handling correction to counter the original disturbance.

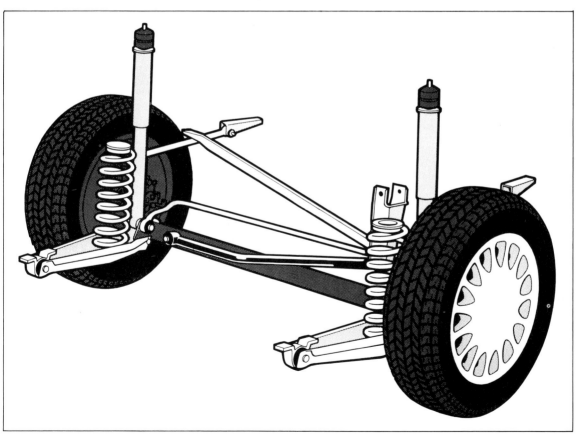

others – or joining them to form an A-arm. Alternatively, all four arms could be left trailing and a Panhard rod used to locate the axle sideways.

The Panhard rod is a long tube – the longer the better – which attaches the axle to the body in a sideways sense. Length of tube is important because, as the suspension moves up and down, the axle-end of an over-short rod moves in an arc, which shifts the axle very slightly sideways to create a rear-steering effect that becomes evident on poor surfaces. If the length of the rod is nearly the width of the track, this effect becomes negligible, a matter of a few millimetres easily absorbed by the tyres. The positioning of the rod forward, in line with or aft of the axle, is more important, as we shall see.

Now that live axles have virtually departed, the techniques of axle location remain important for the Saabs and front-driven Alfa Romeos of this world, among others. There is no drive torque to resist in a dead axle, and it is in theory sufficient to trail the axle on twin radius arms, propped on its coil springs and dampers, and located sideways by a Panhard rod. This essentially is the Saab 900/9000 system, but Alfa Romeo chooses to locate the 33/Sprint dead axle fore and aft by means of Watt linkages – a device originally devised by James Watt to ensure the perfect linear motion of steam engine parts, but one which

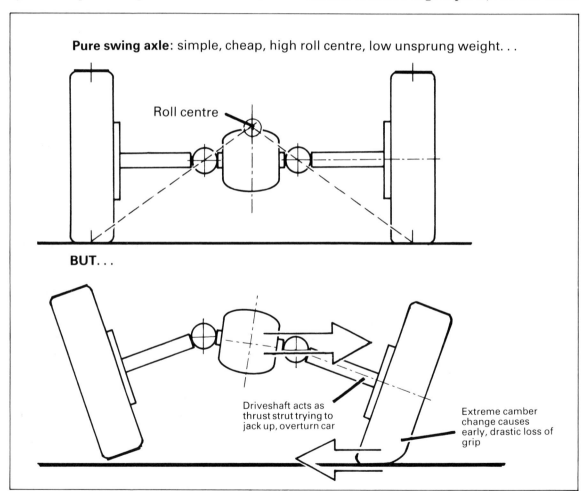

Pure swing axle: simple, cheap, high roll centre, low unsprung weight. . .

Roll centre

BUT. . .

Driveshaft acts as thrust strut trying to jack up, overturn car

Extreme camber change causes early, drastic loss of grip

4:14. The pure swing axle appeared to have many engineering advantages including simplicity, low unsprung weight and a high roll centre. Sadly, they meant little compared with the jacking up tendency encountered if the driver tried to brake and turn simultaneously. The poor straight-line stability of some rear-engined cars, though, resulted purely from the interaction of weight distribution and aerodynamic effects in crosswinds.

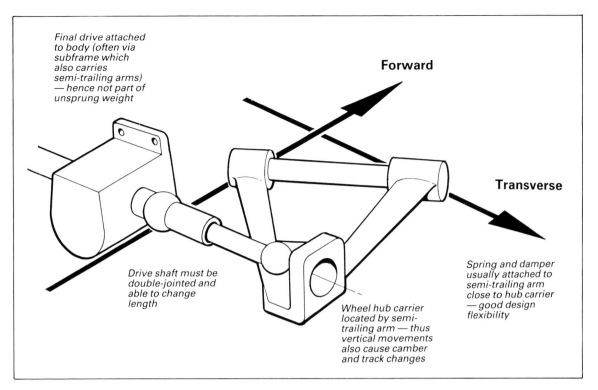

Final drive attached to body (often via subframe which also carries semi-trailing arms) — hence not part of unsprung weight

Forward

Transverse

Drive shaft must be double-jointed and able to change length

Wheel hub carrier located by semi-trailing arm — thus vertical movements also cause camber and track changes

Spring and damper usually attached to semi-trailing arm close to hub carrier — good design flexibility

4:15. Compared with the swing axle, the semi-trailing arm greatly reduces the camber and track change suffered by the wheel but does not eliminate them altogether. The layout has become very popular because it combines relative simplicity and low cost with low unsprung weight and mostly acceptable handling. It still poses problems in high-performance cars.

has proved invaluable to several chassis engineers.

Independent rear suspension

By the early 1950s, the designers of several small European cars had been forced to adopt independent rear suspension as a result of choosing a rear-engined layout. The engines and gearboxes could hardly be left to bounce up and down as part of the unsprung mass, so some kind of independent rear suspension *had* to be adopted by Volkswagen, Renault and the rest. For simplicity and low cost, the arrangement usually selected was the swing axle, whose superior ride comfort compared with the live rear axle could hardly be denied, but whose handling deficiencies were enough to give independent rear suspension something of a bad name.

In the simple swing axle *(fig 4:14)*, the wheel is attached directly to the drive shaft. This is sufficient to hold it upright, or at least at right angles to the shaft: all that remains

necessary is to fit a trailing radius arm to locate it fore-and-aft. It is beautifully simple, has a low unsprung weight and a high roll centre, all very desirable. Sadly, it also has the jacking-up tendency we discussed when looking at double wishbone suspensions with very high roll centres; you can too easily arrive at a position where the opposing cornering forces, outwards through the centre of gravity and inwards through the tyres, succeed in folding the swing axle under the car. The effect is even more devastating than in our double wishbone case because when the swing axle folds, the wheel must perforce fold with it, losing most of its grip. The effect was magnified in the old rear-engined cars because so much of the weight was concentrated where it could do most harm; Mercedes had far less trouble with swing axle rear suspension in their front-engined cars, especially after they redesigned the layout to lower the pivot point (reducing the tyre's ability to exert a folding force) and fitting a transverse spring to transfer loads

55

away from the critical area.

However, the swing axle is now a thing of the past. The modern designer has a wide selection of independent suspension layouts from which to choose, especially if he is working on a front-wheel-drive car.

The first and most obvious move was to overcome the worst deficiencies of the swing axle by articulating the wheel on its drive shaft and providing a second arm, in addition to the original trailing one, with which to locate it. The result was the semi-trailing arm *(fig 4:15)*, attached to the body at an oblique hinge line. It is an arrangement with disadvantages of its own. As it moves up and down, but especially up towards full bump, the wheel suffers track, camber and toe-out changes of

geometry which can have ill effects on the handling, even if they are far less than those of the pure swing-axle. For this reason, the mounting angle of semi-trailing arms in recent year has tended to becomeless oblique and almost fully trailing, minimizing the worst effect even at the cost of increasing the amount of plunge (change of length) which must be accommodated by the drive-shaft.

One may wonder, in the circumstances, why the semi-trailing arm has remained so popular: it is now largely adopted by BMW, Ford, Mercedes, Vauxhall/Opel and Peugeot, for example. The answer seems to be that it is relatively cheap and structurally efficient. A single wishbone-type arm at each side is enough to locate the wheel, and the arm's

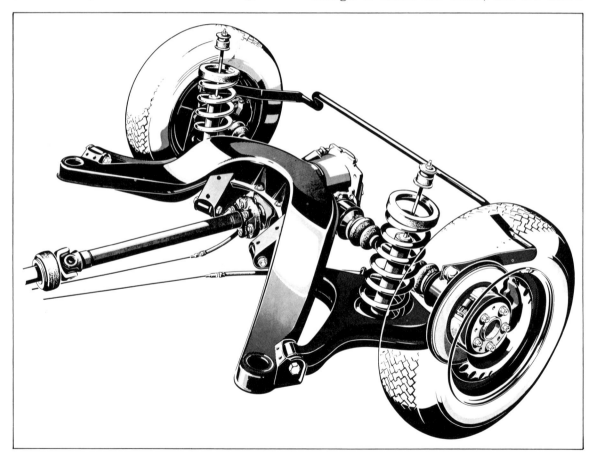

4:16. This typical semi-trailing arm layout comes from the Mercedes 350SLC and shows the way in which a yoke-shaped subframe is used to carry both the final-drive unit and the semi-trailing arm attachments. In this case there is an anti-roll bar running aft of the axle line, while the coil spring/damper unit is concentric and bears on the suspension arm forward of the drive shaft. The shaft itself must, of course, be jointed at both ends, and one of the joints must be able to accommodate small changes in length ('plunge'). The whole assembly takes up relatively little space and production engineers like it because it can be pre-assembled before being offered up to the car.

4:17. The least compromise in rear suspension geometry is achieved by the use of the double-wishbone layout, as exemplified by this assembly from the Ferrari 365 GTC4 which has twin damper units fore and aft of the hub to leave space for the drive shaft between them. Drawbacks of this arrangement which make it not the choice of the designer of mass-production cars include cost, complexity and the large intrusion into what could otherwise be boot space.

inboard mountings at least – usually all of them – can be attached to a sub-frame which also carries the final drive unit. The whole thing can then be bolted to the body at convenient strongpoints, which also afford the designer plenty of scope for achieving good noise insulation through compliance techniques. In other words, the semi-trailing arm is good for cost, for noise and for ease of assembly – not to mention a boot space largely uncluttered except for the tops of the spring/ damper turrets. For a suspension with considerable ride quality benefits and few (now largely conquered) handling defects, that is a list of strong appeal.

There are alternatives to the semi-trailing arm. Two of them are clear enough. Double wishbones and MacPherson struts work just as well at the back of the car as they do in front. Double wishbones suffer the major snag of taking up huge amounts of boot space unless they are very cleverly packaged; Jaguar showed one way in which it could be done in the E-type, using the drive shaft as the upper 'wishbone' in conjunction with a conventional lower one. This arrangement

had the extra advantage that the drive shaft could be of fixed length; one of the problems of splined, plunge-accommodating drive shafts, certainly in the late 1950s, when the E-type was being designed, was that the splines could lock up under hard acceleration, momentarily fixing the length of the shafts with disastrous effects on the handling – as many a Triumph TR4A driver discovered.

The MacPherson strut has proved popular as an independent rear suspension for front-driven cars like the Fiat 127/128 and the smaller Hondas, and in its related Chapman strut form, for some rear-driven cars. Its advantages remain those of extreme structural efficiency and the ease with which it can be fitted round a boot (just as round a front engine bay) with the minimum of intrusion. Its one arguable disadvantage is the tendency of its roll centre to migrate downwards during cornering, which is arguably more serious at the back end since, without close control, it could result in a sudden increase in rolling moment and a switch to oversteer. An interesting feature of the Fiat rear suspensions was their use of a transverse leaf spring to form an element

57

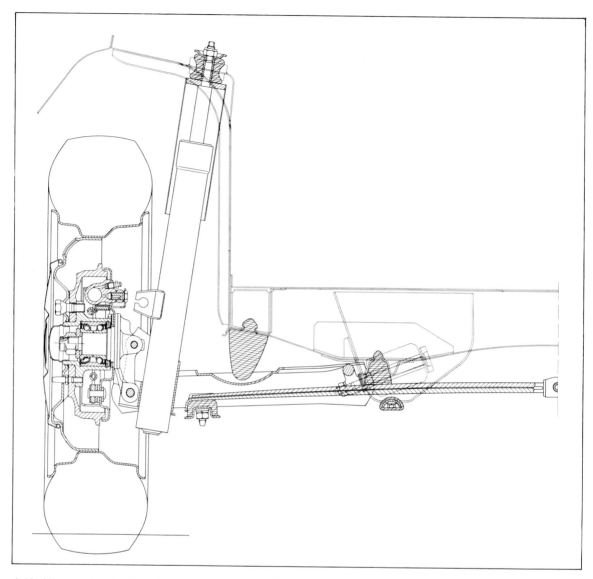

4:18. Very neat use of MacPherson strut suspension at the rear of the Fiat 127 and 128 combined it with a transverse leaf spring anchored at its ends to the pressed wishbones, resulting in a minimum of intrusion into the body. The widely-spaced, rubber-buffered mountings of the spring to the body were cleverly arranged to make it stiffer in roll than in bump compression so that it served the secondary function of anti-roll bar.

of the lower linkage, doing away with the need for the coil spring which is almost invariably wrapped round a MacPherson strut. The leaf spring also, through cunning mounting, acted as the anti-roll bar.

It is, of course, entirely possible in a front-driven car to mount the rear wheels on simple trailing arms. This was done in the Citroen 2CV for instance, as well as the Mini and the Renault 4 and 16. The advantage is simplicity and, if the springing and damping arrange-

ments are carefully thought out, very little intrusion into the luggage space (note that the 2CV had interlinked front/rear springs mounted horizontally, whereas the Mini used compact rubber-spring units and the Renaults employed transverse torsion bar springs). The disadvantage is that the roll centre is low - at ground level, in fact, when in a front-driven car you could really do with a fairly high rear roll centre to kill some of the natural nose-heavy understeer – and that the wheels are forced to roll at the same angle as the body, which reduces their grip.

Nowadays it is rather more common for front-driven cars, especially the smaller ones, to employ some kind of semi-independent suspension – an arrangement in which a pair of trailing arms is joined by a beam that is flexible enough to permit a measure of independent movement, yet rigid enough – in the right sense – to confer most of the advantages of a dead axle. We shall look at this technique in more detail when we come to examine the practicalities of front-driven cars.

The de Dion suspension

There is one type of suspension which might almost be thought of as an axle/independent hybrid. The de Dion arrangement uses a dead axle tube to join a pair of driven wheels *(fig 4:19)*. In other words it offers all the advantages of the axle – low unsprung weight, control of track and camber, and constant roll centre position – plus the ability to drive the wheels. Unfortunately, it is a complicated and expensive arrangement to engineer properly: it calls for variable-length drive-shafts plus careful location of the 'axle' if its advantages are to be fully exploited. Rover explored an alternative in the old 2000, using fixed-length drive-shafts and a slide-jointed de Dion tube. Current de Dion rear suspensions are found in cars as diverse as the smaller Volvos, the Alfa Romeo 75 and 90 and the Aston Martin V8.

Spring variations

As we have already seen, the leaf-type spring dating back to stagecoach days has virtually vanished from the current motoring scene. It evolved, as time went on, to have a smaller number of separate leaves and to be more cunningly mounted. Modern applications on light commercial vehicles use only one or two leaves and avoid inter-leaf friction as far as possible: separate telescopic dampers are much more predictable in their effect and need minimum servicing.

The interest in leaf springs now lies in three things. They have the ability to resist torque

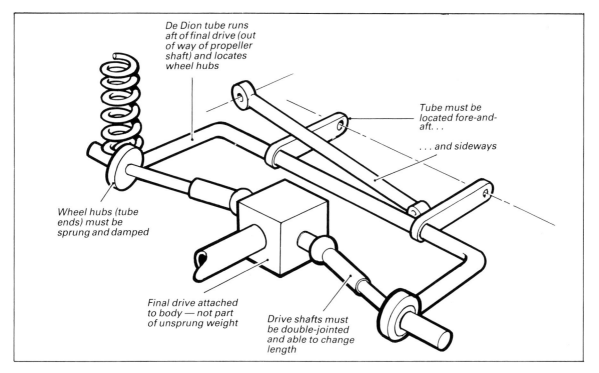

De Dion tube runs aft of final drive (out of way of propeller shaft) and locates wheel hubs

Tube must be located fore-and-aft. . .

. . . and sideways

Wheel hubs (tube ends) must be sprung and damped

Final drive attached to body — not part of unsprung weight

Drive shafts must be double-jointed and able to change length

4:19. The de Dion suspension system, named after a pioneeering French nobleman, employs a 'dead' axle passing behind the final-drive unit to keep the wheels upright and parallel. Either the drive shafts or the axle itself (as in the old Rover 2000) must be able to vary in length, and there still remains the question of how to locate and spring the axle.

4:20. A very simple interpretation of the de Dion idea was found at the back of the DAF 66. Leaf springs locate the axle tube, assisted by a single upper radius arm at the right-hand side. The belt-drive Variomatic transmission feeds power to a conventional final-drive unit and hence does not need to accommodate suspension movement as it did in the earlier swing-axle DAF cars. De Dion suspension was part of the legacy handed on from this model to its Volvo 340-series cousins.

as well as direct weight, a combined function which gives the designer the chance to simplify his suspension layout; they are relatively easy to make variable-rate – that is, becoming stiffer as they are compressed – by making the second leaf a 'helper' on to which the main leaf rolls progressively; and perhaps above all, they are the first type of spring to have been made in production quantity, in ultra-light form, using plastic composite materials instead of steel. This last development, together with its other advantages, may yet secure the leaf spring some future car applications.

However, the coil spring is by far the most widely used in today's cars. Its virtue is that of compactness, especially when wound around telescopic dampers to form integral struts, whether MacPherson or otherwise. Also, by inclining the spring axis, the mounting point can be moved far outboard compared with any leaf spring attachment, adding to the car's roll stiffness. A coil spring can be attached some

way from its wheel, especially on a trailing or semi-trailing arm, so as to magnify its effective rate without detracting from the effective width of the spring base. This enables a small, stiff spring to emulate a softer, longer-travel spring attached directly to the wheel (which is why many spring rates today are quoted 'at the wheel' rather than as they stand).

It has proved possible to make coil springs variable-rate in various ways, by changing the diameter of the spring material itself or by designing the spring so that its coils collapse to become 'solid' – in other words, touching one another - progressively rather than all at once. General Motors has developed the Minibloc spring, used on most modern Vauxhall/Opel models, in which the coil is of beehive form so that it can collapse almost flat before locking.

An alternative spring is the torsion bar, which is really only a coil spring unwound (or is it more logical in reverse?). A handful of designers have used the torsion bar consistently since the 1940s. The Volkswagen Beetle was torsion-bar sprung, and so was the front end of the Morris Minor (and the much less celebrated Marina/Ital series). Renault has frequently used transverse torsion bars and does so with success in the rear suspension of all its smaller cars, as we shall see later. The problem with torsion-bar springing, especially where the bars are installed lengthwise to work in conjunction with transverse arms, is that stressing tends to be awkward and modern standards of compliance and noise insulation are difficult to achieve.

Springs have to work in conjunction with either check-straps or bump-stops, which limit the travel of the suspension system within the length over which the spring can work effectively. Most modern suspension designs use bump-stops to control both bump and rebound movement. With the availability of modern materials, most notably polyurethane elastomer, bump-stops have become longer and more progressive in action to the point where they really qualify as helper springs rather than simple stops.

There have been a number of high-tech spring systems applied to cars, most notably and successfully that of Citroen, which developed a hydropneumatic suspension in the 1950s and has used it on millions of DS, GS, CX and BX models. The Citroen system works on the basis of having four spherical gas springs above columns of incompressible liquid which form the 'linkage' between the wheels and the springs. The passage of the liquid through orifices also provides the damping effect. In essence, the system is extremely simple, though Citroen opted from the outset to add the ability to vary the gas-spring pressure and volume so as to achieve constant spring frequency, constant (and adjustable) ride height, automatic self-levelling and other advantages. A much simpler though similar principle was seen in the Moulton Hydrostatic and Hydragas suspension systems used in most front-driven Austin-Morris models of the 1960s and 70s.

Damper variations

The first separate damping devices used interface friction of the same kind, essentially, which took place between the leaves of multiple springs. They did not, for reasons already discussed, work very well, and during the 1930s the hydraulic damper took over more or less completely. The once-familiar hydraulic units were of the lever-arm type, long since supplanted by the telescopic unit. The last British production cars to use the Armstrong lever-arm damper were the Morris Marina/ Ital and the MG sports cars, both of which survived into the 1970s though their basic designs dated from 20 years earlier.

Today, the telescopic hydraulic damper is almost universal. The only cars not to use this type are those which, like the Citroens, use high-pressure suspension systems with integral damping.

Today's telescopic damper is a sophisticated item of equipment. One of the main aims of any damper design, apart from a long and trouble-free existence, is to dissipate heat as quickly as possible: the damping action of forcing fluid through small holes in internal pistons creates a lot of heat. The damper is, after all, effectively absorbing the energy of the bouncing wheel-and-tyre assembly so as to bring it to rest quickly and positively. It turns that energy into heat, which it radiates away through the damper walls.

If it cannot get rid of the heat quickly enough, 'damper fade' sets in as the internal liquid begins to vaporize. High-performance dampers greatly delay the onset of fade through being filled with inert high-pressure gas to raise the boiling point of the hydraulic fluid – hence the much-bandied, but less frequently appreciated expression 'gas-filled dampers'. Keen, fast drivers often feel the temperature of their tyres after a quick lap or two: feeling the dampers would often be more instructive, though also more painful.

Chapter five

Tyres

Tyres are fundamentally important to car behaviour. All the driving, braking, steering and cornering forces must somehow be transmitted through the four tyre contact patches on the road. Analysis of the way in which this is done has filled books, let alone one chapter of a general work on chassis design and performance.

The tyre is a complex mechanism. If we look at a small section of a tyre, including the road surface contact patch, it must do five things. It must act as a strut holding the wheel rim – and a quarter of the weight of the car – off the road. It must act as a spring to help soften the ride. It must transmit force along the length of the car: braking force on any wheel, traction force if the wheel is driven. It must transmit sideways force to enable the car to turn corners; and it must self-centre if, when used on the front wheels, it is pointing anything but straight ahead.

This is no place to delve deep into tyre structure. Suffice it to say that the modern radial-ply design has proved itself well able to transmit large amounts of traction or braking force while being much more efficient at generating sideways (cornering) force than its predecessor, the cross-ply tyre. Recent tyre developments have concentrated less in this area than on refining the structure of the sidewalls for a smoother spring effect and therefore a better ride, and for a smooth build-up of cornering force when the tyre is turned to a given *slip angle*. A good deal of work has also been done to reduce tyre-generated noise, but that is well

outside the scope of this book.

Nobody can talk briefly and clearly about tyres without first stating some definitions. In the first place, imagine a tyre rolling gently along in a straight line. For most of its trip round in a circle, each block of rubber compound in the tread, and the carcase structure beneath it, is subject to an outward force caused partly by the air pressure within, and partly by centrifugal force. However, when the rubber block rolls into the contact patch it becomes compressed as it passes through, relaxing back into gentle tension on the far side.

The action of turning tension into compression and back again absorbs a certain amount of energy, which manifests itself as rolling resistance. At low speeds, this is the most important force slowing the car to an eventual standstill in a coasting situation (at higher speeds, aerodynamic drag is greater). The rolling resistance is always present, even when the tyre is transmitting tractive effort to accelerate the car. The energy absorbed by the rolling resistance is turned into heat: even though the tyre runs in an ample supply of cooling air, the treads of a hard-driven car are sometimes too hot to touch immediately after it has stopped.

The interesting and vital part of tyre behaviour begins when the tyre is run at an angle to its direction of travel, thus generating a slip angle – the angle between the direction in which a tyre is pointing and the direction in which it is travelling. This is the same situa-

5:1. Even the best tyres are unable to function if they are not in contact with the ground! While the rallying Opel Manta of Jimmy McRae and Mike Nicholson, seen here in full flight, is an extreme case, in most normal circumstances it is the fundamental job of the suspension engineer to ensure that the tyres stay firmly on the road.

tion as when an aircraft flies in a sidewind, pointing in one direction (the heading), but travelling in another (the track). A front tyre assumes a slip angle as soon as the steering is turned from the straight ahead position; what may be less easy to understand is that in any cornering situation, the rear tyres also run at a slip angle, though it is rarely the same as that at the front.

When a tyre runs at a slip angle, it develops two new forces. One is a sideways force at right angles to the tyre, while the other is a twisting force (known as 'self-aligning torque'), which tries to pull the tyre back to a zero slip angle. The origin of both these forces is found in the behaviour of the blocks of tread rubber as they are squeezed through the contact patch. As the blocks enter the patch, they

are forced to follow the tyre's direction of travel rather than their natural path round the circumference of the tread. In other words, they are turned through the slip angle. The further away from their natural path they are forced, the harder they try to return to it, hence the sideways force generated by the tyre and, because the contact patch is no longer symmetrical, the self-aligning torque.

It is conventional, and more helpful to the engineer, to resolve the sideways force generated by the tyre into two components. One is the *cornering force* at right angles to the car's direction of motion, and the other is a *drag force* acting along the direction of motion. Every mechanically sympathetic driver will be aware that the drag acting on the car during cornering is greater than when it is run-

63

5:2. The all-important contact patch is dramatically illustrated by this shot of a Goodyear tyre undergoing aquaplaning tests. A high-speed camera (10,000 frames per second) captures the tyre's passage through a 2mm film of water covering a glass plate let into the test track surface.

ning in a straight line; that his car sheds speed a lot more quickly when it is cornered on a trailing throttle than when coasting straight ahead. At the very least, most of us are painfully aware that tyres wear out more quickly the harder we drive round corners.

The cornering force is the key to all cornering behaviour. The effect of the combined cornering force of all four tyres of a cornering car is to counteract the centrifugal force: or more

strictly, since I was taught mathematics by a wise man who insisted there is no such thing as centrifugal force (and rightly; it is merely a convenient fiction which makes revolving mechanisms easier to understand) the tyres provide the force without which the car would continue straight ahead at a tangent to its corner.

The size of the cornering force generated by a tyre is considerable. An average small fam-

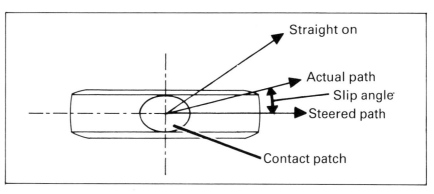

5:3. As soon as the car is turned onto a curved path, the tyres, both front and rear, begin to develop slip angles between the direction in which the wheel is pointing and the path actually followed by the contact patch. That angle, here somewhat exaggerated for clarity, is generated by distortion of the tread, not by loss of adhesion or sliding.

ily car weighing a ton can be cornered at 0.5g without problems, which means the four tyres are exerting a cornering force of half a ton. This would be a great deal per tyre even if all four tyres were contributing equally, but in fact the car leans hard on its outside tyres and especially so on its outside front tyre, which probably has to contribute more than half the total cornering force by itself. Therefore, a single tyre of modest dimensions must be able to generate a sideways force of 300 kilograms or more from a contact patch area of perhaps 40 square inches. Furthermore, if the car is front-driven, it must be able to do so while still exerting enough traction to overcome the air and rolling resistances and the tyre drag.

A number of factors influence the cornering force generated by a tyre, but for any given tyre running at a given pressure, five figures are all-important. These are the cornering force itself, the slip angle, the load on the tyre, the self-aligning torque and the camber angle.

Specific information, complete with real figures, about modern tyres is never easy to come by. I have to thank Michelin for lifting the 'rubber curtain' and providing a pair of diagrams showing how the forces generated by two of their radial-ply tyres (not, for reasons of commercial sensitivity, their very latest ones, and in any case not specifically identified except by size) vary according to condition.

The diagrams relate to a 155R13 tyre *(fig 5:4)* and a 175/70R13 tyre *(fig 5:5)*. These are typical sizes for a medium-sized family car such as the Ford Escort. In both cases the inflation pressure is 2.0bar (29psi), typical for such applications. The 155R13 tyre is a standard aspect ratio design, which means its section height is 82% of its width. The 175/70R13 tyre is a moderately low-profile design with an aspect ratio of 70% – that is, its section height is 70% of its width. The two tyres can be regarded as direct equivalents, and the 70-series tyre is often fitted to up-market versions of a car as one way of upgrading its image and appearance. As it happens this can be done with the minimum of trouble because the tyres have virtually the same effective diameter. Michelin actually quotes a figure of 912 revs per mile for the 175/70R13 compared with 914 revs per mile for the 155R13, and nobody is going to change their speedometer drive gearing on that account!

Tyres are now made with aspect ratios down to 50% or even lower; Formula 1 racing tyres go below 20%. The once-predicted rush to very low profiles for production cars has not materialized though: the feeling seems to be that at aspect ratios below 65 to 70%, ride comfort is increasingly sacrificed because the tyre is less able to act as an auxiliary spring within the suspension system. Tyres typically act as springs with about 10 times the stiffness of the actual suspension spring; stiffening a tyre significantly can upset the ride comfort measurably unless the suspension spring is softened to compensate, and that can cause problems of its own.

Decreasing the aspect ratio also poses the designer the choice between wider wheel rims or larger-diameter wheels. If the existing tyre section width is retained, a lower profile means a smaller rolling radius which is rarely welcome. The tyre is therefore made wider – as in the case of our 175/70R13 – and ideally this calls for a wider rim (Michelin's preferred rim width is 4.5in for the 155R13, 5in for the 175/70). But wider rims are heavier and more expensive, so designers have been known to

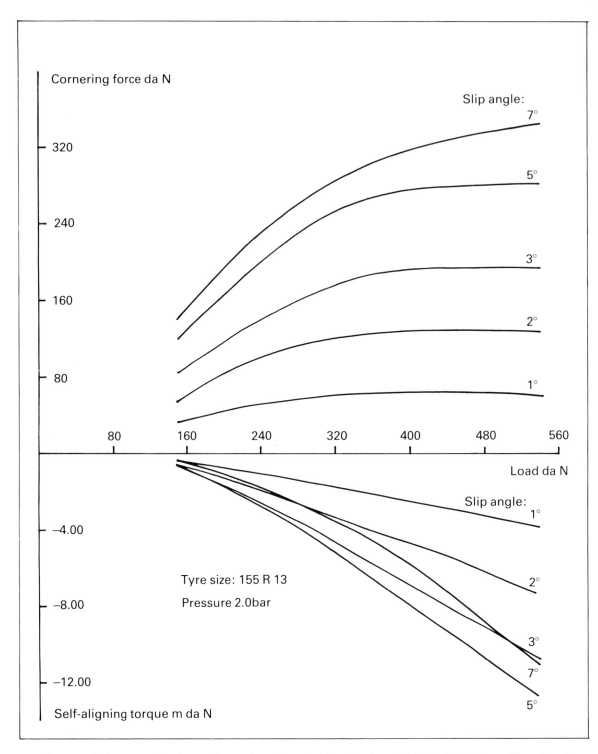

5:4. Curves relating cornering force, slip angle and vertical loading for a Michelin 155R13 tyre. Note that these relationships in a modern tyre are far from being simple straight-line equations. However, cornering force for a given slip angle increases with load, and cornering force for a given load increases with slip angle at least up to an angle of 8 degrees. The Michelin curves do not continue up to the 'stall angle' though it seems likely that this is around 10 degrees.

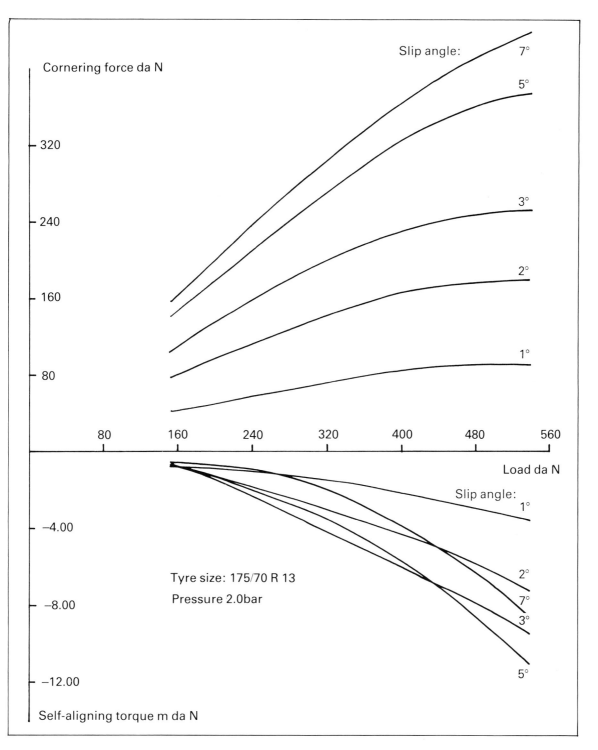

5:5. Curves relating cornering force, slip angle and vertical loading for a Michelin 175/70R13 tyre. Note that the available cornering force for a given load and slip angle is significantly higher than for the 155R13 tyre. While it is not too difficult to push an average family car to its limits on the 155R13, the 175/70R13 provides sufficient potential grip (at least on a dry surface) to permit lateral accelerations well beyond what most drivers would regard as reasonable.

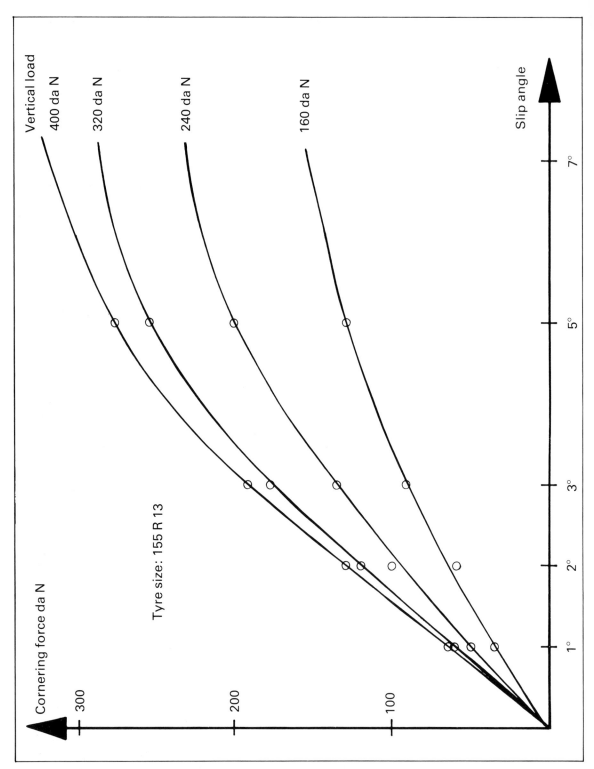

5:6. Curves derived from the original Michelin data with slip angle instead of load plotted along the X-axis. The rate of increase of cornering force falls away as the slip angle is increased, whatever the load. Again, the curves stop short of the 'stall point'.

remain with narrower than ideal rims. Alternatively, wheels can be made bigger. Many cars now fit low-profile tyre options on wheels an inch larger in diameter than the standard fitting. Some make use of the extra space within the bigger wheel rim to fit larger-diameter brake discs.

Putting in the numbers

Michelin's curves are presented to show how the cornering force generated by the tyre varies with the load on the tyre, for different slip angles. It is, of course, also possible to show (for instance) how cornering force varies with slip angle for different loads, and I have used Michelin's figures to derive *fig 5:6*, which presents the results in that way. The companion curves beneath the horizontal axis show how the self-aligning torque varies with the load.

Whatever the form of the curve, the important thing to note is that the relationship between load, cornering force and slip angle is far from linear: you do not always get the same increase in cornering force for a given increase in load or slip angle. As Michelin's curves show, there comes a point, especially at low slip angles, where increasing the load fails to generate any extra cornering force. This effect is far more noticeable for the 155R13 tyre than it is for the 70-series equivalent.

My derived curve in *fig 5:6* shows equally that the rate of increase of cornering force falls away as the slip angle is increased, whatever the load. Although Michelin's curves do not venture beyond slip angles of 7 degrees it is fairly clear that this is not far short of the point at which the tyres reach what the aeronautical engineer would recognize as a 'stall point'. In fact, there is a close resemblance between the cornering force/ slip angle curve for a tyre, and the lift/incidence curve of an aircraft wing: like the lift, the cornering force rises steadily with increasing slip angle until beyond a certain value it first tends to level off, and then to fall away in a condition resembling an aircraft's stall. In other words, the tyre will not go on generating ever-increasing amounts of cornering force the further it is turned: there will come a point where its cornering force remains more or less contant (and less than the maximum) and any further winding-on of lock will achieve nothing except a further increase

in tyre drag. Beyond even that stage there lurks actual loss of adhesion, when the tyre tread elements no longer run through the contact patch in an orderly way, but actually slide across the road surface.

The curves for self-aligning torque show that for both tyres, the torque increases steadily with load, but not with slip angle. It is interesting to observe that the 70-series tyre generates significantly less self-aligning torque (which ought to mean that in a straight 'swap' with no other changes to the suspension or steering geometry, the wider tyre would actually result in lighter steering with reduced feel, despite putting more rubber on the road). Also, the self-aligning torque of both tyres rises to a maximum somewhere between 3 and 5 degrees of slip angle - note that at light loads, the 70-series tyre reaches its maximum sooner – and then falls away towards 7 degrees.

These effects are important. One of the criticisms of radial-ply tyres when they first emerged was that while they gave better response to steering because they generated more cornering force for a given slip angle than a cross-ply tyre of similar load rating, they also let go more suddenly. To return for a moment to the aircraft analogy, it was the difference between a sharp and vicious stall and a gentle one with plenty of warning. Since the first appearance of the Michelin X, its manufacturers have had plenty of time to answer that criticism and the curves shown here certainly suggest not only that the top of the slip angle/cornering force curve is gently rounded to make behaviour in that area less 'sudden', but that warning is indeed provided in plenty of time by the reduction in self-aligning torque, which should be evident as a lightening of the steering (unless, of course, the car designer has managed to mask it in other ways).

Because wider tyres naturally have wider contact patches, these must be shorter to maintain the same contact patch area if the tyre is to be run at the same pressure (the Michelin recommended pressures for both our demonstration tyres are identical when they are fitted as alternatives on cars like the Escort). Shorter, wider contact patches clearly increase grip – or rather, they provide adequate cornering force at smaller slip angles – but they reduce self-aligning torque, and therefore natural stability and steering feel. On the evidence provided by these two tyres, not only is the peak value of the torque reduced but the value goes 'over the top' sooner and begins to fall away as the slip angle continues to build up. The effect is certainly not critical where our 175/70R13 tyre is concerned, but careful thought would seem to be called for before fitting replacement tyres very much wider than the originals.

Balancing the loads

One may wonder, at first sight, why Michelin chose to present their information in the way they did, as cornering force against load. In fact, for the chassis designer, this is often the most useful presentation because in the first instance, it is the load on a car's tyre that changes during manoeuvring, subsequently giving rise to a change in slip angle.

Perhaps the best way to illustrate this is to take a typical Michelin-shod car, a Ford Escort weighing 900kg with the driver only aboard, and see what happens when the car is cornered. Since the Escort is front-driven, it is nose-heavy with just the driver aboard but this does not, as is so often assumed, lead immediately to understeer. Because the centre of gravity is closer to the front wheels they have to provide the greater part of the cornering force; but since they carry the greater part of the load, they automatically provide it – up to a point.

If we assume that the Escort carries 62% of its weight on the front wheels, and neglect the fact that the driver sits off-centre to upset the symmetry of the static weight distribution, then when the car is cornered at 0.5g the weight transfer from the inner to the outer tyres means that all four are now differently loaded: the outside front carries 388kg, while the inside rear is down at 104kg.

We know that given the front/rear weight distribution, we need 280kg of cornering force from the front tyres and 170kg from the back, giving the 450kg necessary to balance the car overall. We also know that the two front wheels have to run at the same slip angle – neglecting the small difference which will exist in practice because of Ackermann-type

steering geometry – and that the two rear wheels must similarly run the same angle (though not, of course, the same angle as at the front).

At this point we need to do some measuring off our available curves to discover that with the 155R13 tyres, a front slip angle of 2.9 degrees generates 185kg of cornering force from the outer tyre and 95kg from the inner one, while at the rear, a 2.6 degrees slip angle produces 120kg and 50kg from the outer and inner tyres respectively. Already, therefore, the shape of the tyre curves has produced a difference between the front and rear slip angles (and, because the front angle is greater than the rear one, the Escort is understeering – but we shall go into that in more detail later on).

Let us, at this stage, contemplate the fact that if no weight transfer occurred from the inner to the outer tyres – if the Escort somehow contrived to have its centre of gravity at ground level – then the inner and outer tyres would generate equal amounts of cornering force. In that situation the front tyres would need to run at a slip angle of only 2.35 degrees. From this we conclude, and should always bear in mind, that *lateral weight transfer at either end of a car always increases the slip angle at that end.* Any weight transfer reduces the ultimate roadholding; that, rather than the risk of overturning, is why racing cars are built with their centres of gravity as low, and their tracks as wide, as human ingenuity and the class regulations will permit.

Having digested that basic rule, suppose we now put a lunatic driver into our Escort and he corners it at 0.75g. This, you might note, is still well within the bounds of safety since, given the Escort's width of track and the centre of gravity height I have assumed, he would need to reach 1.3g before toppling the car, at least on a smooth, level surface (be warned that bumps and camber changes can eat deep into that margin!). Working through the same process, we now find the outside front tyre carrying 443kg of the total load – virtually half of it - while the inside rear tyre carries only 71kg. Of the required 675kg cornering force, 420kg must come from the front and 255kg from the rear.

This time, the results are more spectacular. Working through the curves for the 155R13 tyre produces a front slip angle of 6.6 degrees and a rear angle of 4.45 degrees to produce the necessary balance. Not only is the difference between the two greater, but the front tyres are edging well into the area where cornering force increases much more slowly with extra slip angle.

There is, of course, something missing from this analysis and that is the effect of the front wheels being driven. Before we look into that, however, we should first study the effect on the '0.75g' Escort of switching to the 175/70R13 tyre.

Working through the curves for the lower-profile tyre, using the same tyre loadings because they are determined solely by the weight of the car and the cornering force, we now find that a front slip angle of only 4.3 degrees is enough to give us the required front-end cornering force, while the equivalent rear tyre slip angle is 3.6 degrees. The switch to the wider, low-profile tyre has therefore reduced the difference between the front and rear slip angles – and thus the understeer – and has rescued the front tyres from their slightly precarious position towards the 'stall point' of their curve.

In this particular instance, the self-aligning torque is also similar, though that is fortuitous. Our chosen case has caught both of the self-aligning torque curves 'on the way down', at just about the point where they cross. In the majority of situations, the low-profile tyre would produce less self-aligning torque and therefore less steering feel. It is worth noting that it is the heavily loaded outer front tyre that produces virtually all the self-aligning torque.

Other influencing factors

All the calculations above were based on the simplest possible case, in which the car was rolling round the corner with no power applied. As it happens, even that case is more complicated in reality because without power the car would be decelerating and that, in turn, would throw an extra load on the front tyres.

However, in most practical cases the driver naturally applies sufficient power to maintain speed round the corner – if he can. This means that the contact patches of the driven wheels,

the Escort's front ones, have to transmit drive torque as well as cornering force.

It is more or less inevitable that tyres protest at the idea of doing both jobs. What happens is that any tyre which is asked to transmit torque, or absorb braking forces, 'borrows' some of the capacity to produce cornering force. To a very good approximation, a tyre will produce its total force in any direction to produce a 'force circle' (fig 5:7); by resolving the competing forces within that circle we can deduce by how much the imposition of a driving torque reduces the cornering force in any particular situation.

We shall look at the results of this rule, and its implications for handling, in a later chapter. For the moment it is enough to note that in general, the forces involved in driving the car at a constant speed round a corner build rapidly with the car's speed and the cornering force. The speed is clearly important because the power needed to overcome aerodynamic drag rises as speed cubed; cornering force increases tyre drag because it pushes the tyres towards high slip angles where the drag becomes much more significant.

At moderate speeds and reasonable cornering forces – suppose our Escort is travelling at 50mph while cornering at 0.5g – the drive force is actually very small by comparison with the cornering force, and has only a small effect on it and therefore on the slip angle. To put some typical figures in there, the Escort needs only about 8bhp (at the wheels) to maintain a steady 50mph in still air. The tyre drag round the corner just about doubles that requirement to 15.5bhp, which of course is still well within the most humble Escort's abilities.

When cornering at 0.75g on its narrow tyres, however, the Escort suffers much higher tyre drag, especially at the front. The power needed to overcome the front tyre drag actually exceeds that needed to maintain a steady straight-line 50mph (in fact, it is getting on for twice as much) and the car needs 27bhp at the wheels just to maintain that speed round the corner. Actually, the situation is worse than that because this involves sending a sufficiently high drive force through the front wheels to 'rob' some of the cornering force. To restore that force, the front wheels have to be turned through an even larger slip

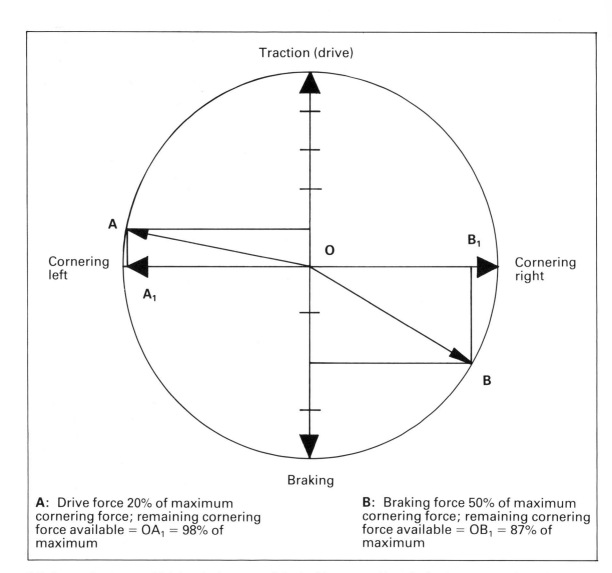

Traction (drive)

A

Cornering
left

A₁

O

B₁

Cornering
right

B

Braking

A: Drive force 20% of maximum cornering force; remaining cornering force available = OA₁ = 98% of maximum

B: Braking force 50% of maximum cornering force; remaining cornering force available = OB₁ = 87% of maximum

5:7. In practice, a tyre which is asked to transmit both sideways and lengthwise forces can only work within a 'circle of forces' as shown. This useful analogue makes clear that the greater the force transmitted in one direction the less the maximum that can be transmitted in the other. If the sideways and lengthwise forces are equal, the maximum the tyre can transmit is about 71% of the maximum in one direction only (since cosine 45 degrees = 0.707). In fact the 'circle' is not truly circular and slightly greater resultants can be generated especially under braking; the technique of 'trail braking' deep into a corner is exploited by many racing drivers for this reason.

angle, which further increases the tyre drag and the power needed, which . . . and the end result of this chasing round in (computerized) circles is that the front tyre slip angle actually needs to be 7.5 degrees rather than our 'zero power' 6.6 degrees in order to maintain a balance.

There is no question that a slip angle of 7.5 degrees is taking the front tyres close to the ragged edge of their maximum grip for that loading situation, and it underlines the fact

that power can quickly increase slip angles and cause control problems of its own. So, of course, can braking – complicated by the fact that hard use of the brakes can cause a major forward shift of the car's effective weight. We shall consider the effect of both power and mid-corner deceleration and braking in later chapters, looking at cars of various configurations.

Apart from the forces at work within the 'magic circle', there are yet other factors which

5:8. The forces on rear tyres and within the rear suspension can be considerable. This Rover 2000 shows how close to the rim a tyre may be deformed in the most extreme driving conditions. The Rover had a form of de Dion rear suspension which ensured that the rear wheels remained parallel at all times: the behaviour of some other types of rear suspension in similar circumstances can give rise to major handling problems. Note in this case that even with the rear tyres provoked to extremes, the Rover is still understeering very strongly.

affect a tyre's ability to produce cornering force. One is inflation pressure. Within limits, the higher the tyre pressure, the greater the cornering force for a given slip angle, under a given load. In this case, however, the limits are severe. Most modern radial-ply tyres are marked with a 'never-exceed' pressure, which is frequently below 40psi (2.7bar), so one's scope for improving performance in that direction is extremely limited. In any case, as we shall see later, chassis engineers frequently use front-to-rear tyre pressure differentials as a means of adjusting handling characteristics, so pumping all four tyres up to the maximum permitted pressure could have unexpectedly dire consequences.

Another major factor is camber angle, though this is not as critical as it used to be. Running a tyre other than completely upright has two effects. It reduces the tyre's ability to produce pure cornering force because the contact patch is subjected to an additional force trying to lift it at one side; but it introduces a secondary side-thrust which arises because when set at an angle, the tyre tries to run round a circle (whose centre is where the axis of the wheel meets the ground) rather than straight ahead.

At one time it was felt that radial-ply tyres could cope much better than cross-ply designs

with camber angles because their more flexible sidewalls would allow the contact patch to lie flat in any case. However, more recent moves towards ever wider tyres and lower aspect ratios have rather disposed of that argument, and on high-performance cars, at least, careful control of the camber angles resulting from suspension movement are as important as ever. As for the use of negative camber to produce a side-thrust in the right direction during cornering, most chassis designers seem now to take the view that it is better by far to keep the heavily loaded outside front tyre properly upright and allow it to do its job as originally intended.

The back tyres are another story: within limits, changes of camber angle at the rear can be exploited to balance a car's handling. Any car which understeers strongly can be given better balance by forcing the outside rear tyre to assume a positive camber angle, since this reduces the tyre's cornering force, which makes it run at a larger slip angle, which reduces the difference between the front and rear slip angles and consequently the understeer. Note, however, that this technique – which we shall look at more closely, especially with respect to front-driven cars – involves a deliberate sacrifice of ultimate grip and therefore must not be overdone.

73

Chapter six

Steering

On the face if it, it would not seem too difficult a task to design a mechanical linkage to pass movements from the driver's steering wheel to the front wheels of the car. Unfortunately, like so many things about chassis engineering, the closer one looks at steering system design the more complicated it becomes.

The task is dominated by three considerations other than the mere transmission of movement. The first is that the effort involved for the driver should not be excessive. The second is that faithful transmission of messages from the steering wheel should not be accompanied by equally faithful feedback of every force exerted on, or every shock and tremor suffered by, the front wheels as they traverse the road surface. The third is that the linkage must be arranged so that the relationship between steering wheel and front wheel movement remains reasonably consistent, even though the front wheels can move up and down, together or individually, by anything up to a foot.

It should be borne in mind that the forces acting on the front wheels include braking torque whenever the brakes are applied, and drive torque in the case of front-driven cars. This is also the place to point out that while *braking* forces are exerted directly through the tyre contact patch (assuming the brakes to be outboard, attached to the wheel hub, as is usually the case), the *drive* force in any independent suspension system is exerted at the wheel hub; only in the case of a live axle does it also act directly through the contact patch.

One of the reasons why pioneer cars had rear-wheel brakes only – apart from some misconceptions about the effect on stability of front wheel locking – was that their designers had quite enough problems arriving at a satisfactory steering system without throwing braking torque into the equation.

Our three initial considerations mean that the simplest imaginable steering linkage *(fig 6:1)* consisting of a drop-arm attached to the end of the steering column, and two track-rods joining the drop-arm to track arms attached to the wheel hub carriers, is not really practicable. In this layout, the hub carriers rotate between a pair of swivel joints, whose centres define the *steering axis* of the wheel (the line of the steering axis is also known as the 'kingpin', because in early steering system designs, though no longer, the wheel swivelled about a pin through the hub).

This simple kind of linkage is found in go-karts, and anyone who has driven one of those will appreciate why something more sophisticated is needed for a car. Considering the ultra-small size and weight of a kart, their steering can be surprisingly heavy and at the same time so 'quick' that newcomers have a problem retaining control. Shocks are also fed back very sharply to the driver's hands, sufficiently so to cause problems of their own, even though karts run only on well-surfaced tracks. Perhaps fortunately, karts have no suspension system as such; if they had, the effects of geometric error due to vertical wheel movement would also be magnified.

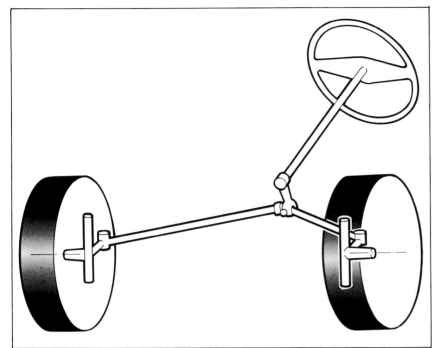

The first requirement of any realistic car steering system, therefore, is some kind of gearbox which will turn something between 2½ and 4 turns of the steering wheel into around a sixth of a turn of the front wheels about their steering axes. In practice, car steering boxes have a ratio of around 20:1, which implies approximately 3 turns of the steering wheel between locks. This gearing has the effect of slowing down the car's response to steering wheel movements and reducing the effort involved to reasonable dimensions. In the last few years, considerable engineering effort has been devoted to variable-ratio steering boxes which become quicker towards full lock while remaining pleasantly light around the straight-ahead position; these have enabled some companies at least to postpone the day when they have to adopt power-assisted steering for medium-sized cars.

The steering box also offers the designer the chance to insulate the steering wheel from the worst effects of feedback from front wheel shocks. At one time, it was felt desirable to use steering box designs which made the steering 'irreversible'; that is, while the steering wheel could move the front wheels, no amount of thumping or heaving at a front wheel could be felt at the steering wheel. Truly irreversible mechanical systems are very difficult to engineer, but much reduced feedback was achieved with steering boxes using worm-and-nut or cam-and-roller mechanical arrangements. These remain in use today, in highly developed form, by some highly respected car manufacturers. The worm-and-nut system, in particular, long remained popular in a refined form in which the 'thread' was formed by a circuit of recirculating ball bearings (in this form the system is in fact generally known as 'recirculating-ball'); with this steering box design, internal friction is very low, a notable advantage for a designer trying to keep down steering effort without adopting excessively low gearing or power assistance.

The drawback of all such systems is that while reducing feedback they also rob the driver of much of his direct sense of feel for what the front wheels are up to – and in particular, how close they might be to the limit of tyre adhesion. They also, by definition, reduce the ability of forces acting on the front wheels to provide automatic self-centring of the steering since their full effect cannot be transmitted back beyond the steering box to help centre the steering wheel.

The modern approach is to adopt steering

box designs which allow a degree of steering feel, and seek to damp down shock feedback through a judicious combination of mechanical advantage, friction, compliance and (sometimes) a separate damper. This change of attitude has resulted in the rack-and-pinion type of steering box becoming overwhelmingly popular. The move has also been helped by the rapid spread of power-assisted steering into virtually all modern cars of over 2-litre engine capacity and 1,000kg kerb weight. So far as the average family car is concerned, the result of rack-and-pinion steering has been to provide the driver with good feel and a positive self-centring action at the expense of a degree of road surface feedback which might have surprised his counterpart of 30 years ago.

The provision of feel itself depends on a number of factors. We saw in the previous chapter that a tyre running at a slip angle generates its own self-aligning torque – it tries to twist back to zero slip angle. At first sight, this ought to be a good and sufficient way of providing both steering feel and automatic self-centring of the steering. Self-centring is an important aspect of a car's overall stability and very few drivers ever consciously think about the extent to which they relax their grip and allow the steering wheel to turn itself back to the straight-ahead when exiting a corner – unless it doesn't happen, or happens unexpectedly quickly.

The problem with tyre self-aligning torque is that by itself it is rarely strong enough to give the self-centring effect the steering system designer seeks, especially if he has sought in the design of his steering box to reduce the feedback of road shocks. It is important, however, to retain the effect of self-aligning torque because what the skilled driver actually senses when he feels the front wheels to be close to losing adhesion, is the flattening out of the self-aligning torque curve as the front tyres near their 'stall point'.

Power-assisted steering poses problems of its own. Hydraulic circuits are indeed irreversible so far as their ability to feed any feel back to the steering wheel is concerned. Most steering systems, however, are power *assisted* which, without delving deep into detail techniques, means that a pathway remains through which a modicum of feel can still be fed to the driver. The art lies in retaining enough of the feel while eliminating enough of the effort to please the customer. Systems which are wholly powered, like Citroen's well-established Varipower, need some provision for artificially generated feel. Citroen, with typical and perhaps slightly exaggerated enthusiasm, made their feel system speed-sensitive and capable of self-centring the steering even with the car at a standstill. Other manufacturers have since added provision for speed-sensitive feel (that is, becoming heavier as speed increases) to otherwise more conventional power steering systems.

Steering geometry

Some means must therefore be found to add to the self-aligning torque, and this is done through the careful positioning of the steering axis relative to the wheel itself. The details of this arrangement are briefly and conveniently referred to as the steering geometry.

In practice, steering geometry is defined by six quantities *(fig 6:2)*. First, there are the angles which the steering axis makes with the vertical, as viewed from alongside the car – the *castor angle* – and from the front of the car – the *kingpin inclination*. Then, since the wheel itself need not necessarily be completely vertical when viewed from the front, there is the *camber angle* which it makes with the vertical. The wheel more often than not makes a very small angle with the true straight-ahead when the car is at rest, either *toe-in*, with the front angled inwards, or *toe-out*, which is more usually found in the front wheels of front-driven cars. In either case, the object is simply to ensure that when the car is running normally with all the slack of the suspension bushes taken up by the tyre drag or drive torque, the wheels point truly straight ahead.

Finally, we need to look at the point at which the steering axis meets the ground, and how that point relates to the centre of the tyre contact patch. The distance of the point ahead of the contact patch centre is the *castor trail*; its distance to either side of the patch centre is the *offset*. If the point lies inside the patch centre, the offset is called positive; outside, it is negative.

The ideal steering geometry would seem at first glance to be one in which the front wheels

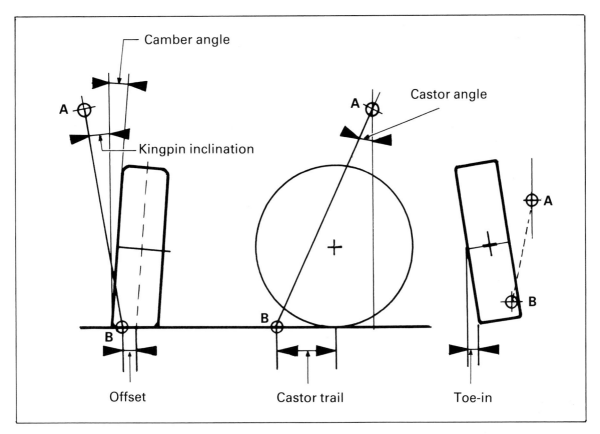

Camber angle

Kingpin inclination

A

B

Offset

Castor angle

A

B

Castor trail

A

B

Toe-in

6:2. Six parameters are needed to define steering geometry completely: two angles to define the inclination of the steering axis across and along the car, two more angles to define the static inclination of the wheel itself, and two distances to define where the steering axis meets the ground relative to the centre of the tyre contact patch.

turn about a vertical axis passing through the centre of their tyre contact patches. In fact this is not so since that would mean self-centring was provided by the tyre's self-aligning torque alone and we have already said this provides insufficient force in itself.

Quite apart from that, such an arrangement makes life virtually impossible for the designer. I have sketched the 'ideal' arrangement in *fig 6:3*, from which it is clear that the only way to set the steering axis absolutely upright and in line with the centre point of the tyre contact patch is to set the steering swivel joints close together and the wheel hub well outboard of centre. To keep things simple, I have not even tried to fit in any brakes.

The real point here is that in such an arrangement the stresses on the bearings in the wheel hub and on the bushes in the steering joints would be impossibly high. It will not, in short, work: there are too many compo-

nents fighting for space at the centre of the wheel. If the layout combined the promise of very light and precise steering (which it does) with stability and good feel (which it doesn't), it might just be worth exercising a lot of ingenuity and some very high-strength materials to try to make it work. As it is, we have to look at the alternatives – in other words, at taking something out of the wheel centre.

It is disastrous, as some of the pioneer designers discovered, simply to move the steering axis (the kingpin) smartly sideways. That makes room for the hub and permits the swivels to be moved further apart, thus reducing the stresses on both. Sadly, it also means that every road shock tries to twist the wheel about its steering axis and in the absence of 'irreversible' steering, is fed smartly back to the steering wheel – not exactly the kind of feel we were looking for. Far from each wheel being naturally self-centring, each will be trying to

6:3. The simplest possible steering geometry would have a vertical steering axis passing through the centre of the tyre contact patch to give 'centre-point steering'. In practice such an arrangement makes life virtually impossible for the designer trying to fit steering and suspension components — let alone brakes — deep inside the dish of the wheel, and an inward inclination of the axis is necessary.

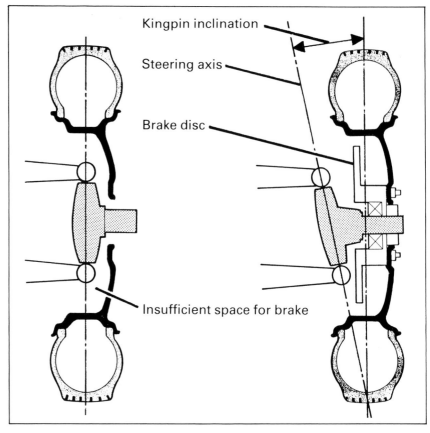

Kingpin inclination

Steering axis

Brake disc

Insufficient space for brake

twist itself round its steering axis in a state of constant conflict with the other. Such permanent tensions are bad news in any kind of engineering, but especially in a system as safety-related as the steering.

As I have already said, the question of steering self-centring is vital. Much of the apparent straight-line stability of a car comes not from the inherent quality of the chassis, but from the tendency of the steering to return itself to the straight-ahead when it has been nudged sideways by a disturbance or, of course, turned to one side by the driver. At the same time, the self-centring effort must not be too strong or it will make the steering needlessly heavy, and it must be sufficiently well damped not to send the car snaking all over the road while the steering oscillates about the centre position.

It follows from what we have already seen that the steering axis must pass at least reasonably close to the centre of the tyre contact patch. If it actually passes through the centre, the result is known as 'true centre-point steering' in which none of the forces on

the tyre are passed back to the steering wheel, other than the self-aligning torque. If the steering axis must pass inboard of the wheel centre in order to make room for the wheel hub in a sensible place, then an approximation to centre-point steering can be achieved by angling the axis outwards, and/or the wheel inwards, so that the axis still passes through the patch.

This outward angling, the kingpin inclination, has an extra benefit as long as it is not overdone. Turning the front wheels from the straight-ahead position involves lifting the front end of the car very slightly: because the kingpin is inclined, the wheel is trying to roll down as well as round the true vertical. The effect could actually be seen in some cars with light front ends and steeply inclined kingpin angles, such as the Hillman Imp. Thus the weight of the car actually tries to return the steering to the straight-ahead position.

That disposes of one of the five quantities in our definition of steering geometry. The second is castor angle. Castor action is familiar to anyone who has pushed a supermarket trolley. By arranging for the wheel to trail behind its steering axis, it will automatically pull itself into line as the vehicle is pushed along. Castor action can be applied in two ways, either simply by moving the steering axis forward of the wheel centre-line to create castor trail, or more subtly by inclining the steering axis at an angle to the vertical, its top inclined rearwards - the castor angle.

The steering geometry of most modern cars includes some measure of both castor angle and trail. The important difference between the two is that castor angle has its own effect

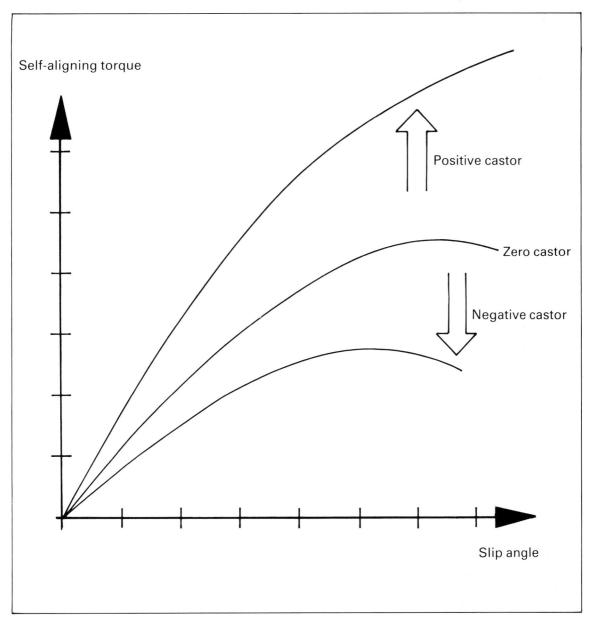

6:4. The castor angle (the angle between the steering axis and the vertical when viewed from the side) has a major effect on the self-aligning torque. Negative castor, in which the top of the steering axis leans forward, reduces the torque and also causes it to 'peak' sooner. Positive castor increases the torque but makes it likely that the 'peak', which is so useful as a warning of impending loss of front-end grip, will in fact be pushed beyond the point at which grip is actually lost.

on a tyre's self-aligning torque and hence on the feel it provides. Increasing positive castor angle not only magnifies the self-aligning torque, but also shifts the point at which the increase in torque begins to fall off – in other words, the point at which a sensitive driver becomes conscious of impending loss of front tyre grip – to a higher slip angle *(fig 6:4)*. Thus, the good designer chooses his castor angle with a view to providing optimum feel for the driver, and if that, together with the effect of kingpin inclination, does not in his opinion provide enough steering self-centring effect for adequate stability, he adds enough castor trail to make up the difference. It has to be said, though, that designers do not always agree about the desirable amount of either steering feel or natural self-centring.

We still have to consider offset and camber. Camber angle, except in very small quantities, is not very popular today. There are two reasons why a designer may adopt a small amount of camber angle. By setting the front wheels at a positive camber angle (with the tops of the wheels further apart) he reduces the kingpin inclination he needs to achieve a given hub clearance. And if he has chosen (or been forced to adopt) a front suspension system which entails big changes in camber angle as the wheel moves vertically he may choose a static camber angle which results in a nearly upright wheel when it really matters, during cornering. Neither is a terribly good excuse; one should always suspect a large static camber angle, positive or negative, at either end of the car, of being an engineering crutch to bolster a bad basic system.

In general, the angles involved in steering geometry are extremely small. Taking a few examples at random, one finds, for instance, that the Mini geometry – whatever the version, according to the workshop manual – includes a kingpin inclination of 9deg 30min, castor angle of 3deg, and camber angle of (nominal) 2deg. Citroen's figures for the supermini Visa II include kingpin inclination 9deg 20min, castor angle 1deg 33min and camber angle 34min. For a rather different type of car, the 'Spridget', BMC quoted 6deg 30min kingpin inclination, 3deg castor angle and 45min camber angle. One can, of course, find maverick geometries – the MGB, for

instance, had an oddly massive castor angle – but there seems to be a wide measure of agreement on the optimum range of values.

Offset considerations

Offset is another matter. Most people can sense the innate desirability of the steering axis passing through the ground in line with the centre of the tyre contact patch, so that forces applied through the patch – including braking forces in the case of front-driven cars, and some wheel out-of-balance forces – generate no upsetting moment around the steering axis. The car designer, however, can point to other considerations.

Where the steering axis is in line with the centre of the contact patch, the front wheel can only be turned by 'scrubbing' the whole patch about its centre. This makes the steering very heavy when the car is at a standstill, and the effect is still evident (if you accept what the best driving-technique books say about *not* heaving the steering at a standstill) at the kind of low speed encountered in parking. One answer is to introduce some offset so that at least part of the contact patch can roll round the steering axis instead of scrubbing. The greater the offset, the lighter the steering is likely to be at low speeds.

There remains the question of whether the offset should be positive or negative. The early users of significant offset, including Ford in the 1950s and '60s, made it positive which had the extra benefit of providing easy hub clearance while keeping kingpin inclination small. Then, during the 1970s, VW-Audi engineers realized that a small amount of *negative* offset, that is, with the steering axis passing outboard of the contact patch centre, could lead to self-correcting behaviour.

The argument is that when a car is braked with one tyre deflated, or one wheel is running on a slippery patch, the difference in drag force pulls the car off-line towards the 'good' front wheel. However, if the steering geometry includes negative offset, the drag pulls the steering in the opposite direction, and hopefully the two effects largely cancel each other out so that the car continues in a straight line. As an argument it sounds crude: the balance ought to depend on conditions. In fact, the idea seems to work in most circumstances, and

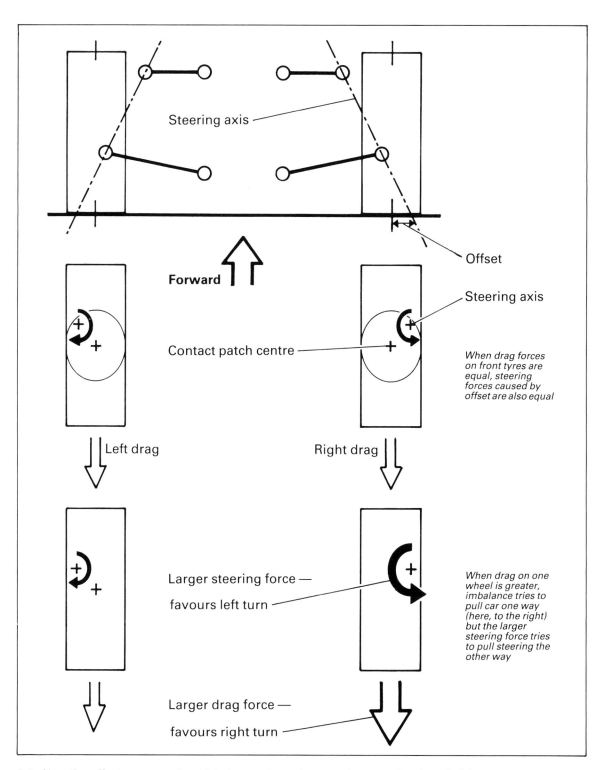

Steering axis

Offset

Steering axis

Forward

Contact patch centre

When drag forces on front tyres are equal, steering forces caused by offset are also equal

Left drag

Right drag

Larger steering force —

favours left turn

When drag on one wheel is greater, imbalance tries to pull car one way (here, to the right) but the larger steering force tries to pull steering the other way

Larger drag force —

favours right turn

6:5. Negative offset geometry, in which the steering axis meets the ground outboard of the contact patch centre, has become popular because it affords a measure of 'auto-stability' when braking with one side of the car on a low-grip surface, or even with one front tyre punctured. It has drawbacks also, including reduced space for the wheel hub and brake.

many manufacturers have now adopted negative-offset steering geometry despite the problems it causes in finding enough room for all the necessary components within the wheel.

One noticeable effect of negative-offset geometry, especially in the first (front-driven) cars to use it, was that it made the steering feel distinctly odd on occasion. In particular, it could be much less willing to self-centre out of tight turns if power continued to be applied. The steering also tended to remain locked over into the turn, or even to try to wind itself into the turn, if one reversed round a curve. In later cars, careful attention to geometric detail ameliorated, but did not entirely overcome these tendencies – which is why some respected chassis designers still fight shy of the whole negative-offset concept.

Ackermann and all that

The steering linkage designer, as I pointed out earlier, needs to make allowance for the fact that the front wheels move up and down. It would obviously be disastrous for the wheels to move in a steering sense (at least, to any significant degree) as they move vertically, and the designer therefore takes care to place the hinge-points of his linkage so that the steering can follow the suspension movement without being unduly affected by it.

In practice, there are very few suspension layouts (parallel wishbones of equal length, as employed by Citroen in the DS, GS, SM and CX is one) which allow the perfect achievement of this objective over the full range of suspension movement *and* the full range of steering movement from lock to lock. The designer responsible for the geometry of the linkage usually has to do the best he can, making sure the ill effects of conflict between steering and suspension movement are minimized. He does not always succeed: there have for instance been cars in which beyond a certain point the steering went 'over centre' towards full lock and needed to be positively pulled back towards the straight ahead. Less serious, though often annoying, is the phenomenon which gives rise to the test driver's technical expression of *bump-steer*, meaning any unwanted steering effect caused (usually) by the lifting of one front wheel over a large bump.

Aside from the question of geometrical conflict, the steering designer must also consider how closely he wishes to conform with classical Ackermann steering. This is the arrangement which makes allowance for the fact that when a four-wheeled vehicle is turning a corner, its inner wheels are running round a smaller radius than the outer ones and consequently need to be turned through a greater angle.

A minor historians' industry has grown up around the fact that Ackermann did not invent the layout, but merely held the British marketing rights on behalf of the real inventor, Herr Lenkensperger. Be that as it may, it was assumed for many years that the steering linkage had also to be arranged in such a way that the extended front wheel axes met on the line of the back axle, towards the centre of the corner. This is indeed the arrangement needed at low speed and with iron-tyred wheels but it makes no allowance for the effects of pneumatic tyre deflection and slip angles – rear as well as front – at higher speeds. Colin Chapman appears to have been the first chassis engineer to question the classic Ackermann assumptions and it is still noticeable that most Lotuses feel somehow 'wrong' at parking speeds, but come to life most wonderfully once they are properly on the move.

Turning circles

Drivers love cars with very tight turning circles even though, as owners of Triumph Heralds discovered, the ability to U-turn in the average backstreet could play hell with the front tyres if it was exploited often enough. In fact, ultra-tight turning circles, which are only going to be used at ultra-low speeds, demand faithful Ackermann geometry if they are to be made to work without a lot of tyre scrubbing; and remaining that faithful implies compromises in other areas.

Besides, tight turning circles call for large angular movements of the front wheels which, in turn, mean large front wheelarches and correspondingly less space within the engine compartment and the footwells. In a front-driven car there is the added disadvantage of subjecting the constant-velocity joints in the drive-shafts to running at extreme angles. For all these reasons, it is a rare car which turns between kerbs in under 30 feet. A short wheel-base helps immensely, all other things being equal, which is why the Mini probably turns more tightly than any rival front-driven car.

The question of steering effects while turning raises a thorny modern question, that of 'torque steer'. There is no doubt that some of the more powerful front-driven cars exhibit undesirable effects in their steering during steady-state cornering and, equally notably, when powering out of a corner. From the driver's point of view, the sensation is that of the power having a direct and unwanted input to the steering, usually in such a sense that straightening up from the corner demands a positive effort and is difficult to achieve with precision.

In theory, driving torque should have no effect on the steering because the offset effects of the two wheels should cancel out, at least so long as the torque is exactly evenly split between the two (it behoves engineers to use great caution when applying limited-slip differentials to front-driven cars!). In practice, it is clear that the more heavily loaded and faster-running outer wheel tends to assume a dominant role, and if the offset at the hub is large – remembering that the drive force acts through the hub rather than the contact patch

– then it will try to wind the steering lock further on. The even more obvious tug felt when straightening up derives from gyroscopic effects: if there is significant offset at the hub, the front wheels are being translated as well as rotated around the steering axis, and it is hardly surprising that the forces caused by their attempted precession are felt through the steering.

This leads on to a word of warning. It is not easy, on most cars, to change the basic steering geometry (though it is not impossible, especially if one 'fiddles' with the lower link arrangements of MacPherson struts), but it is very easy to change the offset, almost unwittingly: it is an almost inevitable consequence of fitting wider wheels to accept wider tyres, let alone of fitting something like spacers in search of wider track. It should (I hope) be obvious by now that changing one or two parameters of a front suspension geometry *could* have unexpected and unpleasant consequences. It does not necessarily follow, but you could, for instance, end up with radically different, possibly non-existent steering feel and reduced self-centring, to say nothing of magnified torque-steer effects and road shock feedback. Almost certainly, of course, you will also increase the stresses on your wheel bearings.

Chapter seven

Handling

We cannot stress too often that handling and roadholding are two different things. Now that we have looked at all the elements that go to make up a car's suspension design, we may perhaps consider the difference between the two more precisely.

Any car's roadholding depends on whether its four tyres can between them generate enough sideways force to counter the cornering force which results from the car's mass subjected to a lateral acceleration. If the total grip exceeds the cornering force, the roadholding is satisfactory, as long as the car can also be controlled, which is where we move into the realm of handling. It would not be very satisfactory if nearly all of a car's grip was generated by the front tyres, for instance, because it would take a driving genius to prevent the back end from overtaking the front. That, however, is not poor roadholding: that is bad handling. The roadholding potential was there, but the car could not be controlled to take advantage of it. We should never talk about one end of a car (usually the back end) having 'poor roadholding' because it slithers wide in the wet.

Let us, first of all, decide what we mean by 'potential' grip or roadholding. We have already seen, in Chapter 5, that a tyre generates cornering force according to the load upon it, the slip angle at which it is operating and the camber angle it makes with the vertical. It follows that a tyre reaches its limit – its maximum potential grip – when it is sitting on top of the cornering force/slip angle curve for

whatever load/camber combination is being imposed upon it. The only other maximum which may intercede is when the resulting cornering force is so high that the car falls over sideways first; in any modern saloon car that is almost impossible to achieve on a smooth surface and on standard tyres.

The load, as has been pointed out previously, is a function of the weight of the vehicle, the cornering force, the height of the centre of gravity and the width of the wheel track. There is, of course, no point in loading your car to increase the load on its tyres. Extra weight inside the car creates its own demand for cornering force and you will not so much as break even: all other things being equal, the lightest car will corner quickest. You may, within limits, think about increasing tyre pressure, but we disposed of that in Chapter 5.

No; in order to realize your car's full cornering potential it must be capable of running its outer front and rear tyres at the top of their respective cornering force/slip angle curves – and the summits of those curves must be of equal height, in other words the front and rear tyres must be loaded equally (assuming they are the same size).

There is little apparent point in looking at the tyres on the inside of the corner because the outward shift of loading due to cornering force will have left them lightly loaded and making scant contribution to the proceedings. However, on the basis that every little helps, it is as well to make sure the inside wheels are doing nothing absurd. The lower your centre of gravity and the wider your wheel track, the less weight transfer will take place from the inner to the outer tyres and the greater the contribution the inner tyres will make to the roadholding. Even so, it does not seem to matter all that much if one (non-driven) wheel is lifted completely clear of the road surface; racing Ford Lotus Cortinas and Hillman Imps regularly lifted an inside front wheel round sharp corners, and it is fairly easy to lift the inside rear wheel of a VW Golf GTI, for instance, if it is driven with real enthusiasm. In general it remains true that the greater the weight transfer from the inner to the outer wheels, the less will be the maximum potential grip, and anything which adds to this adverse weight transfer (including, as we shall see, such devices as anti-roll bars) subtracts from a car's ultimate cornering ability.

The main emphasis, though, should be on solving a dual problem – balancing the loads on your outer tyres for maximum roadholding, then making sure your handling is good enough to enable you to reach that condition, maintain it with as little danger as possible of overdoing it, and finally return to straight-line running with the minimum of extra grey hair.

Setting the scene

We set our scene in Chapter 5 by looking at a Ford Escort-sized car in the context of tyre performance. We saw that given the Escort's weight distribution and choice of (155R13) tyre equipment, a point was reached at or about a cornering force of 0.75g where the demand for cornering force from the front tyres, plus their need to transmit enough driving force to maintain a speed of 50mph through the corner, led to a front slip angle in excess of 7 degrees. We saw that such a slip angle brought the front wheels close to the summit of their cornering force curve, and possibly edged them over it.

We also saw that the front slip angle was considerably greater than that of the rear wheels and, from examination of the various cornering force curves, we can see that the rear tyres are performing some way short of their full potential. The immediate conclusion is that if they could be persuaded to run at a higher slip angle, they would generate more cornering force. Yes, but if there was more

7:1. Where a car is rear-driven, as in the case of this rallying Vauxhall Chevette, it matters relatively little if the inside front wheel lifts completely clear of the ground during cornering. Indeed, most rally drivers often depend on the wheel being in the air to help them cut the apex of a corner. If the inside rear wheel also leaves the ground, as in this case, the effect can be a little more startling, though in any modern competition car, traction is maintained through the use of a limited-slip differential.

7:2. Another good example of the lifted inside front wheel technique is provided by Chris Sclater in a works Nissan Violet. Note that the front inside wheel is well clear of the ground but the inside rear wheel is barely (and probably only momentarily) clear, pointing to the priority the chassis tuner has accorded to good traction. The heavily laden outer front tyre is the governing factor so far as the handling is concerned in this situation: clearly close to the limit, the Violet is evidently understeering, though not to excess.

7:3. Where a car is front-driven, it is necessary to ensure that the inside *rear* wheel leaves the ground first in extreme situations, demonstrated by these racing Renault 5s. However alarming it may look, such antics have almost no effect on the car's handling beyond a step-change in the rear roll stiffness which many drivers find hard even to detect. The important thing is to maintain traction and front-end grip, and to ensure that the outer rear tyre develops enough sideforce to prevent the car whipping into oversteer. These Renaults are obviously well towards the understeer end of the handling scale.

7:4. Extremes of handling quality: in a scene from 1960s American club racing, a Lotus Elite demonstrates almost perfectly neutral handling under power out of a chicane, while the following Porsche 356 is suffering the trauma so often associated with rearward weight bias and swing-axle rear suspension.

rear-wheel cornering force the car would be unbalanced unless there was also more cornering force at the front – and we cannot achieve any more front cornering force because we have already hit the limit there. Are we, therefore, condemned to waste part of the potential cornering ability of our rear tyres?

The answer is yes – and no. Before we begin to look at the tricks used by chassis designers to achieve a better balance, and at the reasons why they choose not to seek the theoretically best balance in a car, not to mention brief consideration of the techniques available to the driver to make the most of whatever balance he ends up with, we need to consider the whole question of handling more formally – starting with one of the most vexed definitions in the whole of enthusiast motoring.

Handling – limiting factor?

What, then, is handling? Much earlier, we defined good handling as a car's willingness to do what the driver intends it to do, smoothly, quickly and without unpleasant surprises. Any driver – not just the average driver-in-the-street – appreciates a car which always behaves as he expects it to (consistency is always important), and which does things at a comfortable speed. Where drivers differ is in their assessment of what constitutes that 'comfortable' speed. No driver likes a car which finishes responding to a steering movement while he is still working out whether that response was shaping up the way he meant it to; but some drivers are slow-witted, tired or lacking in confidence, while others are wide awake, quick-witted and entirely aware of what they are after.

In practice, the difference between these two types of driver is that the former gets on much better with a car that understeers moderately, while the latter prefers minimal understeer and may even prefer neutral or marginal oversteer. Unfortunately, that commits us to defining those two much-discussed characteristics, understeer and oversteer.

People have tried to define these in all manner of ways, from whether the front wheels are pointing into or out of the corner, to how much the driver has to turn the steering wheel to achieve a given result, to the celebrated contention that understeering cars go through the hedge nose-first, while oversteering ones leave the road tail-first. That doesn't square with the experience of Porsche 911 repairers who find themselves far more concerned with nose jobs than bent rear bumpers, but in any case the only way to define handling properly is to look at causes rather than effects.

When we were looking in detail at tyre characteristics, we found that the cornering force developed by a tyre in any situation depends on several factors: slip angle, load, inflation pressure, camber angle and transmitted drive or braking torque. The proper definition of handling uses only the slip angle. A car *understeers* through a corner if its front tyres run a larger slip angle than its rear ones. Otherwise it *oversteers*, except in the rare event when the front and rear slip angles are identical, in which case we have a *neutral steer* situation.

It is not true that oversteer necessarily involves the tail hanging out or the application of opposite lock, though it often does. Nor is it true that oversteer is necessarily an unstable condition leading to difficulty of control, although once again, it often does. It *is* true that any car cornering in a stable manner points 'into' the bend *(fig 7:6)*. This is inevitable because since the back wheels are (usually) constrained to point in the same direction as the car body, the back tyres can only develop a positive sideways force (towards the centre of the corner) if the car's attitude is nose-in, and the rear tyre slip angle is the difference between the direction in which the car is pointing and the direction in which it is travelling. The direction in which it is travelling is, of course, the tangent to the curve at that point.

For the front wheels, however, the slip angle is that same difference *plus or minus any angle which the driver applies with the steering*. In an understeering car, the driver will have added more lock so that the front

wheel slip angle is greater than at the back. In an oversteer situation he will have subtracted lock – in other words, wound it off. This certainly means that the front wheels are pointing less into the corner than the rear ones, but it does not necessarily mean that they are actually pointing *out* of the corner – which is what most people mean by 'opposite lock'.

What is certainly true about genuinely opposite-lock cornering is that it is slow, however spectacular it looks. This is because if the front wheels are pointing out of the corner rather than into it, they are developing a cornering force in the wrong direction. Yet again we have to remind ourselves that a car corners quickest when its two outer wheels are operating close to the peaks of their cornering force curves – helped as much as possible by contributions from the inner wheels. That certainly isn't happening when the front wheels are pulling one way and the rear wheels the other.

Nor should opposite-locking be confused with the 'four-wheel drift'. The true drift, as so many good pictures of Nuvolari, Fangio or Moss showed in the days before superwide tyres and ground effect killed the technique, involves running all four tyres at very high positive slip angles, set up by persuading the car to adopt a large into-corner attitude *without* applying opposite lock. Fundamentally, there is nothing difficult about drifting as a driving technique except for the little matter of getting into and out of it in one piece. More scientifically one might say that steady-state four-wheel drifting is fine: it is the concomitant transient manoeuvres when entering and leaving the corner that separate Fangio and Moss from the rest of us.

Having disposed – I hope – of some of the hoarier myths surrounding handling, the first really important question is: what, exactly, *is* optimum handling? We have already said that it depends who and what kind of driver you are. Top racing drivers are reputed to prefer mild oversteer because they find it easier to set up an oversteering car to a balanced cornering situation with all four tyres developing strong positive sideforce. Most average road-going drivers are less concerned with the ability to corner consistently hard. The overwhelming evidence is that most people find cars feel more

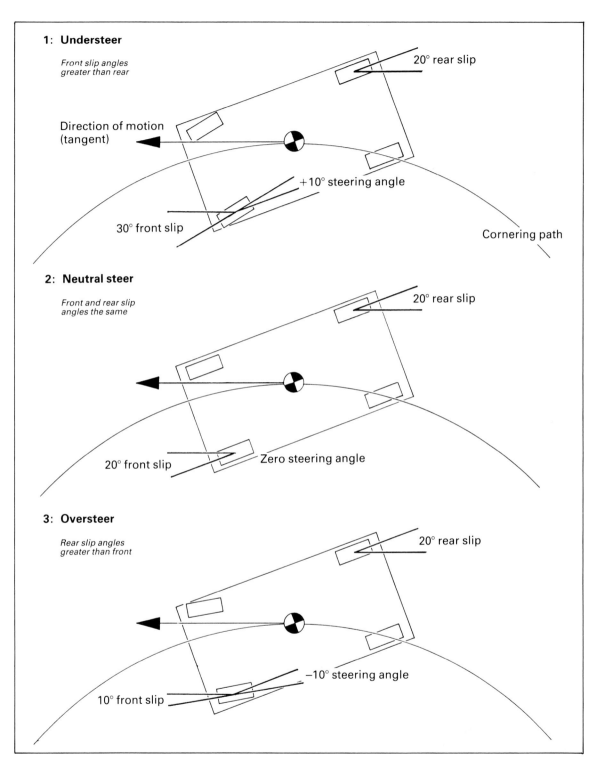

1: Understeer

Front slip angles greater than rear

20° rear slip

Direction of motion (tangent)

+10° steering angle

30° front slip

Cornering path

2: Neutral steer

Front and rear slip angles the same

20° rear slip

20° front slip

Zero steering angle

3: Oversteer

Rear slip angles greater than front

20° rear slip

−10° steering angle

10° front slip

7:5. Understeer or oversteer is defined by the difference between the front and rear slip angles. In each of these three examples — angles greatly exaggerated to make them visually obvious — the back tyres supply the same cornering force while that provided by the front tyres varies. The cornering force keeps the car on a curved path against its natural tendency to proceed in a straight line along the direction of motion, at a tangent to the curve.

7:6. This trio of racing Alfas, besides providing another example of front wheel lifting, illustrates clearly that cars on a stable cornering line point into the bend, even when understeering: the middle car of the bunch is *not* going to hit the corner markers in spite of the direction in which it appears to be aimed.

stable, predictable and easy to drive if they understeer moderately.

Understeer or oversteer can vary in severity. We saw from the Escort example of Chapter 5 that at 0.5g cornering force the front slip angle was a small fraction of a degree larger than the rear slip angle, indicating very moderate understeer. When the cornering force was increased to 0.75g the front slip angle was more than 2 degrees greater than at the rear, indicating quite severe understeer, which was still further increased if the driver applied enough power to hold his speed, let alone accelerate, through the corner.

Understeer in moderation is a safe and stable kind of handling. Its benefit is that in most circumstances, changes initiated by the driver – more or less power or steering lock, or even the application of the brakes – will simply change the degree of understeer. In addition, the behaviour of an understeering car when it reaches the limit of its roadholding is, as our Escort example showed, that it will simply refuse to corner any harder no matter how much extra lock is applied; eventually, if the driver refuses to take the hint, the front wheels will actually begin to slide. It is, how-

ever, more likely that the driver will back off the accelerator, and this in most cases leads to a safe recovery, as we shall see later.

The drawback of understeer, for the really keen driver or one involved in competition, is that it prevents the rear tyres from achieving their full roadholding potential. Again, as the Escort showed, some of it is wasted. What is needed to maximize the available grip is something close to neutral steer. Unfortunately, cars with neutral or oversteer characteristics lack the safe stability of the understeerer. In particular, their behaviour at or close to the limit is less predictable, though, as that ancient definition of oversteer implies, it is quite likely to take the form of loss of adhesion at the back of the car; and the plain fact is that the vast majority of drivers find this condition more alarming and difficult to cope with than limiting understeer.

The chassis engineer therefore faces a two-fold task. First he has to decide, in the light of the market at which the car is aimed, how strongly it should understeer (nobody these days deliberately designs a car to oversteer, and it is questionable if anybody ever did – deliberately). Then he has to decide how to achieve that desired result.

The task is not simple. The engineer is faced not simply with the car as it stands, but with one which may be driven one-up or heavily laden, which the driver may accelerate or brake round corners. So far as is possible, the engineer will seek to ensure the car's handling remains safe in all these circumstances while at the same time retaining as much of its potential roadholding as possible. Where handling and ultimate roadholding come into contact, though, the production car designer will favour safe and predictable handling, in other words, consistent understeer. To achieve this, he has various means at his disposal.

Ringing the changes

At this juncture we need to return to our cor-nering Ford Escort. We have seen the way in which, when driven one-up, it suffers increasing understeer as the cornering force is increased, until at around 0.75g on 155R13 tyres it approaches the limit of front tyre grip. We have also seen how switching to the equivalent 175/70R13 low-profile tyre restores the situation to a large degree, greatly reducing the understeer at 0.75g (though it is still greater than at 0.5g on the original tyres) and pulling the front tyres back down the cornering force curve from the peak so that they have further grip in hand.

It is instructive to look at the situation when the Escort is running fully laden, weighing 1,300kg with the aid of three hefty passengers and a bootful of luggage. One result of this extra weight in the back seat and boot is that the centre of gravity shifts aft so that the

7:7. The author demonstrating almost perfectly neutral steer in a Lotus Elan Plus 2 through Becketts Corner at Silverstone. The front wheels are pointing virtually straight ahead, yet the body roll angle indicates moderate to high cornering force, generated equally by the tyres at each end of the car running identical slip angles.

91

7:8. A racing BMW coupe, again showing near-neutral steer, though at a much higher cornering force than the Elan Plus 2. The body angle to the direction of travel (and thus the actual tyre slip angle, front and rear) is much more obvious and the inside front wheel is sufficiently unloaded to ride up the kerb without affecting the car's handling to any significant extent.

7:9. Extremes of oversteer behaviour can easily be provoked in rear-driven cars on snow or ice. The rallying Lancia Stratos here is well into the opposite-lock phase. Skilled drivers can hold this kind of attitude all the way through a long corner, but it is not the fastest way round: the front tyres are probably generating sideforce out of the corner rather than into it, and a neutral-steer attitude would improve the situation. Note the narrow, high-pressure tyres used to achieve maximum grip in sheet-ice conditions.

7:10. The four-wheel drift technique involved making the car adopt a large into-corner attitude angle without applying opposite lock so that all four tyres ran at high positive slip angles. A Mark VII Jaguar, all 34cwt of it, on 1950s tyres, provides this demonstration at Silverstone.

front/rear weight distribution becomes 50/50.

Now we ought to suspect from earlier calculations that this more even balance would improve the handling within our definition, by loading the rear tyres more heavily and making better use of their potential – by lifting the peaks of their cornering force curves in fact. What is immediately obvious is that in the power-off situation the handling must be neutral because we are demanding the same cornering force from each end of the now perfectly balanced car, its front and rear tyres equally loaded. Looking at our curves, we discover that at 0.5g sideways acceleration, we need to run both front and rear tyres at a slip angle of 3.25 degrees to achieve a balance. That is, both front and rear tyres are now running greater slip angles with the car fully laden.

When we increase the sideways acceleration to 0.75g we find that the tyres simply cannot cope. No matter how far you go along the cornering force curves for the outer and inner tyres, the cornering force never adds up to as much as we need. The car will, assuming the driver can control it in such conditions, begin to slither gently sideways at about 0.7g lateral

acceleration.

We have one immediate weapon in our armoury to counter this situation, and that is the 175/70R13 tyre. Returning once more to the curves suggests that the fully-laden Escort can pull 0.75g lateral acceleration on these tyres at a slip angle, front and rear, of just under 5 degrees which leaves plenty of extra cornering force still in hand – though it has to be said that the forces build up so quickly towards very high levels of lateral acceleration that the ultimate limit may not be as high as you think.

Having looked at one particular case, we ought now to study the general theory that nose-heavy cars naturally understeer, and tail-heavy cars naturally oversteer. They do, but not because of their basic weight distribution. Extra load on one end means a higher cornering force is needed, but the load itself means the tyres generate extra cornering force automatically. Understeer and oversteer arise because tyre characteristics are non-linear: the increase in cornering force is not directly proportional to the increase in load.

The best way to study the situation is to take a car and look at the effect on the power-off handling characteristic if weight is shifted from one end to the other. I have carried out the exercise on an imaginary car with deliberately simple though realistic numbers – weight 1,000kg, track 50in, centre of gravity height 20in, lateral acceleration 0.75g. Using our Michelin data for the 155R13 tyre, the results are as follows, as the front/rear weight ratio shifts from 65/35 (typical of a very small front-driven car) to 40/60 (in which case the car would certainly be rear-engined):

Weight Distribution F/R	Front Slip Angle	Rear Slip Angle	Difference
65/45	7.4deg	4.5deg	2.9deg (understeer)
60/40	7.2deg	5.0deg	2.2deg (understeer)
55/45	6.5deg	5.1deg	1.4deg (understeer)
50/50	5.7deg	5.7deg	Zero (neutral steer)
45/55	5.1deg	6.5deg	−1.4deg (oversteer)
40/60	5.0deg	7.2deg	−2.2deg (oversteer)

It must be said, of course, that 0.75g is a high lateral acceleration by normal driving standards, but with modern tyres one has to use something like this figure before truly significant differences start to show up. The other point to be made immediately is that allowance should also be made for the force transmitted through the driven wheels.

As I said in Chapter 5, the force needed at each wheel to maintain a small car at a steady 50mph round a corner, even when it is pulling 0.75g lateral acceleration, is not large by comparison with the cornering force. In round figures, each driven tyre needs to transmit about 300 Newtons while the front outer tyre of the nose-heaviest example car is generating a cornering force over 10 times larger. If you find this difficult to credit, remember that a car capable of accelerating at a consistent 0.75g *in a straight line* would reach 60mph from rest in under 3.7sec and would certainly deploy more power than the 16hp implied by our 300 Newtons per tyre at 50mph.

It follows, therefore, that while the drive force has an effect, it is not large unless the driver chooses to make it so – if he tries to accelerate round the corner – and even then the average family saloon has too little torque to spare, except perhaps in first or second gear, to make a huge difference to the handling. As long as the driver is happy to maintain his

50mph, then the effect of adding a drive component of 300 Newtons to a cornering force of 3,000 Newtons is to demand a total force of only 3,015 Newtons from that tyre. It will add something to the slip angle at which that tyre is running, but not a lot – unless the tyre is already close to the top of its cornering force curve.

However, there is no denying that the driven tyre runs a higher slip angle, however slight, than it would if it were undriven. Thus front-wheel drive increases the slip angle of the front tyres and so increases any tendency to understeer, while rear-wheel drive increases the slip angle at the rear and so *decreases* any understeering tendency. Four-wheel drive, as long as the torque is evenly split between front and rear, should have no effect whatever on the handling.

What we may conclude is that, in theory, maximum roadholding is achieved in a front-driven car if it is slightly tail-heavy, and in a rear-driven car if it is slightly nose-heavy. In each case the application of drive force pushes the driven tyre that little bit further up the cornering-force curve so that it exactly matches – if we have done our sums right – the undriven outer tyre sitting on the peak of *its* curve. In subsequent chapters I shall examine in detail the implications of this conclusion for front, rear, and four-wheel driven vehicles. At this stage we need merely observe that many rear-driven cars are indeed slightly nose-heavy while, so far as I know, there is no such thing as a tail-heavy front-driven car unless one counts something like a Mini Traveller with half a ton of cement sitting above its rear wheels. We should also observe that the weight distribution that is good for handling is by no means always the best for traction.

Changing the handling

So far, we have been looking at the merest basics of handling – at the interplay between a car's static balance, the load transfer during cornering, the tyre characteristics and the drive forces. There are, however, several things the chassis designer can do to change a car's handling balance without going so far as to move the engine from one end to the other, or widen the track by a foot.

The simplest trick of all is to run different

7:11. This Renault 5 Turbo, cornering fast on tarmac, is understeering very slightly. Handling balance in this rear-engined and very powerful derivative of the Renault 5 supermini is achieved in part by fitting considerably wider tyres at the rear than at the front, thus increasing the tendency to understeer to compensate for the oversteer effect of the rearward weight bias. The driver in this shot is trying hard enough to have lifted the inside front wheel just clear of the ground; an interesting contrast with the front-driven Renault 5s shown earlier in this chapter.

tyre pressures front and rear. A glance at a tyre data book will show how few cars actually run exactly the same pressures all round. The recommended pressures for our earlier example, the Ford Escort, are 23psi front and 29psi rear. We have already seen that the higher the tyre pressure, the greater the cornering force for a given load and slip angle. It follows that by decreasing the front tyre pressures, we incline the handling towards understeer. On the face of it therefore, far from trying to counter the basic understeer of the nose-heavy, front-driven design, Ford engineers are trying to make the Escort understeer even more.

Before we jump to any such conclusion, remember we are only at the beginning of the story. In theory, a designer could exert a major effect on the handling by fitting different sized tyres front and rear, but the practical difficulties confine this approach to supercars and pure racing cars. Obviously, the fitting of a larger tyre subjected to the same load on its corner of the car, will result in a larger cornering force for a given slip angle. Thus, the fitting of larger tyres at the back end of a car – as is usually the case – reduces the rear slip angles and consequently increases the understeer. This is not what you might expect at first sight, especially in a Formula 1 car; but remember they need to transmit huge

amounts of drive force, and to allow for the effect that force has on the rear wheel cornering force.

The road car designer still has four shots left in his handling locker. He may incline the roll axis; he may fit anti-roll bars; and he may engineer the rear suspension so as to deliberately introduce either a camber change, which modifies the rear tyre sideforce in a cornering situation, and/or an extra steering effect through the rear wheels as the car rolls – hence the term 'roll steer'.

If the roll axis is inclined front to rear, the end of the car at which the axis is lower will try to roll further, because the weight at that end is further above the axis. But because the body can only roll at one angle, the result of this imbalance is that the other end of the car is forced to take a greater share of the rolling force. If the roll axis slopes up towards the rear, then some of the rolling force set up at the front will be reacted at the rear, which means the rear outer wheel will be more heavily loaded, and the inner wheel correspondingly less loaded. This increase in lateral weight transfer at the rear means the rear tyres have to run at a higher slip angle to achieve the necessary cornering power, so understeer is reduced. An axis which slopes down from front to rear will increase understeer. As a technique, changing the slope of

95

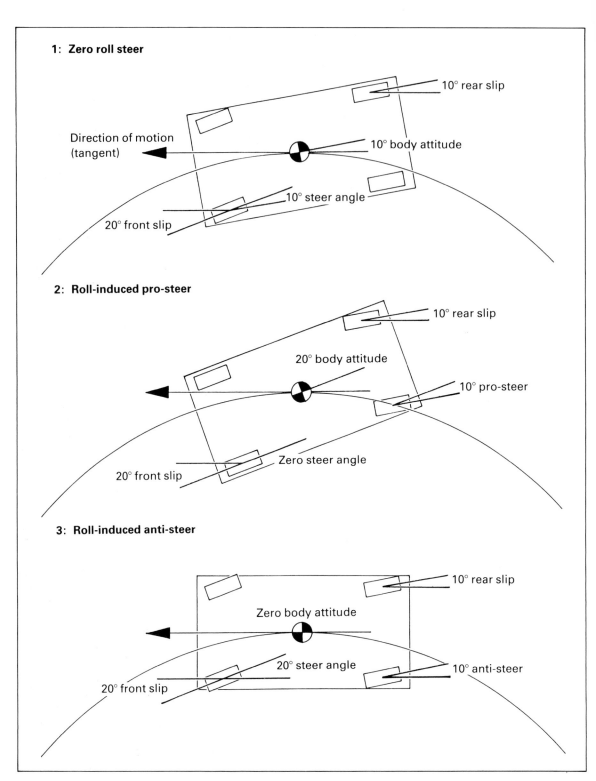

1: Zero roll steer

10° rear slip

Direction of motion (tangent)

10° body attitude

10° steer angle

20° front slip

2: Roll-induced pro-steer

10° rear slip

20° body attitude

10° pro-steer

Zero steer angle

20° front slip

3: Roll-induced anti-steer

10° rear slip

Zero body attitude

20° steer angle

10° anti-steer

20° front slip

7:12. The influence of roll-steer — the engineering of the rear suspension deliberately (or by accident!) to introduce a steering effect into or out of the corner — is transient: its only result in steady-state cornering is to alter the attitude of the car, making it point more or less sharply into the bend.

the roll axis (by changing the height of either the front or rear roll centre) is quite an effective way of modifying the handling. One of the subtly illegal tweaks sought out by scrutineers in production car racing is a relocation of wishbone or transverse link attachment points to the body and/or wheel hub carrier!

The action of the anti-roll bar is similar. The law of action and reaction means that while the bar tries to prevent the body rolling, the body tries to lift the inner wheel in the corner and squash down the outer one. Again there is a shift of load towards the outer wheel and the slip angles at that end of the car are increased. Consequently, a front anti-roll bar will increase understeer and a rear anti-roll bar will reduce it.

Camber change occurs during cornering with most forms of independent suspension. As we have already seen, negative camber – with the top of the wheel leaning inwards – increases cornering force while positive camber reduces it. It follows that a fairly easy way for a chassis designer to reduce understeer is to arrange for the outer back wheel to suffer a positive camber change when the car is cornered. It is an effective method but, like the fitting of a rear anti-roll bar, it deliberately sacrifices some of the potential grip of the back tyres.

The idea of roll steer needs to be examined closely. One's immediate thought is that by introducing a measure of rear-wheel steering, understeer will be reduced or increased according to which way the rear wheels turn. This is not actually true. If we consider a car cornering with no roll steer effect, the picture is the familiar one of the rear wheels running at a slip angle, and the front wheels running at *their* angle which comprises the slip angle plus the steering angle. If we now turn the rear wheels as though to steer the car into the curve, what will happen is that the car will indeed turn tighter; but assuming the radius of the curve remains the same, the driver will have to unwind a little steering lock and the car will then settle down to exactly the same lateral acceleration as before. The weight distribution has not changed, which means in turn that we still need the same cornering force from both the front and the rear tyres; consequently they must run at the same slip angles as before.

In *fig 7:12* I have drawn an extreme example to make the situation clearer. The weight distribution and cornering force demand a front slip angle of 20deg and a rear slip angle of 10deg. So long as the rear wheels are parallel to the car's centre-line, the body must therefore point 10deg into the corner. If we then introduce 10deg of pro-turn roll steer into the rear wheels, the same balance is achieved with a body attitude of 20deg, and the front wheels parallel with the centre-line, that is, with no steering input at all! Quite apart from the question of roll-steer, the example also serves to show why rear-wheel steering is not a good idea for anything quicker than a fork-lift truck, and it gives the first clue to the ideas behind the late-1980s development of proper four-wheel steering.

What this all means is that roll-steer is a transient effect. Its only influence on steady-state cornering behaviour is that pro-turn roll steer increases the attitude of the body, but reduces the necessary steering input, and *vice versa*. It also serves to remind us yet again that steady-state understeer and oversteer are functions of weight distribution, weight transfer, tyre characteristics *and nothing else*. The only proviso we should add is that one of the factors which can change a tyre's characteristic curve, along with tyre pressure, is camber angle. The value of roll-steer is not, therefore, as a modifier of understeer, but rather – and significantly – of transient behaviour. Without actually changing the steady-state behaviour, roll-steer can encourage a car to turn-in more quickly or more sedately, and reduce or increase the amount of steering lock required.

Roll-steer effects may be introduced in a number of ways. One of the simpler examples is the axle, live or dead, located by trailing radius arms *(fig 7:13)*. If the arms slope slightly downwards when the car is at rest, the action of the body rolling will push the outer arm more nearly level, increasing its effective length, while the inner arm will be lifted to a steeper angle and so effectively shortened. The inner end of the axle is therefore pulled forward and the whole axle slightly skewed so that it steers the car into the corner; this is pro-turn effect.

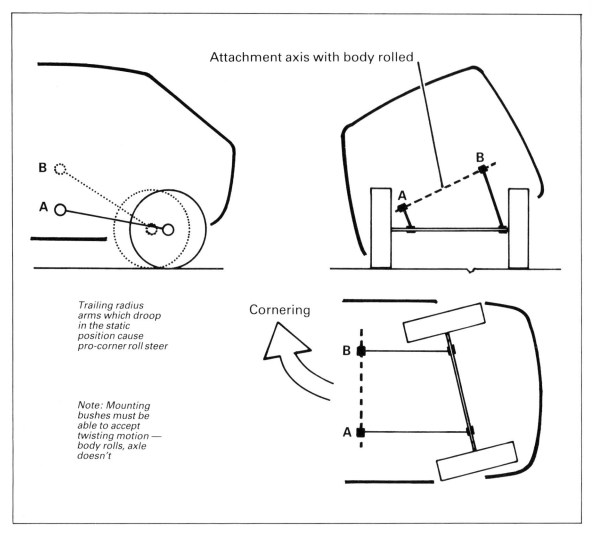

Attachment axis with body rolled

B

A

Trailing radius arms which droop in the static position cause pro-corner roll steer

Cornering

Note: Mounting bushes must be able to accept twisting motion — body rolls, axle doesn't

B

A

B

A

7:13. If a dead rear axle is located by trailing arms, then a roll-steer effect will be generated by the arms pulling the axle at a slight angle as the car rolls. The angles of the arms when at rest determine whether pro-steer or anti-steer results. This effect can be exploited for modifying the transient behaviour according to whether the car is lightly or fully laden.

This kind of arrangement can be self-correcting for load if it is carefully engineered. A heavy load in the back of the car will flatten the radius arms more nearly horizontal, and this will reduce or even reverse the effect; the heavily-laden car will turn in more slowly and the inertia effects of the extra load will have less influence on the stability.

Roll-steer effects can also be built into independent rear suspension systems. Some degree of roll-steer is inevitable with semi-trailing arms, for instance, and its direction and strength can be adjusted by suitable choice of semi-trailing angle and the static angle of the arm. An arm which droops at rest will have an anti-turn effect, while one which is set level to begin with will work in the pro-turn sense. Again, changes of geometry with load can be used to effect an automatic correction for any change of transient handling characteristic with load.

Designers are by no means unanimous in their approach to roll steer. Quite apart from its effects on transient handling, it offers contradictory advantages in the steady state. Pro-turn roll steer reduces the necessary steering input, which has an appeal for the man who is trying to hide slightly heavy steering; anti-

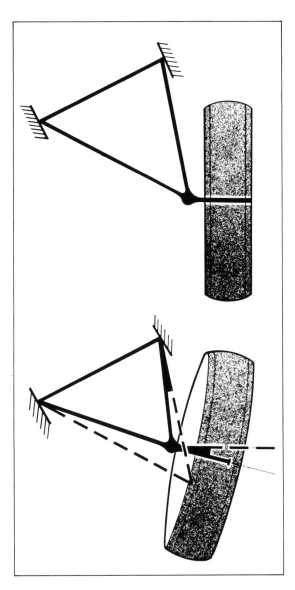

7:14. Semi-trailing arm rear suspension always has some roll-steer effect, though its size and sense will depend on the inclination of the arms in their static position and the angle of their pivot axis to the car's centreline. Once again, the effect can be used to help compensate for changes in load.

turn roll steer reduces the body attitude and therefore the angle through which the body itself has to be turned when entering or leaving the curve, or to change direction through an S-bend.

It is, perhaps, small wonder that some designers call plague on both notions and engineer for zero roll steer – though most of them are surely tempted to run the options

through the ubiquitous computer to see what happens. In any case, though, roll steer has to be used with caution and certainly not to excess. Strong or gusting sidewinds cause body roll in cars travelling in a straight line and thus roll steer inevitably degrades sidewind stability – though if the car's natural aerodynamic stability is good, as it is likely to be in a nose-heavy front-driven car for instance, the disturbance is likely to be too quickly and positively damped to pose a major problem.

Transient handling

When we talk of understeer or oversteer, we usually have a mental picture based on steady-state cornering: the car proceeding on its smooth path round the bend with its front and rear slip angles properly established. But to reach that stage, a car has to turn into the corner, to make the transition from running straight to running round the curve. At the exit from the corner, the car must be straightened up again. Two opposite-hand corners may follow one after the other, so that the car has to switch directly from cornering one way to the other. It may be necessary for the driver to correct his line in mid-corner, either because its radius changes or because he got it wrong in the first place.

One of the in-phrases of late-1980s motoring is 'turn-in', which so far as I am aware, was not used in its present sense 20 years ago. Be that as it may, it has become a convenient shorthand for summing up the transient behaviour of a car.

Turning into a corner is a complicated process. The driver may see it simply as turning the steering wheel and feeling the car responding, but there is far more to it than that. In the first place, the front tyres need to build up their cornering force. This can only happen when all the tread components in the contact patch have had the chance to rearrange themselves from a straight-running into a cornering pattern, and this logically requires that the tyre must roll forward the length of its contact patch before the full cornering force is established. That is why wide, low-profile tyres with short, wide contact patches give the impression of more eager turn-in (it is not, in fact, merely an impression).

Then again, the car must be started into its turning motion. The turning of the front wheels and the build-up of the front end cornering force is the first stage of this process. The way in which the message gets through to the rear wheels to set up slip angles and cornering force at the back end of the car also has a major influence on the speed of turn-in. Donald Bastow, in his mathematical analysis of transient behaviour, showed that in cars with a low polar moment of inertia, the build-up of rear cornering force starts (though at a lower rate) as soon as the front wheels are turned. In cars with a very high polar moment, the rear tyres actually begin by generating an anti-turn cornering force – which is then reversed as the pro-turn force builds up in turn. This not only slows the turn-in process but gives a feeling that the back end of the car is 'floating'.

The choice of tyre equipment and the size of the polar moment of inertia are therefore critical to the speed with which a car turns into a corner, and how it feels as it does so. It is as well to remember, as we observed earlier, that a very low polar moment also encourages pitching on poor surfaces: yet again, the designer has to seek the right happy medium.

We have already looked at the possible influence of roll-steer upon transient handling. Another factor that affects turn-in is the ratio of roll stiffness to roll damping. There will always be a tendency for the body roll angle to lag behind the turn-in: the sideways acceleration forces build up as the car begins to turn, but they take time to get the sprung mass on the move. If the springs are soft and the roll damping is weak, the inertia of the body will also take it past the steady-state roll angle and a moment may arrive when the rolling body is actually adding even more to the weight transfer to the outer wheels. This will momentarily magnify the handling characteristic, making an understeering car understeer even more and *vice versa*. Even in a neutral-steering car the extra weight transfer will degrade the roadholding and call for the momentary application of extra steering to increase the slip angle. The worst possible case would be a very heavy body (in other words a high spring mass) on very soft springs, with little roll damping.

There is another transient condition which it is vital to understand, and that is the effect of acceleration or braking. Except in very powerful cars, acceleration forces are small compared with cornering forces, as we have already seen; they may still be enough to tip the handling balance, especially in rear-driven cars – to the extent that skilled drivers can exploit the effect and unskilled drivers can be caught out by it. Braking forces are another matter altogether. A driver who would never exceed 0.5g lateral acceleration except in the direst emergency will quite often achieve 0.5g in straight-line braking. Most modern cars will exceed 0.9g in limiting braking and there are plenty that will achieve better than 1.0g (given the effect of the tyre tread 'keying into' the road surface, there is no truth in the old theory that no car can exceed 1g braking; racing cars, especially on 'soft' compounds, often do so by a very large margin).

In braking, as in cornering, there is a weight-transfer effect – in this case towards the front end of the car. As in cornering, the effect depends on the weight itself and the height of the centre of gravity, but also on the wheelbase rather than the track. Since the wheelbase is usually about twice the track, the transfer effect is roughly halved, but because braking deceleration can be large, its effect remains highly significant.

Forward weight transfer places an extra load on the front tyres. If the car is cornering, this means they can develop more cornering force for their existing slip angle. At the same time, the rear tyres are unloaded and develop less cornering force. In addition to all this, all four tyres are being asked to transmit a large force to slow the car, and this robs all the tyres of cornering force. What has happened in effect is that the act of braking has both added to (through weight transfer) and subtracted from (through the applied braking force) the cornering power of the front tyres. At the rear, however, both effects subtract from the cornering power.

Whatever the case, the car if left to itself will seek to achieve a new cornering balance between the front and rear slip angles. It may be, however, that the new demand may be

7:15. Real situations are often more complex than the steady-state constant-radius cornering of the theoretical model, so that a car's transient behaviour is an important part of its handling. An S-bend faces this Elan and its driver with the urgent need to switch from turning left at a very high cornering force to turning right equally hard, creating rapidly changing conditions for the tyres and suspension to cope with.

more than the lightly laden rear tyres can produce and the wheels will then slide sideways unless the driver reduces the steering lock to compensate. Such indeed is the danger of spin-

ning through clumsy braking in mid-corner that generations of (road) drivers were taught *never* to brake while cornering; and it is one of the effects against which the chassis designer

7:16. While competition and test-track scenes provide the extreme cases useful to illustrate the subject of handling, the same principles apply in less dramatic form on the road. As this Scorpio turns in to a corner, lateral weight transfer increases the load on the outside front tyre which is visibly distorting as it adopts a slip angle. The rapidity and vigour with which the cornering 'message' is transmitted to the other end of the car is an important factor in how the handling feels to the driver.

must guard.

Acceleration has the opposite effect. The weight shift is rearwards, which improves the cornering power of the rear tyres at the expense of the front ones. The acceleration force will also reduce the cornering power of whichever wheels are driven; thus in a front-driven car, acceleration doubly reduces the front end cornering power while increasing it at the rear. In a rear-driven car, on the other hand, the effects tend to cancel each other out, the rearward weight shift increasing the rear cornering power while the actual driving force decreases it.

It is worth noting, as a postscript to our thinking on basic handling, that speed itself plays a part in cornering behaviour. Even when you are cornering at a steady speed, a higher speed will involve a greater traction force to overcome the higher aerodynamic drag. Thus, all other things being equal, a front-driven car will tend to understeer more the faster it is driven round a corner, while a rear-driven car will understeer less. Even without considering aerodynamic effects (which are certainly beyond the scope of this book) it is not mere imagination which leaves the driver feeling his car's handling is 'different' when he has taken a corner at unusually high speed.

Chapter eight

In detail: front-wheel drive

Some time in the early 1980s, the turning point was finally reached when the majority of cars being manufactured had front wheel drive. By the time General Motors and Toyota had switched the majority of their production to front-drive, the issue was beyond doubt. It may well be that Toyota's switch to a front-driven Corolla replacement swung the balance. No doubt one day some historian will work it out. From the point of view of the chassis engineer, it meant that the layout which had started tentatively in the 1920s and 30s, and struggled to gather pace until the launch of the Mini at the end of the 1950s, had become the working norm rather than the exception.

What does front-drive mean for the suspension specialist? Fundamentally, that he is dealing with a nose-heavy car. The average front-driven car carries over 60% of its weight on the front wheels in the 'kerb' condition, though the balance shifts aft, especially in a small car, when four people and some luggage are aboard. That rightly implies a second problem. The car is basically nose-heavy, but the load on the back wheels of a typical supermini may double between the extremes of driver-only with a near-empty fuel tank, and four occupants, luggage in the boot and a full tank. That wide variation causes problems in the design of the rear suspension which we shall look at later.

The choice of front-drive causes some preoccupations in the steering department, too. The concentration of weight on the front wheels leads to heavier steering, and it is noticeable that all the larger front-driven cars either have power-assisted steering or uncomfortably low-geared manual steering, as in the Audi 80 and Vauxhall Cavalier. Beyond that there looms the question of whether all the drive torque can be transmitted satisfactorily through the front wheels. There is evidence of a practical limit to front-wheel drive torque and two cars at least, the Audi 200 Turbo and Saab 9000 Turbo, exhibit control problems in the wet because wheelspin is too easily provoked. Short of this actual limit, other powerful front-drive cars have raised questions about torque-steer. In practice this appears to result from a combination of gyroscopic effects and the increased friction in bushes and bearings in the steering linkage under their very high loads.

However, the designer also has a few things going for him. Most notably, the nose-heaviness of front-driven cars places the centre of gravity well ahead of the centre of aerodynamic pressure so that they are naturally very stable in crosswinds. This asset has occasionally been squandered by over-ambitious suspension design, especially the provision of over-generous roll-steer, but it remains a powerful plus point for the layout generally.

Inevitable understeer?

It is usually accepted that front-driven cars understeer. We have already established, in Chapters 5 and 7, that this is not because they are nose-heavy as such; if weight distribution was the only thing that mattered, everything would cancel out because while the front tyres would need to generate more sideforce – being closer to the centre of gravity – they would be able to simply because they carried more load. However, that simple picture would only apply if tyres had truly linear characteristics, and they do not. Thus we discovered that even in the idealized 'zero power' situation, a nose-heavy car will indeed demand that its front tyres run at greater slip angles and that it will consequently understeer.

The chassis engineer of a front-driven car therefore begins with something that understeers naturally. Then, because the front wheels are driven, it understeers even more because, again as we have seen, the feeding of drive torque to the front wheels reduces the amount of cornering force the tyres can develop for a given slip angle. So you apply more slip angle and there is your additional understeer. The saving grace is that in most circumstances, the addition will not be large; but even so the more torque you ask the front wheels to transmit, the greater the understeer will be, all other things being equal. The main task of the chassis engineer is, of course, to ensure that other things are not equal.

One's first thought is that if the front-driven car naturally understeers, then a certain degree of oversteer tendency should be built into the chassis to compensate. As we have seen, the practical means by which the chassis engineer can do this (neglecting things like different-sized wheels front and rear, or joke tyre pressures) are to incline the roll axis downwards to the front, to fit a rear anti-roll bar, or to design the rear suspension to develop positive camber.

If the roll axis is inclined downwards to the front, then some of the sideways weight transfer effect will be shifted from the front to the rear wheels. Since any load transfer from an inner to an outer tyre results in a reduction of the cornering force available for a given slip angle, this rearward shift of the transfer will reduce the front wheel slip angle and increase that at the rear. In other words, it will reduce the understeer. What we have achieved, in the language of our cornering force curves, is to make the two summits of more equal height.

What we have also done, though it matters less, is to increase still further the inner-to-outer load transfer on the rear wheels. This can quickly result in the total unloading of the inner wheel so that it lifts completely clear of the ground, an effect commonly seen in some briskly-driven front-wheel-drive cars. Once the inside wheel lifts there can be no more weight transfer at the rear, and the experienced test driver can often feel that a wheel has lifted on the steering pad because the understeer then begins to build more quickly. The point at which the wheel lifts actually causes a discontinuity in the car's handling characteristics, though it is rarely critical.

If an anti-roll bar is fitted at the rear, its action in resisting body roll again increases the inner-to-outer weight transfer between the rear wheels, reducing their effective cornering power and causing them to run at a greater slip angle. Understeer is consequently reduced.

Of these two techniques, the inclined roll axis is the better bet from an engineering point of view because it improves the situation at the front (by reducing the load transfer that would otherwise have taken place) while pushing the rear tyres closer to a limiting situation. The rear anti-roll bar merely reduces the back-end cornering power and while reducing understeer, also sacrifices some of the car's ultimate roadholding. This is why, in practice, you rarely find a front-driven car with only a rear anti-roll bar.

The rear suspension may be set up to work on the problem by using its movement under the influence of body roll to alter the cornering power of the rear wheels by changing their camber angle. Pure trailing-arm rear suspensions, for instance, force the rear wheels to lean over at the same angle as the rolling body, and the resulting positive camber angle greatly reduces total cornering force at the rear. Consequently, the rear tyres have to run greater slip angles to achieve the necessary cornering force and understeer is reduced. This was, of course, the approach adopted for the Mini, all recent Citroens and most Renaults. The Citroens, from DS to CX, were a special case because their use of double-wishbone front suspension geometry with equal-length arms meant that all four wheels leaned to the body roll angle and the handling balance was adjusted primarily by the relative stiffness of front and rear anti-roll bars.

Before we go on to look at front-drive suspension systems in more detail, we should remind ourselves of the consequences of acceleration and of braking in mid-corner. With front-drive, any application of power increases the tendency to understeer, and if sufficient power is applied actually to accelerate through the corner, the rearward weight transfer increases the understeer still further. This may prompt the wild thought that what we really need to achieve ultimate roadholding in a front-driven car is a vehicle that basically oversteers so that it is brought back to neutral steer when power is applied.

Two things are wrong with this argument, or three if you count the effect on engineering sanity of a rear-engined, front-driven car.

First, such a contraption would have disastrous traction, and second, it would be bound to exhibit wicked oversteer under braking, if not merely on a trailing throttle. When braking, as we discovered earlier, the effect on the front wheels is that the forward weight transfer at least partly compensates for the way the cornering power is reduced through the tyres having to apply a braking force. The rear wheels, on the other hand, suffer reduced cornering force on both counts. The result is that understeer is greatly reduced. Also, the actual load on the rear wheels may be reduced to the point where both – or possibly just the inside rear – lock up, with serious consequences for stability.

Yet again, it helps to put some real figures into the situation. We saw in Chapter 5 that if

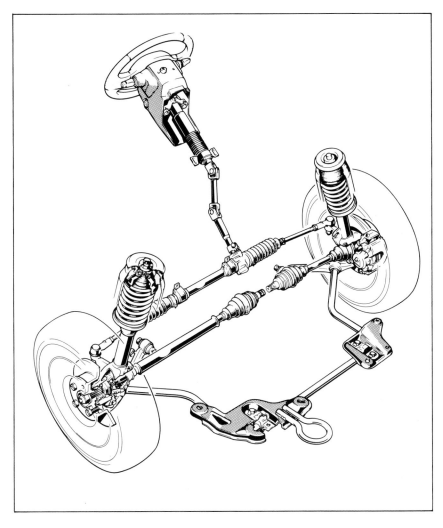

8:1. The front suspension of the front-drive Ford Escort uses MacPherson struts, and makes an interesting contrast with that of the Sierra illustrated in Chapter 4. Again the lower members are effectively wishbones formed by transverse links plus the cranked ends of the anti-roll bar. In this case, however, the anti-roll bar runs across the front of the car and the steering rack is aft of the axle line. Also, the bottom ends of the struts have to be engineered to leave room for the drive shafts to pass through.

our driver-only, 900kg Ford Escort on Michelin 155R13 tyres is cornered at 0.5g, it understeers gently. If we now brake it at 0.5g while still cornering at the same lateral acceleration, then the forward weight shift means that the loads on the tyres alter to the point where the outside front is supporting 460kg – more than half the entire weight of the car – while the inner tyre supports 261kg. At the back, the outer tyre load is now 166kg and the inner load is away down to 73kg.

Even before we start to think about the effect of braking effort, the more heavily loaded front tyres need to run at only 2.35 degrees slip angle (instead of 3.05 degrees) to maintain the same front cornering force, while the more lightly laden rear ones move up from 2.6 degrees slip angle to 4.6 degrees. Already, therefore, the Escort is oversteering. If we now apply the circle-of-forces rule to discover the total force each wheel must generate and the necessary slip angles, we reach a final answer of front 4.3 degrees, rear 6.4 degrees. The action of the braking force has pushed all four wheels further up the cornering force curves and in the case of the rear wheels they are getting perilously close to the top – the point at which the back end will begin to slide wide.

In practice, simultaneously cornering and braking a car that hard amounts to fairly brutal treatment. That is not to say you would not do it if, breaking the first commandment of driving ('Thou shalt not drive faster than will enable thee to stop safely in the bit of road thou canst actually see is clear') you swing round your favourite blind bend to discover a tree has fallen across the exit line. The chassis designer tries to bear that in mind. There is a limit beyond which one can practically guarantee to spin any front-driven car by simultaneously braking and cornering hard but the engineer can seek at least to prevent the car from spinning within the limits of lateral acceleration regarded as high by the average driver – which is to say, about 0.5g.

Ideally, he would like to achieve this kind of safety without making the car understeer excessively when it is accelerating round a bend, which is what he will do by making the basic understeer so strong that the braking effect merely reduces it. There are ways of doing this with the aid of variable-rate springs

– the object being to reverse the usual effect of an inclined roll axis and force lateral weight transfer back to the front tyres – but a more usual approach is to ensure that in such a 'panic' situation, the front tyres themselves will be close enough to their own maximum cornering power to ensure the back end does not lose grip all by itself. Now, perhaps, we begin to understand another possible reason for Ford's odd-looking choice of tyre pressures for the Escort, referred to earlier. Leaving the more heavily-laden front tyres at a lower pressure than the rears means that in a savage brake-and-turn situation, there is a much better chance that the car will remain balanced even if it is with reduced grip at both ends. You may, of course, choose to pump up the front tyres for the sake of reduced understeer in normal running, but you will only have yourself to blame if you find out the hard way why the recommended pressures are as they are. Along with such handling considerations, of course, arrangements are also made to prevent the rear brakes locking when the rear wheels become lightly laden, by means of pressure-limiting valves which may be made directly load-sensitive.

In some cases, braking is not necessary in order to provoke changes in a car's handling. If slip angles are large and tyre drag is high, even the deceleration caused by lifting off the accelerator in the middle of a corner may be enough to cause an awkward weight transfer and all its subsequent problems. This is no academic question, as anyone who drove an early Mini (especially a Cooper or Cooper S) will recall. There was indeed a transition from power-on understeer to power-off oversteer, and it could be abrupt to the point where you could lighten the back end enough to unstick the rear wheels altogether. Eventually, of course, the rally and racing Mini drivers learned the art of letting the tail swing out so far before pinning it down with re-applied power, leaving the car sufficiently sideways for speed to be scrubbed off quickly and safely, but this was hardly a technique to be recommended for public roads.

The Mini appeared deliberately to ignore one of the chassis tuning techniques I mentioned earlier. Its roll axis actually inclined downwards to the rear because its double-

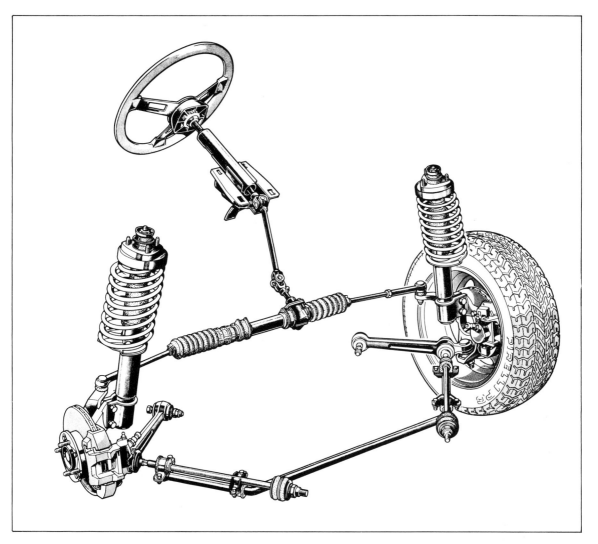

8:2. Fiat's approach to the front-drive MacPherson strut, as applied to the Strada Abarth 130TC, is in most respects very similar to Ford's. One major difference is that the lower wishbones are formed by two dedicated locating members, leaving the anti-roll bar as a separate component which does not contribute to wheel location.

wishbone front suspension had a roll centre above ground level while its simple rear trailing arms gave a centre at ground level. Those trailing arms did, however, ensure that when the body rolled the rear wheels adopted the same roll angle, reducing the cornering power of the back tyres. The roll axis inclination actually increased the considerable natural understeer; the camber change reduced it. The end result was still a quick switch to oversteer when a driver who was trying hard released the accelerator. Any braking while cornering made things even worse, though from the outset the Mini was equipped with a

rear brake pressure limiter. Preventing premature locking of the back wheels is one thing, but it does nothing to overcome problems inherent in a car's handling.

The Mini survived and remained popular because its ultra quick steering allowed the average driver to pay off lock briskly and avoid disaster, and in any case drivers soon learned – aside from genuine emergency situations – how the car needed to be driven to avoid premature greyness. You simply did not lift off the accelerator in mid-corner or, if you had to, you eased your foot up rather than immediately remove it. Alternatively, you simply wound on even more lock without lifting off, knowing that the rapid build-up of understeer and tyre drag would kill the speed almost as quickly. For the first few years of its life it was enough that the Mini would go round most corners with power on faster than almost any rear-driven contemporary. Even so, the Mini was a warning to other chassis engineers, and for the most part, later designers took different routes, especially in rear suspension design. The emphasis switched from using every possible means to tame the power-on understeer, to striking a balance between that and ensuring a less dramatic response to lifting off the accelerator in mid-corner.

The key to success in this objective has not been to throw away all the original Mini thinking, but to remove one of the factors which made the understeer/oversteer switch so rapid and alarming. Most modern front-driven cars ensure, above all, that the outside rear wheel remains substantially upright in any cornering situation, avoiding the extra loss of back-end sideforce caused by camber change. Also it has often been found worthwhile to use anti-roll bars at both ends of the car to limit roll angles without stiffening the springs to a ride-ruining extent, leaving the rear bar effectively the stiffer so that basic understeer is still counteracted. This technique has proved effective even though it

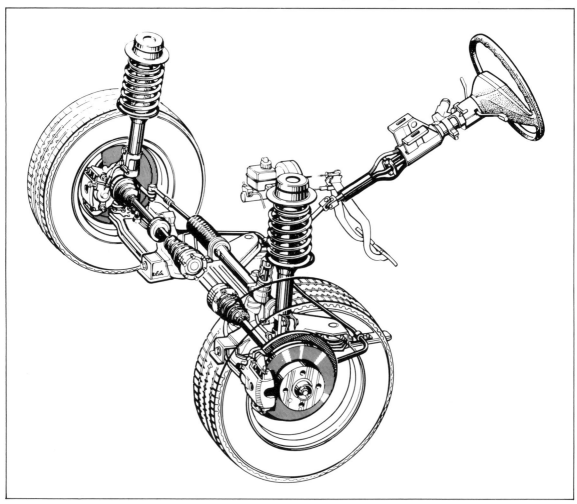

8:3. A third example of the use of MacPherson struts for a front-drive car is the VW Golf — this is the GTi 16V version. The location of the lower end of the strut is the responsibility of a proper wishbone-like member, and both the anti-roll bar and the steering rack lie aft of the axle line.

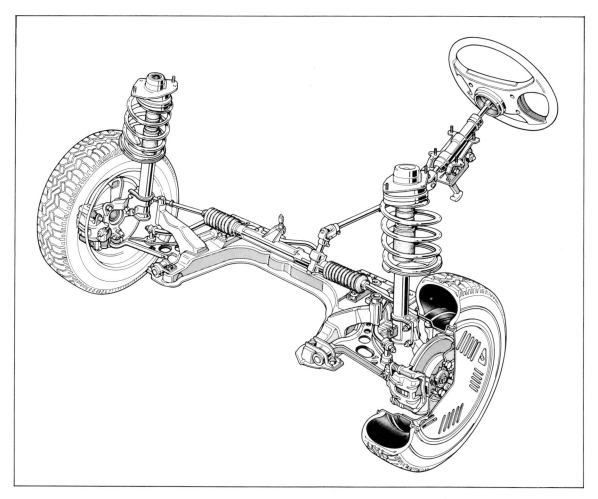

8:4. Fresh thinking from Fiat is evident in the MacPherson front suspension of the Tipo, which is innovative in its use of nodular cast iron for the wishbones. Their swept-forward shape in conjunction with carefully designed mounting bushes allows compliance for noise and vibration absorption without undue steering deflection. Wishbones and steering rack are attached to a subframe.

may result in the inside rear wheel lifting well clear of the ground during enthusiastic cornering.

Front suspension

There are really only two choices of front suspension layout for any car these days, front-driven or otherwise. Most of the earlier front-drive designs – the Citroen *Traction Avant* and DS, the BMC Mini and ADO16 1100/1300, the Renault 4 and 16 – used double-wishbone geometry, even though Citroen managed to make it look rather odd. The adoption of transverse rather than in-line engines, especially with end-on gearboxes, has tended to eat into the space needed for the upper

wishbone, and as a result more designers seem now to favour the MacPherson strut, on the evidence of cars like the Fiat 127 and Uno, Ford Fiesta and Escort and Volkswagen Polo and Golf. The transverse engine at least makes it easy and natural to install a steering rack immediately aft of the engine, where it is very well protected against frontal impact. It should be noted, though, that Honda, pioneers and apparently devoted users of the MacPherson strut from the earliest Civics onwards, have recently reverted to double wishbones for the Accord and Legend. This they have done by ingeniously removing the upper wishbone to a point well above the wheel, almost to the position that would be occupied by the turret at the top of a MacPherson strut.

The only problem posed by the front-drive is that of finding space for the drive-shafts along with everything else. If anything, that has favoured the MacPherson strut because the conventional coil spring in a double-wishbone layout has to bear on the upper wishbone so as to leave passage for the drive-shaft between that and the lower one. The result is a very short spring, which has to be operated on a long lever arm to achieve a reasonable spring rate when measured at the wheel. Perhaps in consequence, many of the front-driven designs that use double wishbones have featured other types of spring: rubber in the Mini, lengthwise torsion bars in the Renaults, and hydropneumatic in the Citroens for instance. Conventional coil-spring layouts were possible, however, as Renault showed with the 12/18 and Saab with the 96/99/900 series.

Citroen's almost deliberately odd-ball approach resulted in the DS and SM having double-wishbone geometry, but formed from two massively curved arms, which swung back to mountings on the main bulkhead structure. While you might argue the weight savings and losses of such a layout, it was dreadful from the compliance point of view, and when it replaced the DS, the 1974 CX had its curved arms trailing from the nose structure. There could be little doubting the weight penalty of *that* layout, and eventually the BX emerged with MacPherson struts! Even odder was the 2CV layout, with massive single leading arms attached to the front of the chassis-platform assembly. This, too, gives no chance to build in compliance, and it also calls for large changes in drive-shaft length as the 2CV rolls through its considerable angles. The 2CV, DS, SM and CX had one common factor in that their suspension geometry obliged all four wheels to lean over at the body roll angle. By accepting the adverse camber change they sacrificed ultimate roadholding potential, but against that, they avoided the worst effects of lift-off oversteer and also enjoyed very 'pure' steering geometry, free of bump-steer and fight-back effects.

The designer has comparative freedom to choose his front roll centre height with double wishbones and, in a front-driven car, will normally seek to place it close to ground level so that the roll axis may slope nose-down or, at the very least, be level. The upwards migration of the roll centre caused by roll will 'disincline' the roll axis and so increase understeer but against that, the actual rolling moment will certainly be reduced, which is probably the more desirable effect.

Where the MacPherson strut is used, the main difference between the various layouts in current use lies in the design of the bottom end. There is no real alternative to running the strut down to a clamp which attaches its lower end to the upper part of the hub carrier. The outer end of the drive-shaft runs below the clamp, and below that is the lower wishbone or equivalent carrying the lower swivel which, together with the upper end of the strut, determines the actual line of the kingpin. The strut need not actually follow this line, and the coil spring certainly will not, since it was found many years ago that offsetting the lower end of the coil reduced the tendency of the strut to suffer 'stiction'. Angling the coil axis relative to the strut resulted in a much better low-speed ride in cars where this had previously been an apparently intractable problem.

The actual form of the lower wishbone varies widely. Some designers favour a strong, wide-based genuine wishbone, as in the Lancia Delta: others make the wishbone narrower-based, as in the Fiat Uno, while Ford retains its long-standing principle of using the trailing ends of its front anti-roll bar together with simple transverse links to form an effective wishbone. This is an area where cost is always balanced against the need for adequate strength and reliability. Increasingly, the need for adequate compliance is also being taken into account, and this will certainly influence the design of the lower member, which is almost entirely responsible for fore-and-aft wheel location.

With the MacPherson strut there is again considerable scope to vary the roll centre height, and no problem exists in placing it at or even below ground level for a downward-inclined roll axis. When the car rolls, the MacPherson roll centre tends to drop even lower: while this shifts even more of the lateral weight transfer towards the back, the ever-increasing depth of the roll centre also means

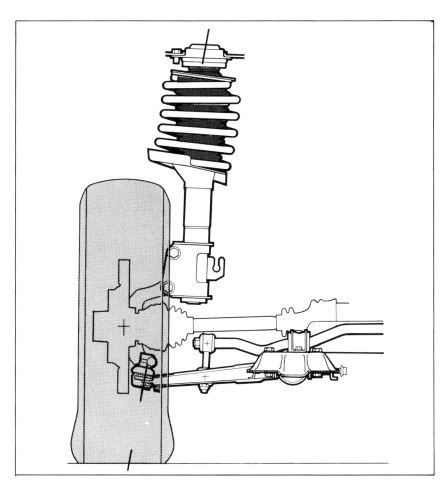

8:5. Massive front suspension of the Saab 9000 serves to illustrate how a MacPherson strut, brake disc, hub bearing and drive shaft are accommodated in the space within, beside and above the wheel. The strut top mount and lower ball joint define the steering axis. Note that the coil spring is offset to be concentric around that axis rather than the damper strut itself.

there is more weight to transfer. In practice, engineers who use both MacPherson struts and double wishbones seem to find ways to minimize their disadvantages.

Rear suspension

There is a temptation to think that because all the main mechanical components of a front-driven car are at the front, the rear suspension has nothing more to do than hold up the back end of the cabin. That is a dangerous idea. Without simplifying the case too much, you might almost argue that while the front wheels of a front-driven car determine its roadholding (because they are more heavily laden and able to generate far more sideforce) the rear wheels determine the handling.

As I have already pointed out, there is a particular problem in designing rear suspensions for front-drive cars in that the load on them can vary greatly according to the car's occup-

ants. A typical supermini might weigh 1,700lb with driver alone and fuel for a short drive. Of that, perhaps 600lb will rest on the rear wheels compared with 1,100lb on the front. Now load two fat friends into the back seat for another 350lb, place their suitcases under the hatch (say 30lb each) and put another 8 gallons of fuel in the tank (60lb). Almost the whole of the extra 470lb load falls on the rear wheels.

The first question the designer has to face is what kind of spring rate he is going to use. If he chooses a soft spring to achieve the right kind of ride frequency when the back wheels are lightly laden, those hefty back seat passengers are likely to end up feeling seasick, and besides, they will make the back end of the car sink by several inches when they get in – quite possibly down to the bump stops. Some early front-drive cars, especially the BMC ADO16 (Austin/Morris 1100) with its Hydrolastic sus-

8:6. The 'Omega' rear suspension of the Lancia Y10 and the later Fiat Panda is an example of how a light tubular axle beam need not necessarily pass straight from one hub to the other. Location is by a central bush, which must be compliant enough to permit the relative movement of body and axle in roll, and two angled trailing links.

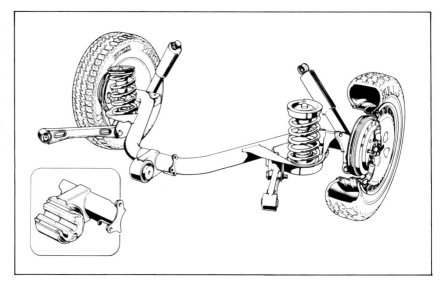

8:7. The Vauxhall Astra/ Opel Kadett rear suspension is typical of the torsion-beam layout now found in so many of the smaller front-driven cars. The beam actually joins the two trailing arms a short way aft of their body attachment points, creating a shallow H-shape in plan view. The cross-section of the beam is carefully calculated to permit the trailing arms to move relative to one another vertically while maintaining rigidity in other senses. An interesting detail of this suspension is the use of conical 'Minibloc' springs, which compress virtually flat under full load, minimizing the use of space.

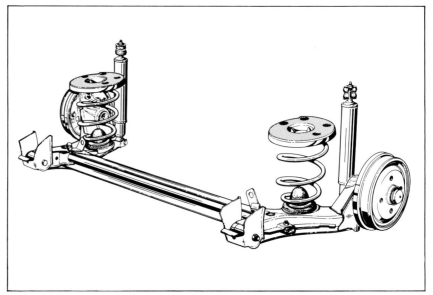

pension linked front to rear, became all too familiar for their habit of lifting their headlamp beams to the heavens when people were sitting in the back.

If, on the other hand, the rear spring rate is optimized for the fully-laden case, the ride will feel terribly rough when the driver is on his own. The designer must also bear in mind that unless the front and rear suspension frequencies are reasonably well harmonized, the car is likely to suffer severe pitching motion on poor surfaces.

It is a situation which calls for compromise, and most of today's designers use variable-rate spring arrangements of one kind or another. Variable spring rate can be achieved either in the construction of the spring itself, or by operating the spring through a linkage, which decreases the spring's effective lever arm as the car is loaded and so increases its stiffness. Some of these latter arrangements have formed part of ingenious 'folded' trailing-arm rear suspension systems which have their dampers installed vertically or nearly so, and leave the rear load platform completely free of suspension intrusion. An increasingly popular alternative to clever spring or linkage design is the use of very long bump-stops, usually of

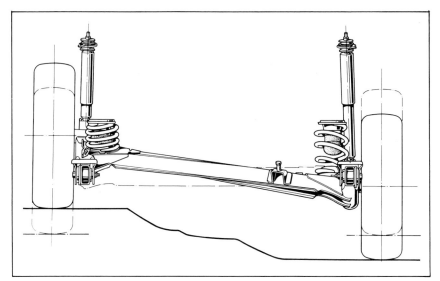

8:8. The operation of the torsion-beam layout is illustrated by this drawing of the Fiat Uno's rear suspension in a rolled position. As one wheel rises and the other droops, the axle beam is twisted, doubling as an anti-roll bar, while the wheels are kept parallel and upright.

polyurethane elastomer, which themselves provide a progressive rate spring effect as they collapse. In the Austin-Rover Maestro for instance such bump-stops come into play after only 2 inches of a total 8-inch rear suspension travel.

Once the designer can call upon a variable-rate spring – a typical figure, taken from the Renault 5, is 140lb/in unladen and 175lb/in fully loaded – he can aim far more closely for a constant ride frequency, which he can then match with that at the front. His other problem, that of a tail-down attitude when the car is fully laden, is also reduced though by no means eliminated; the only way this can be done is by providing some means of actually adjusting the rear suspension height to match that at the front. This leaves the car sitting

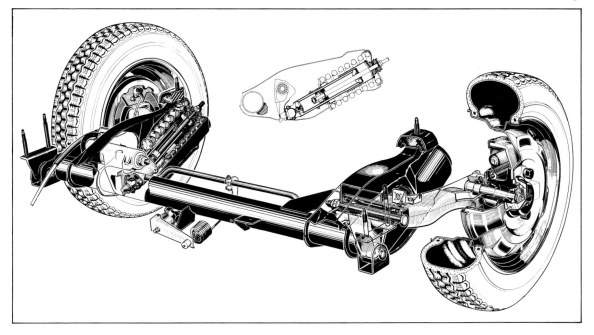

8:9. The Peugeot 305 Estate introduced a novel rear suspension layout which permits the car's load platform to be completely flat and unobstructed between the wheelarches. The trailing arms, carried at either end of a simple tubular crossmember, operate the compact coil spring/damper units via lever arms. The anti-roll bar is conventional.

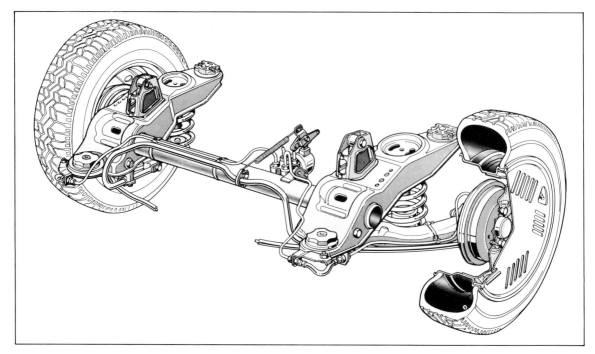

8:10. Again partly to minimize intrusion into the boot area, Fiat have chosen simple trailing arms for the rear suspension of the Tipo, mounted on a subframe composed of two pressings joined by a transverse tube. Flexible mounting of the subframe for noise suppression allows the trailing arms to be carried on taper roller bearings for precise control of wheel tracking.

lower on its springs so that it can take advantage of the stiffer spring rate. An alternative is offered by Citroen, whose high-pressure hydropneumatic suspension system offers constant ride height as well as level (in fact the ride height is adjustable for fording and rough-road ground clearance) together with near-constant ride frequency. Despite the fact that Citroen has proved its system in millions of cars over a 30-year period – and managed to produce those cars at competitive prices – no other manufacturer has yet taken up the principle.

Rear systems

While the choice of front suspension layout might be effectively limited to two, the range of options at the back of the front-driven car is extremely wide. They extend from simple trailing arms through semi-trailing arms, double wishbones, MacPherson struts and dead axles to that 1970s newcomer, the torsion beam axle.

We have already discussed the trailing arm and it still has its many proponents, most notably including the major French manufactur-

ers, at least for their smaller cars. In summary, the advantages of the trailing-arm layout are simplicity and the positive camber-change which helps reduce the basic understeer characteristic. Trailing arms have also readily lent themselves to space-saving rear suspension arrangements such as those found in the Peugeot 205 and Renault 5, in which all the components are assembled to a sub-frame which fits entirely beneath the load compartment floor. Against that, trailing arms give a ground-level roll centre, which does nothing to counteract basic understeer.

The light 'dead' axle also finds favour with Alfa Romeo and Saab, for instance. Compared with the trailing arm arrangement, the dead axle has a higher roll centre, which encourages inclination of the roll axis to reduce understeer. It also prevents wheel camber change, so that rear tyre cornering power is consistently high, which means that while in one sense it is better at reducing understeer, in another sense it does less to help – classic swings and roundabouts, except that the purist engineer (like Alfasud's Hruska) may prefer the dead axle because, unlike the trailing arm, it makes no deliberate sacrifice of rear tyre cornering power. If the designer favours roll-steer, the dead axle can be made to provide it by way of inclined trailing arms. It has to be said, though, that it is more difficult to find room for a dead axle at the back of a car where other engineers are seeking maximum space and minimum clutter.

Double wishbones have scarcely found favour with front-drive designers because their adoption would represent a deliberate sacrifice of that great front-drive virtue, a simple and spacious back end. They would also very probably cause structural headaches. One of the few front-drive production cars with what is claimed to be double wishbone rear suspension is the Honda Accord, in its 1986 model-year relaunch, though in fact this system is rather more complicated since the lower 'wishbone' is cleverly split into two separate linkages, one controlling camber while the other looks after castor angle.

The MacPherson strut has found a lot more favour with the designers of front-driven cars. It was used on all the early Hondas, for instance, (and was retained for the Legend) and was a feature of Fiat's successful early front-driven models, the 128 and 127. Its appeal for rear suspension use is much the same as for the front: it wraps neatly round the corners of the cabin 'box', feeds its loads into structurally convenient, widely separated points, and controls wheel camber angle within close limits. Its problem of roll centre migration downwards is more of a problem at the back end though, because the movement will tend to increase understeer with body roll as well as increasing the actual rolling moment.

Ford adopted a hybrid suspension geometry for its front-driven Escort, combining semi-trailing and MacPherson features. As in the strut design, the wheel is clamped to the damper casing to control the camber angle. Lateral wheel location is provided by a 'wishbone' (offering a footing for the coil spring which is not wrapped round the damper) with a single locating bush inboard, while fore-and-aft location is by a radius arm. This combines with the transverse member to form an effective semi-trailing arm, which dictates the geometry of wheel movement except in

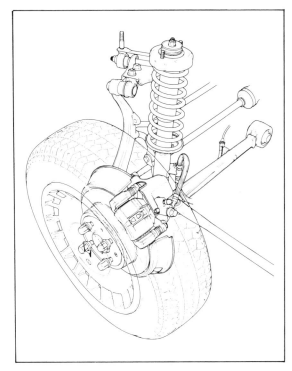

8:11. Honda refers to the Prelude rear suspension layout as double-wishbone, but in fact it is rather more subtle than that: the upper member is a wishbone locating the top end of the long, sweeping wheel hub-carrier extension, but the lower transverse and trailing members are attached independently rather than being joined to form a wishbone as such. Each member is thus responsible for controlling wheel movement in a particular plane. This version is also equipped for four-wheel steering, of which more anon.

camber. As a result, there is some carefully calculated roll-steer effect. Apart from saving space, the object of the layout was apparently to create scope for noise suppression through compliance; as far as the roll centre is concerned, the geometry remains MacPherson, with the same potential problems of roll centre migration.

Other companies, notably Lancia and some of the Japanese manufacturers, have adopted a form of MacPherson strut in which the lower end of the strut is located by two transverse links in parallel. By attaching these links asymmetrically with respect to the wheel hub (and thus the point of application of the cornering force) their inboard mounting bushes can be persuaded to compress in such a way as to give a roll-steer effect. This is claimed to improve stability when the wheel passes over

8:12. Renault 30 rear suspension was MacPherson
strut in principle, with the
wheel hub rigidly attached
to the base of the damper
strut. However, the location
of the lower end of the strut
was interesting, with
angled body mountings for
the transverse members,
which were attached to the
hub carrier independently
of the trailing arms to give a
complex multi-link effect.

8:13. The Ford Escort uses
MacPherson struts at the
rear as well as the front.
Transverse wheel location
is by large pressed-steel
members located well
towards the centre of the
car; fore-and-aft location is
by simple trailing links. As
in the Renault 30, the coil
springs are separated from
the dampers to minimize
turret intrusion into the
load space. The combined
effect of the transverse and
trailing links is to locate the
lower end of the strut by a
semi-trailing arm.

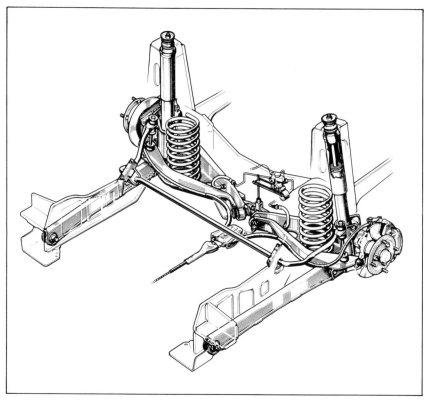

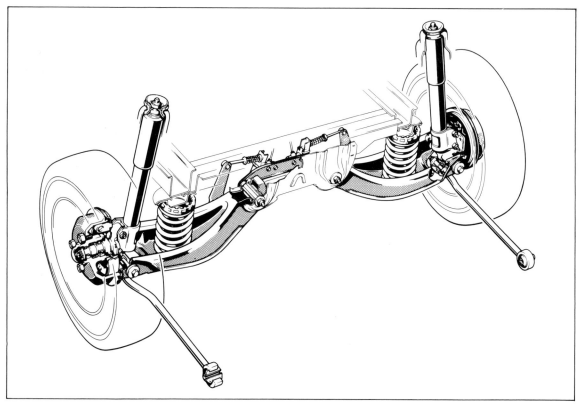

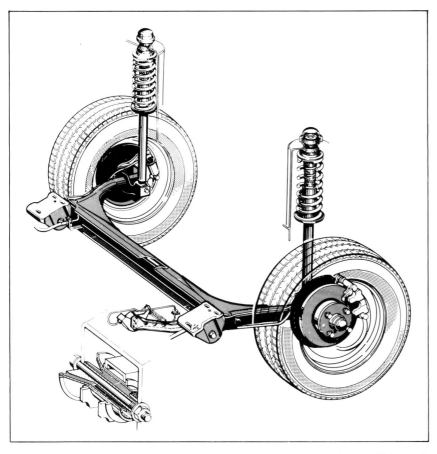

8:14. Volkswagen Golf rear suspension is another of the torsion-beam type (in fact VW pioneered the system). However, in this case the beam joins the trailing arms very close to their body attachment points rather than forming an H-shape as in the Opel Kadett rear suspension. Note, in the inset view, how carefully the mounting bushes in modern suspension systems are designed to achieve stiffness in some directions while retaining flexibility (and noise insulation) in others.

a single bump.

A major development of the 1970s, initiated by Volkswagen but widely copied, is the torsion-beam axle. When the Golf first appeared, it was equipped with a trailing-arm rear suspension in which the arms were joined by a semi-rigid transverse beam. It quickly transpired – to judge by the evidence of its widespread copying – that this was a brilliant notion. In particular, it combined two of the better features of the trailing arm and the dead axle: the forced camber-change of the former, but the higher roll centre of the latter. It thus incorporated both of the features which reduced basic understeer.

The system also had structural advantages (it was devised by Volkswagen in the first place as part of the outstandingly successful weight control programme for the Golf). The torsion beam absorbed some of the stresses which would have had to be fed into the body with pure trailing arms; it also acted as the rear anti-roll bar, adding yet another understeer-reducing element. As the system has been progressively developed, different manufacturers have used torsion beams of different cross-section, and mounted them at different points along the trailing arms so that the rear suspension member resembles a flat 'H'. Some engineers indeed refer to the layout as the 'H-beam'. It is clear that the tuning and positioning of the torsion beam are critical to suspension performance, and especially to the car's behaviour in the mid-corner lift-off situation. The Golf and Polo are noteworthy for their evident positive rear-wheel camber during cornering, and for their willingness to lift the inside rear wheel, yet they do not appear to oversteer violently, even in the most extreme situations.

Chapter nine

In detail:
rear-wheel drive

Rear-driven cars ought to have advantages from the point of view of the chassis engineer. To begin with they are better balanced, and we should by now be entirely aware that the more weight is concentrated at one end of the car, the more lateral weight transfer takes place there to upset the balance of cornering power. Ignoring the effects of drive or braking force, and the chassis engineer's manipulation of tyre pressures, roll axis and roll stiffness, a nose-heavy vehicle will understeer and a tail-heavy one will oversteer.

A really good rear-driven car should approach a 50:50 front/rear weight distribution when empty, and the front seat occupants at least will do little to upset the balance. Most rear-driven cars actually still have a nose-heavy weight bias, but certainly not to the extent of front-driven ones. Rarely, as in the Alfa 75 and 90 and the Porsche 924/944/928, the most even possible balance is sought by moving the gearbox aft to lie in unit with the final drive rather than the engine.

Also, because the weight distribution is more even to begin with, rear-driven cars suffer less from variations in rear ride height caused by back seat passengers and luggage. This is not to say they do not suffer from them at all, as many a heavily laden sales rep's Ford Sierra testifies: but the chassis engineer is spared the worst agonies of trying to pick a spring rate that will cope with all load conditions and still give a reasonable ride, or having to spend extra effort (and money) developing a system with variable-rate springs or at least

an effectively variable spring rate.

An undoubted rear-drive advantage is the relative freedom to lay out the front suspension and steering geometry for optimum handling, without having to worry about fitting wishbones round transverse engines, or minimizing the effects drive torque may have on the steering. Against that, the rear suspension instead has to find room for drive-shafts, and the means of resisting both drive and braking torques when these are applied – unless the brakes are mounted inboard, when the torque is reacted directly through the body. It can amount to a complicated task, not least because the brakes of a rear-driven car carry a larger share of the load. Thus, compared with the apparent simplicity and lightness of the rear suspension in a front-driven car, that of a rear-driven vehicle is bound to be more complicated and heavier.

The handling balance

The apparent beauty of a 50:50 weight distribution is that assuming your tyres are all the same size, the even split means each tyre can develop its maximum cornering potential. There will be no question of one tyre reaching its 'stall point' while the other has more to give. In reality, though, we have to consider the transmission of drive torque even when a car is being driven round a corner at a steady speed. When the car is rear-driven, the rear wheels are robbed of some of their cornering power by the need to transmit drive. Consequently, the 50:50 weight distribution is not ideal after all because it would mean the rear wheels reaching a limit first. For perfect balance under power, the designer should arrange for the weight transfer at the rear to be less than at the front, and the easiest way of doing this is, of course, to make the car slightly nose-heavy.

As a means of maximizing the possible cornering force this is still less than ideal. It means we are using lateral weight transfer deliberately to degrade the front-end cornering performance in order to balance out the effect of drive force at the back. In any case, we cannot always achieve that balance, but must engineer the suspension to achieve perfect balance in one hopefully typical and useful case, while ensuring reasonable behaviour across the whole range of possible circumstances.

The rear-driven car has some things on its side. As I pointed out when looking at front-wheel drive, there is a drawback to driving through the more lightly-laden pair of wheels; traction is inevitably reduced. In the case of rear-drive, however, that disadvantage is minimized because the weight transfer during acceleration is from front to back. Thus, the harder the rear wheels drive, the more heavily they become loaded and traction remains reasonable.

When it comes to cornering under power, my earlier remarks about driving forces normally being much less than cornering forces still apply. Exactly how much less depends on the torque output of the car (more strictly, its torque-to-weight ratio) and its gearing. Very powerful rear-driven cars exercising maximum torque in second gear can usually 'outgun' their tyres. The Porsche 928S4, for example, demands a back-end cornering force of about 620daN at 0.75g lateral acceleration (of which the outer tyre would probably have to generate 450daN) and at peak torque in second gear it can apply over 700daN of drive force through those same back tyres.

Those tyres are naturally of considerable size – their 245/45VR16 dimensions make a notable contrast with the 155R13 of our original Michelin example – and undoubtedly they are capable of exerting formidable cornering forces. Given the Porsche 928's outer rear wheel loading of 635kg at 0.75g, it seems

likely that our low-profile example tyre, the 175/70R13, could just about generate the kind of cornering force involved, though only by running very close to the peak of its curve, and probably with its carcase overstressed into the bargain. The actual Porsche tyre obviously has a lot in hand, but the lesson remains. The ratio of cornering force, at around 450daN for the outer tyre, to the maximum available driving force of 350daN, assuming the drive remains evenly split between the two rear tyres, suggests the resultant can be rotated a long way round the 'circle of forces'. This in turn rightly implies that the driver can modify the handling significantly by applying power, but what will happen when he does?

Clearly his imposition of driving force will 'borrow' from the rear tyre cornering force so that the tyres must run at a greater slip angle to maintain the handling balance. The car therefore moves towards, and quite possibly into, oversteer. The front and back tyres are still generating the same cornering force because the balance and weight transfer remain the same. The greater slip angle of the rear tyres implies a more nose-in body attitude through the corner, which in turn means that to maintain their original slip angles and cornering forces, the front wheels must be moved closer to the straight-ahead – some steering lock must be wound off.

If the driver fails to do this, the imbalance of cornering force will cause the car to tighten its line so that the lateral acceleration increases. Eventually it will settle down on its tighter line. Every experienced driver knows that he can 'steer' a car with the accelerator once it is cornering: in a rear-driven car extra power makes it turn tighter, while lifting-off relaxes the turn, all without the driver moving the steering wheel. With front-drive the reverse applies: extra power widens the turn, releasing the accelerator tightens it.

Mechanically, what happens with rear-drive is that the car assumes a more nose-in attitude in keeping with its new, higher lateral acceleration. So long as the driver does not move the steering, both slip angles must of necessity increase by the same amount – the angle through which the body attitude moves. This angle will be the one at which the front and rear cornering forces re-establish a balance, depending on the tyre characteristics and the extra load transfer front and rear. It would take a computer about as long to work out what that angle ought to be as it takes the car.

What is interesting about this is that if the car was neutral steering to begin with, it will still be neutral steering because the front and rear slip angles, which were equal to begin with (the definition of neutral steer) will still be equal (because they have been increased by the same amount). Similarly, if the car was understeering or oversteering to begin with, it still will be. The effect of adding power has simply been to make the car turn tighter while exhibiting the same handing characteristic. In fact, the tighter turn, which increases the lateral acceleration, means that the handling characteristic is magnified: an understeering car will understeer rather more strongly and an oversteering car will oversteer more.

How does this square with the ready notion that 'applying power pushes a rear-drive car into oversteer'? Easily enough. If the driver of our car is actually following a bend of given radius and applies the power to try to get round it a little faster, he will have to pay off lock to avoid running off the nearside. As soon as he does that, the rear slip angle is indeed increased more than that at the front, and the car moves towards oversteer.

The lesson of this is that the technique of adjusting the cornering line with the accelerator alone is inherently safe *only as long as* the driver resists the temptation to add steering wheel input. Mixing power and steering is what leads to problems. Pile on the power, start to nose-in, correct with steering, pile on a little more power, correct with a little more steering and you can very quickly find yourself in a genuinely opposite-lock situation. And as I pointed out several chapters ago, even if you have the skill to cope with an unstable situation, you are no longer cornering anything like as hard as the fundamental grip of your tyres would allow you to, because by then the front tyres are trying to pull you out of the corner rather than helping you round it. Some of this argument also, of course, applies to front-wheel drive; the only real difference (except for the reversed sense of reaction to increased or decreased power) is that the even-

tual limit is set by terminal understeer: pile on the power, extra lock to pull tighter, back to the original line, still more power, still more lock.

To complete the handling picture we need also to look at the effect of braking. As we observed in the previous chapter, braking, like deceleration only more so, causes a forward weight transfer which, in turn, loads the front wheels more heavily, increasing their cornering power while decreasing that at the rear. At the same time, the need to generate braking force to slow the car robs all four tyres of cornering power. Thus far the picture is common to all types of car. Where the rear-driven car scores over its front-driven rival is, first, that its more even weight distribution throws less of a braking load on the front tyres, and second, that it is much less likely to suffer a violent change of handling characteristic when moving directly from acceleration to braking in mid-corner.

When the front-drive man lifts off and hits the brakes, the removal of driving force from the front wheels allows them to develop greater cornering force. The arrival of the extra load transferred forward increases this effect. The front tyres are likely to find improved cornering power even allowing for the effects of braking force, while the back tyres find themselves simultaneously unloaded and braked.

The difference with the rear-driven car is that while the forward weight transfer helps the front tyres to find extra cornering power, backing off the accelerator helps the *rear* tyres by removing the driving force. Because both front and rear wheels have something going for them, the handling reaction to braking in mid-corner will be much less exciting – which is not to say you will not notice it. Very hard braking will still be an overriding effect pushing the car towards oversteer.

Now, perhaps, we begin to appreciate why all serious racing cars are rear-driven. Not only can the designer set up a reasonable cornering balance, ensuring that, at full power in hard cornering, the car will just about neutral steer – a trick which would be very difficult to achieve in a practical front-driven car. Even more to the point, the rear-driven car is more easily controllable because its reaction to changes of power setting, or even braking, in mid-corner is far less violent.

The problem for the racing car designer, as for his opposite number in the road car department, is to ensure as far as possible that engineering for one particular case does not cause problems elsewhere in the range of drive power and lateral acceleration. Racing cars, for instance, were once known to oversteer through long, very fast curves because even at maximum speed, they could not generate the 'design point' lateral acceleration which caused the lateral weight transfer, which reduces the total cornering power of the front tyres in line with that at the rear. Today, aerodynamics and ground effect has changed all that, but the basic point remains.

It is relatively easy for the rear-wheel designer to tune his chassis for an ideal cornering balance, for moderate understeer, at a given design point. His weapons once again are roll axis inclination and the ratio of front-to-rear roll stiffness, adjusted by means of anti-roll bars. If he feels the car as presented to him by the body team is undesirably nose-heavy which would lead it to understeer more

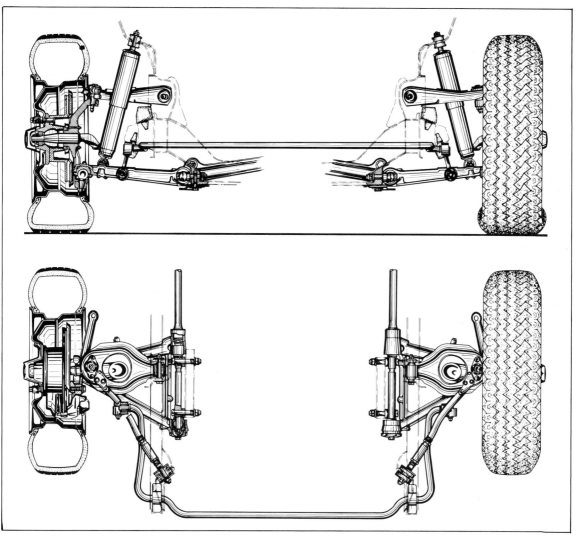

9:1. Double-wishbone front suspension of the Alfa Six was classic in most respects. The upper wishbone comprised a joined drag link and transverse link, the latter a broad pressing pierced to make way for the damper. The lower member was a 'proper' wishbone directly attached to the lengthwise torsion bars which formed the springing medium. The anti-roll bar also picked up on the lower wishbones.

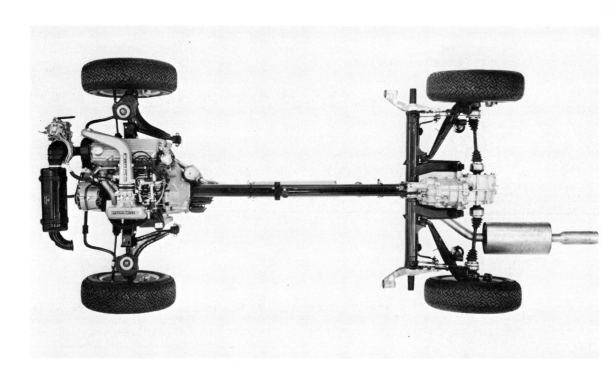

9:2, 9:3. The Porsche 924 chassis, seen from above, shows its MacPherson strut front suspension and semi-trailing rear layout. The lower members of the front suspension are notable for being rather oddly-shaped wishbones, with one attachment point virtually opposite the wheel hub and the other a long way aft. Note the rear-mounted gearbox, in unit with the final drive for better static balance. The Porsche 928 chassis, below, is superficially similar to that of the 924, but turns out to be completely different in principle. Front suspension in this case is double-wishbone, the upper wishbone broad-based enough to allow the damper to pass through its fork. The rear suspension, though still basically semi-trailing, uses the 'Weissach' front attachment points, which embody an extra member designed to deflect under load in such a way as to result in a directly compensating wheel movement, resulting in superior stability.

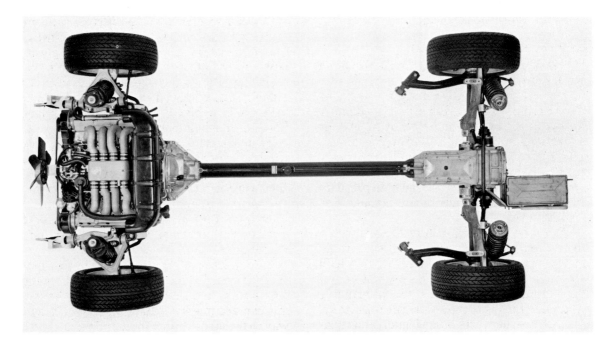

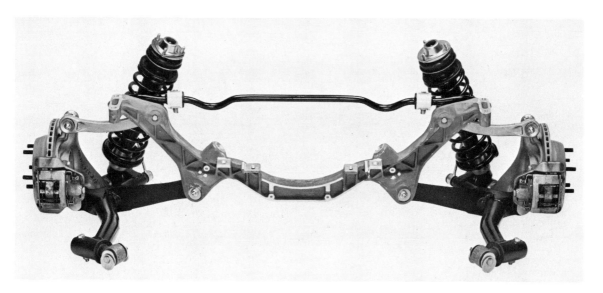

9:4. A more detailed shot of the Weissach rear suspension in the Porsche 928, built up on its subframe. The specially designed 'deflection pots' in the lower arms are nearest the camera. Note that in addition to the semi-trailing lower arms, there is an upper transverse member to achieve positive control of wheel camber angle as in a double-wishbone layout.

than he wishes, he can adopt the same techniques as his front-drive counterpart: slope the roll axis nose-down, reduce the recommended rear tyre pressures, or fit a rear anti-roll bar. What he can be sure of is that, compared with a front-driven rival, his rear-drive design is much less likely to exhibit handling problems when the driver departs from the design point. That is one of the virtues of better static balance.

Exploiting the potential

At this point, having drawn the picture of an 'ideal' rear-driven car as something modestly nose-heavy, we have to confront the evidence of the Formula 1 racing car which is evidently tail-heavy. The situation with any racing car is that it needs to deploy a lot of driving force – that is what racing is all about. The only way that force can be transmitted through the rear wheels (since we have already disposed of front-drive as a rational racing layout) is to use huge tyres.

We might then think about using those huge tyres on all four wheels, but that would demand a slightly nose-heavy car, which would be bad for traction (to say nothing of aerodynamics). So we study the alternative solution, which is to make the car tail-heavy, but with the rear tyres much bigger, and capa-

ble of producing much more cornering force, than those at the front; and we find it works. Not only does it work, it makes the task of mechanical design much easier, reduces overall weight by doing away with the propeller shaft – to say nothing of subtle tweaks like using the engine as a stressed unit – and reduces the polar moment of inertia to help the car turn-in that much quicker.

Given a carefully chosen difference in tyre sizes, the natural tendency of the tail-heavy car to oversteer is overcome. Any lingering traces you can tame sufficiently for your brave and (hopefully) highly skilled drivers with the aid of a nose-down roll axis. The inclination is very easily achieved because the back axle line is so much higher and the whole car basically wedge-shaped, and you would hardly think of using anything but double-wishbone suspension, which makes the roll centre positions very easy to adjust. You can then use the stiffness of the front and rear anti-roll bars to provide the fine trim according to the needs of a particular circuit or the whim of the individual driver.

The evolution of the modern racing car carries lessons for the designer of road-going sports cars. In essence, the thread of the racing car argument is that the most efficient way to persuade the smallest and lightest pos-

9:5. Volvo's new independent rear suspension, the first to come from a company formerly dedicated to the virtues of the well-located live rear axle, is an extremely complex arrangement in which massive trailing arms are supplemented by three separate transverse links to ensure full control of wheel movement in any situation.

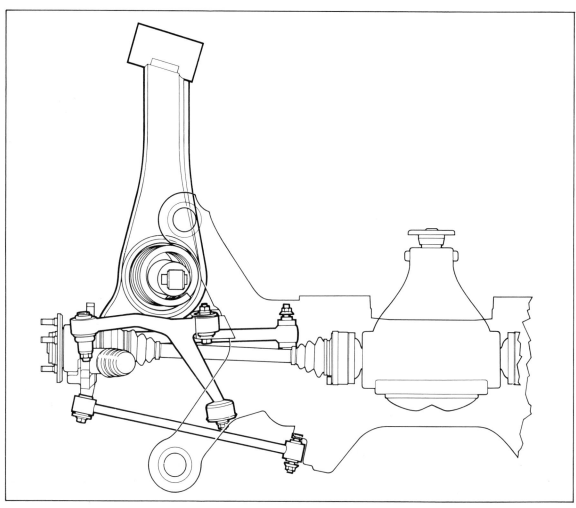

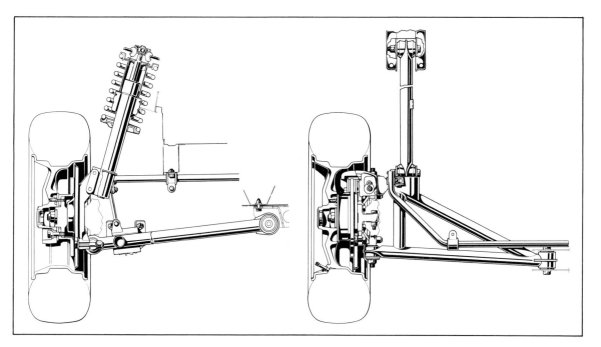

9:6. MacPherson suspension at the rear of the limited-production Fiat Abarth 124 Rally, with the lower end of the strut located by a triangulated transverse link and a trailing arm. Long links minimize camber angle change with long suspension travel, an important consideration for rough-road motoring.

sible chassis to cope with huge amounts of power while retaining good handling is to build a mid-engined device with the back wheels much larger than the front ones. Unfortunately, some road-car designers have been so enamoured by this package as to build mid-engined devices which deploy perhaps a fifth as much power as a modern Formula 1 car, and have equal-sized tyres at all four corners. The mid-engined layout is 'modern' because the racers use it, and technical doubters can be referred to the great gods Polar Moment and Crisp Turn-in.

As used in road-going sports cars the mid-engined layout gives tail-heavy static weight distribution. *Autocar* test weight results include 44.6/55.4 front-to-rear for the Ferrari Mondial, 42.6/57.4 for the Fiat X1/9 and 44.2/55.8 for the Toyota MR2, for example. It has been argued that the occupants of a mid-engined car sit slightly forward of the static centre of gravity and shift the weight distribution closer to a perfect 50:50, but that argument doesn't withstand close scrutiny: the occupants of the little Fiat and Toyota sit with their 'H-points' very close to, even aft of, the static centre of gravity.

Thus the road-going mid-engined car is tail-heavy. That means its rear tyres are going to be subjected to the effects not only of the drive force, but of the greater part of the lateral load transfer. Both will reduce the cornering power of the back wheels relative to the front. Left to themselves, such cars would oversteer readily were it not for chassis tuning, notably by adding front roll stiffness to give an understeer effect – creating extra weight transfer to rob cornering power from the front wheels as well! The conclusion must be that the mid-engined sports car is not an altogether serious machine. It may feel great, courtesy of light steering, good traction and that quick turn-in, but if it has equal-sized tyres front and rear it cannot, in fact, make best use of all their potential grip. Mid-engined cars properly shod with bigger rear tyres (as is the aforementioned Ferrari Mondial, for instance) are another matter, but the buyer then has to address the impracticality of different-sized tyres, to say nothing of the layout's other drawbacks.

We should, perhaps, passingly refer to the rear-engined layout since a few such designs are still available. It would not be fair to

9:7. Rear suspension design introduced by TVR in 1986 employs wide-based hub carriers and lower links, assisted by trailing radius rods, to eliminate any suggestion of rear-wheel steering. The wishbone geometry is completed by fixed-length drive shafts. Inboard brakes, in addition to reducing unsprung weight, simplify the job of fitting a sturdy hub assembly deep in the hollow of a wide road wheel.

include the Porsche 911 or the Renault GTA in this category since both have taken great care – the Porsche through 20 years of assiduous development, the Renault through careful engineering from scratch – to overcome the worst of the problems (and not least, again, by fitting bigger tyres at the back).

Failing such attention, any tail-heavy car will oversteer unless something drastic is done to stop it. Some of my readers will surely recall the Hillman Imp, which actually handled in a reasonably well-balanced manner, but only with the aid of tyre pressures of 18psi front, 30psi rear, and swing-axle front suspension, whose deliberate aim was to make the front tyres' cornering power vanish as fast as that at the rear.

Actual oversteer aside, the main problem of a rear-engined layout from the chassis point of view is that aerodynamic stability in cross-winds will almost inevitably be poor, while it is also vital to guard against the 'jacking up' of the rear end, caused by the weight of the engine fighting the side force of the rear tyres along an inclined drive shaft. It is also necessary, though difficult, to guard against premature locking of the front wheels in 'panic' braking, when a stab on the brake pedal may apply full force to the front brakes before the forward weight transfer has had time to take

effect. Other members of a saloon car design team – like the product planner who wants the biggest boot and the engine man who wants the simplest and most effective cooling system – will, of course, have their own reasons for disliking mid or rear-mounted engines, but these are not our current concern.

Suspension practicalities

Any discussion of rear-drive suspension design ought, therefore, to be centred around the classic front-engine layout, which is still manufactured in considerable numbers. The larger and more expensive cars – all BMWs, Jaguars, Mercedes, Rolls-Royces, for instance – retain it for two good reasons quite apart from the benefits of an even weight distribution for handling balance and cornering ability. It also gives the designer freedom to choose closely matched spring rates and do wonders for ride quality; and the majority of such cars offer engine torque outputs large enough to cause problems when taken through the front wheels, as we have already seen.

Front suspension

Just as with front-driven cars, there seem now to be only two practical choices of front suspension design even when the layout is rear-driven. Shall it be double wishbones or MacPherson struts? Most of the real 'quality' manufacturers remain faithful to double wishbones: Aston Martin, Jaguar and Rolls-Royce would probably not even consider the alternative. It must have been a blow to the faithful, though, when Mercedes went over to the MacPherson arrangement – and Porsche has used it on all its more recent models.

The reasons for choosing wishbones are the now familiar ones – to anyone who has ploughed through the preceding chapters – of wide choice of detailed geometry and the favourable migration of the roll centre. People are less specific about the years of work they have put into developing double-wishbone systems which combine accuracy with com-

pliance, but that is another important factor. So is the *relative* freedom from the need to squeeze every last pound of structural weight out of such cars, a need which always favours the MacPherson strut.

Among the more weight and cost-conscious manufacturers, however, the MacPherson strut has certainly gained ground of late. Ford, after a period of disenchantment with the strut, brought about it seems by persistent wheel-balance problems leading to steering shake (which caused a switch to double wishbones for the later-mark Cortinas), have returned to the MacPherson arrangement for the Sierra and Granada/Scorpio. General Motors in Europe has also adopted the strut for the Omega/Carlton. BMW has never used

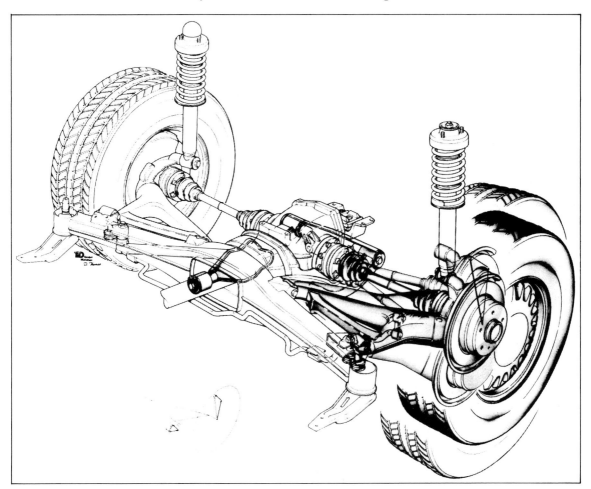

9:8. BMW's adherence to the semi-trailing rear suspension layout came to an end with the introduction of the new 7-series, in which extra members were introduced to achieve a more desirable wheel movement and more predictable handling, even at the expense of extra weight, complication and expense, and an extra noise path into the body.

127

anything else for its current series of cars. Volvo switched to struts with the 200-series introduced in 1974. Peugeot used struts for the 504/505. Thus there can be no doubt that, at the moment, the MacPherson strut arrangement is in the majority among Europe's remaining rear-driven cars.

The appeal of the MacPherson strut should by now be well rehearsed for readers. Good camber control and structural convenience appear increasingly to outweigh fears about the less favourable direction in which the roll centre migrates when the body rolls. There is the extra virtue (which seems to have influenced Mercedes) that the strut arrangement lends itself to 'self-correcting' negative-offset steering geometry.

Like those who remain faithful to wishbones, the strut users have devoted a lot of time to the question of compliance and noise insulation. It is easy enough to mount the lower transverse links or wishbones on a subframe, which may then be bolted to the body on extra insulating mounts, though care is needed to make sure the 'squidge' of those mounts does not allow the frame to move in such a way as to upset the suspension geometry. Yet even this fear can be turned to advantage, and General Motors, in the Omega/Carlton, has devised a lower-arm mounting bush arrangement which, through carefully controlled distortion, has much the same steering self-correction effect as negative offset.

Increasingly, too, MacPherson strut suspensions are emerging with much stronger-looking, more positive transverse members locating the bottom end of the strut. It becomes important, when you are working with the deliberate intention of allowing certain suspension mountings to deform in particular ways, that you do not allow the suspension members themselves to deform and upset the balance. At the same time, renewed attention is being paid to the mounting of the upper end of the strut, where worthwhile reductions in noise transmission – and lighter steering – have resulted.

Whatever the chosen suspension layout, rear-wheel drive has the apparent advantage of affording the designer much more freedom of steering linkage layout. In practice, this gain is probably counteracted by the awkwardness of the in-line engine, which cuts across most of the convenient rack-mounting lines. What is certainly true, however, is that rear-drive obviates the problem of drive torque effects being fed into the steering, as well as those of insufficient traction – leading to control problems of its own – for high-powered cars in slippery conditions.

Rear suspension

Virtually every modern rear-driven car now has independent rear suspension. An exception was Volvo, whose 700-series cars were launched with a live axle located by one of the most complex trailing-arm and Panhard rod linkages ever devised. Volvo's reason for retaining the axle was its entirely predictable qualities (constant track and camber, constant roll centre position, constant ground clearance beneath the final drive), which the company felt were sufficiently vital in Scandinavian conditions to warrant accepting the extra unsprung weight and its adverse effect on ride. But Volvo too has now followed the majority and developed an independent layout.

The most common form of independent rear suspension used with rear-driven cars is the semi-trailing arm. Such systems are now employed by BMW, Ford, Peugeot, Rolls-Royce and Vauxhall/Opel among others. The appeal of this arrangement is one of cost and structural convenience: it is certainly the cheapest means of achieving a satisfactory independent arrangement, and also probably permits the lightest structure. On the other hand, it has its notable drawbacks, including track and camber change and roll-steer effects. This has driven some former users, notably Mercedes and more recently BMW in its new 7-series, to consider ways of controlling the camber more positively by adding extra articulation at the hub and extra control arms. The improvement in consistency of handling behaviour, especially close to the limit, is very noticeable, though it has to be said that those who still use the simple semi-trailing arrangement have increasingly found ways to take the sting out of its behaviour in adverse circumstances.

Full control of camber angle can, of course,

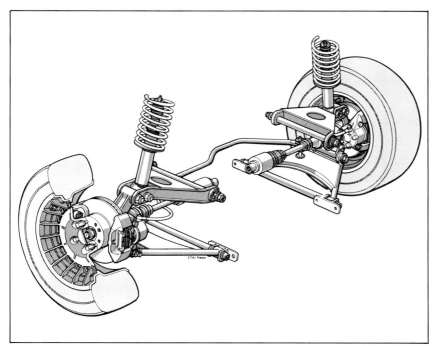

9:9. The Renault 5 Turbo uses a proper double-wishbone rear suspension, as befits its status as virtually a specialized competition car. Both wishbones are wide-based and the spring/damper units act on the upper wishbones, making way for the drive shafts beneath. The amount of space taken up by this layout is evident.

9:10. Mercedes-Benz too have moved on from semi-trailing arms with this multi-link layout for the rear of the 190/190E. Five separate links provide close control of wheel movements and the geometry includes both anti-squat and anti-dive provisions.

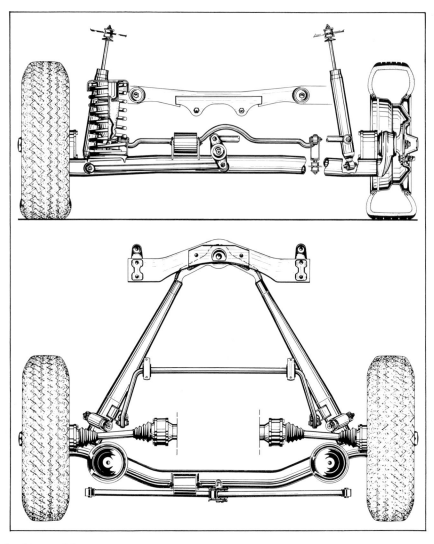

9:11. The Alfa Six, like its smaller predecessors the Alfetta and Giulietta, used a de Dion rear suspension. The massive tube, running aft of the final-drive unit, is located by the two semi-trailing arms (converging to a single mounting hinge-point) plus a transverse Watt linkage. Note the anti-roll bar working between the two semi-trailing arms, and the separate mounting of the coil springs and dampers, the one forward, the other aft of the drive shafts.

be achieved with proper double-wishbone suspension, but for most designers, this has proved too expensive and space-consuming to be considered. Exceptions include Ferrari, which almost inevitably uses 'proper' wishbone arrangements, and Jaguar, which devised a neat arrangement for the E-type in which the fixed-length drive-shaft formed one of the transverse members. The system was successful enough to be carried across into the original XJ6 saloon (whose boot space did suffer as a result, it must be admitted), where it gave outstandingly consistent handling to high limits. The basic arrangement has been retained for the new XJ6, launched in 1986, though the geometry differs in many subtle ways, and a very high degree of fore-and-aft compliance has been achieved with no loss of accurate location.

The wishbone's great rival, the MacPherson strut, has been used at the back of several rear-driven cars. Two of the most notable were the Datsun 240Z and the Fiat 130. It is easy enough to see the appeal of the strut for this application, and it is perhaps surprising that it has not been tried as a replacement for some of the semi-trailing arm suspensions when new-series designs have been considered. An alternative to the genuinely independent arrangement is the de Dion suspension. This has found a few adherents, notably Alfa Romeo and Aston Martin, who appreciate that it combines the virtues of the rigid axle with much reduced unsprung weight.

Chapter ten

In detail: four-wheel drive

The appeal of four-wheel drive was originally that of extra traction. With all four wheels driven, there was less chance of wheelspin in slippery conditions, and less chance of being bogged down with a pair of wheels helplessly spinning. Even so, the real value of those qualities in off-road driving was sometimes not appreciated. As one French authority has put it, the true value of four-wheel drive is that it enables you to pick your way slowly and carefully in places where a two-wheel-drive vehicle would have to take a run at an obstacle and risk breaking itself.

That, however, was in the past. The reason why four-wheel drive has been so much discussed and adopted in recent years is that its value for high-performance road driving has been recognized. The Jensen FF of the 1960s sparked the first interest, and the Audi Quattro fanned the flame back into life. Now few major manufacturers consider their ranges complete without a road-going four-wheel-drive car.

The *disadvantages* of four-wheel drive are obvious. To a large degree it combines the worst of both worlds. For the chassis engineer there is all the complication of front-wheel drive with its constraints on front suspension layout and its need to provide space for drive-shafts, and of rear-wheel drive with its weight penalty and its call for a long central propeller shaft and a complicated rear suspension complete with drive shafts. Then there is the additional weight and complication of providing some means of splitting the drive to front and

rear, and the threat that these arrangements will pose extra problems of noise and vibration. If these drawbacks are worth accepting, then the advantages of four-wheel drive must indeed be formidable. Those advantages are two: better traction and better handling balance.

The appeal of traction is obvious. It means that more drive torque, in fact roughly twice as much, can be transmitted in slippery conditions without suffering wheelspin because each wheel transmits a quarter of the torque instead of half. Quite apart from the straightforward advantage this confers on wet or icy surfaces, it has a special appeal to the manufacturers of cars whose torque output is reaching the limit of what can be taken comfortably through two wheels – especially two front wheels. It was no mere chance which saw Audi start to push the Quattro concept so hard, as anyone with wet-weather experience of a front-driven Audi 200 Turbo would acknowledge.

We began each of the two previous chapters with a discussion of handling balance, and we shall do so again here. We have seen how the weight transfer effect, plus the need to transmit the drive force, adversely affects the ability of the front tyres of a typical front-drive car to provide cornering force and that consequently – assuming the wheels and tyres are all of the same size – some of the potential grip of the rear tyres is always wasted. By the same token, we have appreciated that the nose-heavy rear-drive car spreads the prob-

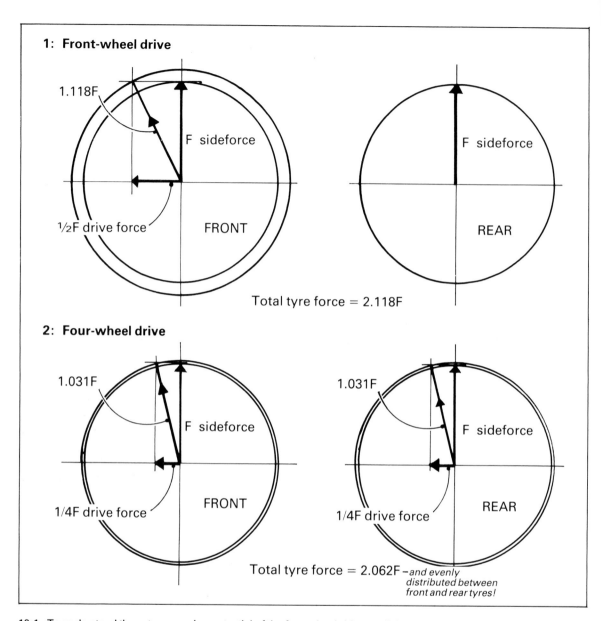

1: Front-wheel drive

1.118F

F sideforce

½F drive force   FRONT

F sideforce

REAR

Total tyre force = 2.118F

2: Four-wheel drive

1.031F

F sideforce

1/4F drive force   FRONT

1.031F

F sideforce

1/4F drive force   REAR

Total tyre force = 2.062F *–and evenly distributed between front and rear tyres!*

10:1. To understand the extra cornering potential of the four-wheel-drive car, it is necessary to look at the way cornering and drive forces are distributed within the 'force circles' for the front and rear tyres. In effect, asking all four tyres to share the drive force results in a net gain in cornering force compared with a car which concentrates all its drive force at one end.

lem between its two ends, with the lateral weight transfer sapping cornering force at the front while the drive force does so at the rear – but that a better balance and easier control results. What is the position with the four-wheel-drive car?

A four-wheel-drive car with a 50:50 front/rear weight distribution and a 50:50 front/rear split of drive torque falls between the two extremes and should likewise be able to exploit all the potential tyre grip. This is logical because the transmission of drive torque no longer affects the basic balance of the car: the front and rear wheels sacrifice the same amount of sideforce to the need for torque transmission.

The same theory predicts that such a car will be less twitchy than its front-driven equivalent when subjected to power changes in mid-corner, but less easily controlled than the

132

rear-drive car. This again is logical. The four-wheel-drive car should show no change of handling characteristic with the drive torque removed, though it will still tend more towards oversteer when power-off because of the weight transfer effect of deceleration.

This implies that the four-wheel-drive car should allow its driver to use most of the potential tyre grip without encountering so many problems of control in the situation which causes so much trouble to the quicker drivers of front-driven cars: the realization that the corner tightens unexpectedly, and you have entered it much too fast. The four-wheel-drive car should not be understeering so much to begin with, nor should it twitch so hard towards oversteer when the driver backs off.

If this is really so, it is good news for the chassis engineer because it enables him to endow an evenly-balanced car with high usable cornering power. The even balance means he is able to provide a decent ride without having to endure the conflict of matching spring rates or accepting too much pitching movement; the four-wheel drive gives the cornering power without the problems.

As it turns out, this prediction is well in line with reality, up to a point. The four-wheel-drive Audis quickly showed, and other models have confirmed, that drivers were able to corner more quickly in most circumstances than they could in a two-wheel-drive car. Many people drew the wrong inference: that four-wheel drive actually increased the ultimate cornering power of the car in some way. It does, but only to a limited extent. Its achievement is to 'rob' the tyres of the least amount of cornering power necessary to transmit all the drive force.

The simple diagram *(fig 10:1)* will suffice to show the real situation, and the advantages of four-wheel drive. I have shown the tyre 'force circles' for the two outer tyres of a perfectly balanced car, calling for equal cornering force from both ends. If the cornering force of each tyre is F and the front tyre is also required to transmit a driving force of 0.5F, then its total resultant force will be 1.118F. In other words the circle needs to be nearly 12% bigger and the front tyre will have to run at a larger slip angle to keep the cornering force constant. The car will therefore understeer; and the total force generated by the tyres is 2.118F.

If, instead, each of the wheels is asked to transmit a driving force of 0.25F – the four-wheel-drive situation with an even torque split – then two resultants emerge, each of size 1.031F. Both tyres have to run at the same slightly greater slip angle in order to keep the cornering force constant, so the handling remains neutral; and the total force generated by the tyres is 2.062F. In other words, by switching to four-wheel drive we have saved ourselves the need to generate around 3% of the total force.

That is an appreciable amount in engineer-

10:2. The value of four-wheel drive in ordinary road cars may be questionable in many circumstances, but the system comes into its own on unmade roads, as shown by this Audi Coupe GT quattro, and on slippery surfaces where traction is at a premium.

10:3. The more powerful the car, the more point there is to having four-wheel drive so that the power can be put down on the road without encountering wheelspin problems. Despite the control problems which have been experienced at the very limit of cornering power, four-wheel drive has become virtually essential for any car, like this Audi Quattro, destined to win a loose-surface rally. On tarmac, depending on conditions, the advantage is much less marked.

ing terms (and as the drive forces become larger, the savings become greater). On the other hand, the way some people started out to drive the Audi Quattro, you might have thought the gain in potential roadholding was more like 30% than 3%. They forgot that the cornering power of any car depends on the grip exerted through those four patches of rubber on the road. Four-wheel drive simply sacrifices less of it to the exigencies of chassis engineering. What the Quattro *did* do, because its handling in most conditions was so consistent, was to make that slightly improved cornering power much more readily accessible to the average driver of a slightly nose-heavy car.

The corollary is that beyond a certain point, fast Audi Quattro drivers, including the works rally men, confirmed that understeer took charge suddenly and conclusively. There would come a stage beyond which the car would run wide, and carry on running wide seemingly regardless of corrective action. To understand the reason, we must first bear in mind that because four-wheel-drive cars are less sensitive to changes of power than two-wheel-drive ones, a driver gets into the habit of adjusting his cornering line much more with the steering and less with delicate manipulation of the accelerator.

What appears to happen is that the driver pressing on round a slippery bend eventually discovers the four-wheel-drive car's limit when he turns the steering a little bit too far. He pushes the front tyres past their 'stall point' and they lose sideforce, making the car understeer violently. The correct reaction, in theory, is to unwind the steering again and 'unstall' the front tyres, but the *natural* reaction, given that the car is already understeering ever wider of its intended line, is to lift off the accelerator. This restores some side force to the front tyres but unfortunately it also reduces the slip angle at the rear. In fact, because the rear tyres are not 'stalled', their slip angle decreases even more when the drive torque is removed, and the understeer becomes stronger still. Thus, once the limit of adhesion has been passed, which in practical circumstances will usually be front-first, the four-wheel-drive car will tend to plough straight ahead until it has scrubbed off enough speed for the driver to straighten up and sort things out more or less from scratch.

This behaviour is closest to that of the rear-driven car when control is lost through understeer, when lifting off increases the rear sideforce while doing nothing whatever for the front. The difference is that the rear-drive car is actually more likely to lose control through oversteer brought on by the use of too much power, reducing the rear side force; lifting off the accelerator is then the natural and effective correction.

One might also observe that because the Quattro is by no means 50:50 weight-balanced, but substantially nose-heavy because of its front-drive origins, while its drive torque split *is* 50:50, it retains a tendency to understeer anyway. This is a deliberate acknowledgement of the average driver's handling preference, even though it sacrifices a little of four-wheel drive's ultimate advantage. It is still the case that the 50:50 torque split means the use of more or less power has no (or almost no) effect on the handling; the Quattro's gentle understeer should be totally consistent – until the limit of front end adhesion is finally breached.

We are, however, getting close to discussing exotic rally driving techniques rather than looking at chassis design and its effect on handling. The important thing to remember – and it is worth reiterating – is that four-wheel drive makes it possible to approach optimum roadholding in an evenly balanced car. If problems arise, it is not so much because of any inherent defect of the four-wheel drive concept, but because average drivers are not – or not yet – used to having such ready access to extreme cornering power.

Chassis variations

At this point we need to look at two fundamental choices facing the chassis engineer of a

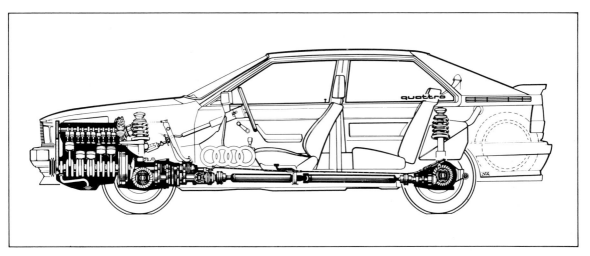

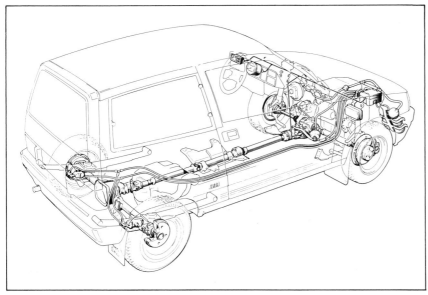

10:4, 10:5. All the four-wheel-drive saloons (as different from vehicles of the Range Rover type with a predominantly off-road purpose) seen so far have been adaptions of existing two-wheel-drive designs. The case of the front-drive car with the engine lengthways ahead of the front axle, like the Audi (above), is the simplest: MacPherson suspension, using front suspension components reversed, replaces the undriven lightweight beam axle at the back. Tranverse-engined designs are adaptable too: the Lancia Y10 (left), like its Fiat Panda cousin, swaps a live axle on leaf springs for the 'Omega' beam and coil springs.

135

four-wheel-drive vehicle. The first is whether or not to have a centre differential and, if it is fitted, whether to make it lockable. The second is whether to accept the apparently natural 50:50 torque split, or choose to bias the drive towards front or rear.

It is entirely possible to have a four-wheel-drive car with no centre differential of any kind, but merely, in effect, a rigid propeller shaft link between the front and rear differentials (rigid in torsion, that is: all such links need joints to enable them to line up with the two differentials and the output shaft as they move in relation to one another). If there is no centre differential, the front and rear wheels will try to run at the same speed and on good, high-friction surfaces this can lead to 'wind-up' in the transmission and in turn to jerky progress and undue strain on the gears. Vehicles which lack a centre differential are usually provided with freewheel hubs to allow 'unwinding' to take place on good surfaces, or carry a warning to confine the use of (selectable) four-wheel drive to loose or slippery surfaces on which the wheels will be able to do their own unwinding, of a kind.

It follows that a centre differential is essential if four-wheel drive is to be used effectively on good road surfaces; it also implies that where cars are provided with centre differential locks, these should only be used sparingly and with due thought for the consequences.

In the first place, we need to remind ourselves that, barring limited-slip devices, a conventional differential is merely an ingenious mechanical device for allowing relative movement between its two outputs (the drive shafts to the wheels) while ensuring a 50:50 split of its input torque between them. Thus a four-wheel-drive car with three such differentials, one central and one at each end, will always feed 25% of its torque to each wheel, even if all four wheels are rotating at different speeds. In normal driving circumstances this is close to what we need to exploit all the roadholding potential of a perfectly balanced chassis. The only possible improvement would be a system which somehow managed to split the torque between the inner and outer wheels in the same proportion as the load imbalance caused by lateral weight transfer while cornering.

If, however, just one of the wheels sinks in a mud patch or stands on a patch of ice, the car will be immobilized, or nearly so, because if one wheel cannot absorb any appreciable torque without spinning, no significant amount of torque will be delivered to any of the others. Even with four-wheel drive, you will be left with one wheel spinning and the engine screaming its head off. The answer lies in lockable (or limited-slip) differentials. If a rear wheel (say) is spinning, a locked centre differential will ensure that torque reaches the front wheels so that you can drive away. This is fine so far as it goes, but, as is so often the case, it brings two snags of its own.

In locking the differential, you destroy its ability to split input torque evenly. If the front end of the car will not accept the torque because of the spinning wheel, then all the torque will be fed to the back end (or, of course, the other way round). That means the drive shafts and differential gears have to be stressed on the basis that each wheel may be fed 50%, rather than 25%, of the available torque – so they have to be made bigger and heavier.

The other snag is that by locking the centre differential, you interfere with the natural 50:50 split of drive torque between the front and rear ends. In the Audi Quattro, therefore, which is substantially nose-heavy, the car will take more of the drive torque into its front wheels when its centre differential is locked, and will behave much more like a front-drive car than when the differential is free. That is, it will understeer more under power, and twitch more readily towards oversteer if the throttle is closed during cornering. It will then be more difficult to exploit the full roadholding potential – especially as the chassis is engineered for the 50:50 torque split.

One of the fraught areas of 4WD chassis engineering is braking, and especially anti-lock braking. Normally, ABS senses the impending locking of individual wheels and releases and re-applies the brakes accordingly. If the wheels are linked together by a four-wheel drive system with a locked centre differential, however, a situation could arise where the application of braking to the front wheels by the ABS could result in rear wheel locking.

The greater debate in four-wheel-drive circles in the 1980s has been whether it is better to have a 50:50 torque split or to arrange for the greater part of the torque to go to one end of the car. This is certainly not the place to delve into the details of how the uneven torque split is achieved; but BMW and Ford both used a form of central epicyclic gearbox to split their torque 33% front, 67% rear for their four-wheel-drive models (versions of the 325, and the Sierra and Granada/Scorpio, respectively). It is worth remembering that while Audi started its work from the basis of a front-driven car, BMW and Ford both used rear-driven models as starting points.

The BMW/Ford arrangement means their cars are nose-heavy but with a rearward drive bias. This means they more nearly approach the original rear-drive concept. If the driver applies more power, the rear wheels will be required to transmit more of the drive force than the front ones. This will increase the rear slip angle more than the front – but against that, the underlying weight distribution should ensure that the car is understeering to begin with. The end result is a car which reacts in much the same way as the rear-driven one, but less positively. Throttle- steering round corners is still possible, but more power will be needed for a given change of line; the division of torque between the wheels will allow more of the tyres' potential grip to be realized, though not as much as with the theoretically perfectly balanced design.

When thinking about the origins of four-wheel-drive models, it is interesting to realize that every current 4x4 car (as distinct from purpose-built off-road vehicles) extending now from Alfa Romeo to Volkswagen with contributions doubtless to come from Volvo and quite possibly even from Yugo, appears to have a two-wheel-drive equivalent which formed its engineering starting point. The pattern which seems to have emerged thus far is that the rear-drive derivatives, including Mercedes as well as BMW and Ford, have favoured a rear-biased torque split while the front-drive developments have gone for either 50:50, or an automatically variable split.

What seems to emerge from all this is that the variation of torque split can be exploited to achieve any particular pattern of handling. Rear-biased split gives handling like that of a rear-driven car, though less extreme. An exactly 50:50 split has little direct effect on the basic handling (as determined by the weight distribution, chassis tuning and tyre characteristics) at all. It follows, though so far as I am aware nobody has yet deliberately done it, that a front-biased split would reflect the characteristics of a front-driven car, but in a less extreme way. This might be quite an attractive package, but the closest anyone has come to it so far is Volkswagen with the Golf Synchro, in which a viscous coupling replaces the differential in the driveline to the rear wheels, connecting them only when it senses that the front wheels are running faster than the rear (in other words, that they are spinning due to insufficient grip).

The former Group B works rally cars ,which used four-wheel drive were mostly equipped with the means to allow the driver to select torque split at will, within fairly wide limits. The general idea was clearly that if the driver felt the car was understeering too much he could direct more of the torque to the back wheels, and if the tail felt over-twitchy he could direct more of it forwards. It is worth noting that because of the weight transfer effect during acceleration, which loads the rear wheels and makes them more capable of transmitting drive force, the best traction is obtained with a rearward torque split. This was certainly an extra attraction for BMW and Ford in choosing their rear-biased split for production 4x4 models.

Practicalities

In general, it is easier to make a front-driven car into a 4x4 model than a rear-driven one. It is easiest of all if the engine is in-line and overhung ahead of the front axle line and the transaxle, as in the Audi, the Subaru and the Alfa 33. Some form of drive can then be taken directly from the rear of the transaxle, via a new propeller shaft to a final-drive unit at the rear, and thence through drive shafts to the rear wheels. For some time there appeared to be a problem in deriving a fore-and-aft drive to the rear wheels from a transverse front-drive engine and gearbox, but this is now done quite simply (though with clever detailing) by installing a bevel output gear to mesh with the front final-drive pinion.

From the suspension point of view, the front

10:6. The packaging of four-wheel drive for an originally rear-driven car is often rather more difficult. This cutaway of the transmission arrangements of the 4x4 versions of Ford's Sierra and Granada Scorpio shows the chain needed to step the drive sideways to the front propeller shaft, and the left-hand drive shaft passing through the engine sump. The hub assembly of the MacPherson front suspension on these models was designed from the outset with four-wheel drive in mind, it would appear, so that clearance for the universal joint was not a problem.

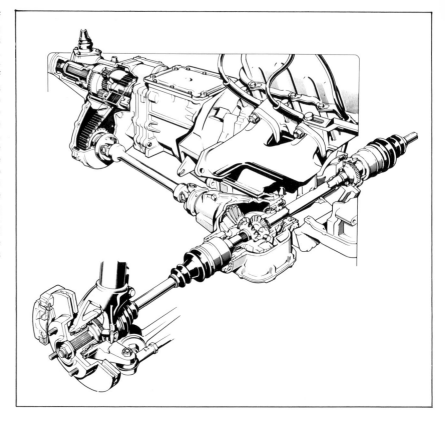

end of a converted front-drive car can remain the same. The rear needs substantial reworking in any case, but especially if the original form of rear suspension was not well suited to the addition of drive shafts – as in the case of pure trailing arms, for instance. There have been many solutions to this question. The original Audi 80, for instance, which had a torsion-beam rear axle, adopted MacPherson struts at the back (having already used them at the front). The front-driven Audi Coupe has a dead rear axle with radius arms and a Panhard rod; the 4x4 Quattro again has rear MacPherson struts. The larger Audi 200 quattro, however, has a rear suspension with double-wishbone geometry.

There have been simpler ways of doing the job. Conversions of the Renault 18 Estate to 4x4 configuration, for instance, carried out originally by specialists, but adopted by Renault itself during the latter stages of the car's life, replaced the front-driven car's dead axle (located by trailing arms and sideways by trailing A-bracket) with a live axle! Other forms of rear suspension are better suited to

accept drive shafts without modification. Subaru's long-running series of 4x4 saloons and estates, for instance, run essentially the same semi-trailing arm suspension as their front-driven counterparts.

However the conversion is carried out, the task is never entirely straightforward. The addition of 'works' at the back increases the weight on the rear wheels, so ideally the spring rates and travels, and the damper settings, have to be rethought. The new arrangement must also be able to cope with reacting the drive torque.

When the 4x4 conversion starts with a rear-driven original the task of the chassis engineer is actually rather more simple – which certainly cannot be said for his colleague the transmission engineer! This is because all modern cars use one of two front suspension designs, the MacPherson strut and the double wishbone. Both of them are well suited to the addition of drive shafts and react drive torque without difficulty. The main complication is likely to be the rearrangement of the bottom end of a MacPherson strut, or the relocation of coil springs if the originals ran between double wishbones, to make room for the drive-shaft to pass through. The BMW 325iX and the Ford Sierra and Granada 4x4 models all use Mac-Pherson strut front suspension; Ford in particular was able to call on its existing expertise in front-drive MacPherson strut suspensions, gained from the higher-powered versions of the Escort. In fact, the maximum torque transmitted through the front end of a 4x4 Sierra or Granada, one-third of the peak torque of the 2.8-litre V6 engine, is actually much less than that of the Escort XR3i, for instance.

Off-road considerations

Almost throughout this chapter I have concentrated on road-going four-wheel-drive vehicles rather than the cross-country type pioneered by the Jeep and Land-Rover. That is not to say technical development has stood still in the latter area. All through the 1950s and 1960s there were few changes: the accepted formula was live axles and multi-leaf cart springs at each end. Few concessions were made to ride comfort. The late Peter Wilks, mastermind of Land-Rover development and later of the Range Rover, once told me that the design objective of the Land-Rover suspension was to ensure the driver broke before the vehicle did!

Peter's tongue was in his cheek, even when he said that, late in the 1960s, because the Range Rover was close to announcement, complete with long-travel coil-spring suspension and a far higher standard of ride comfort. Other manufacturers have since emulated that approach and now even the Land-Rover 90 has coil springs. The main debate now is whether independent suspension is advisable for off-road vehicles. The problem is, of course, that if you drop the nose of a vehicle with independent front suspension over a hummock, either the final-drive casing will hit the ground or the bump-stops will have to be set so low in order to prevent it that they will seriously limit spring travel. This in turn could encourage the chassis designer to adopt downward-sloping suspension arms and drive-shafts, which would then pose a 'jacking up' problem in fast cornering (or even in slow cornering, across a steep enough slope). The Rover approach has been to minimize the unsprung weight by using light-alloy rather than iron castings for transmission casings and other components; it is one of the areas where the future may see composites playing an important role.

As a final thought, we might consider why, if the perfectly balanced car with 50:50 drive torque split to a four-wheel-drive transmission makes the best possible use of the available tyre grip, the system has not been adopted for racing cars. In fact it has been tried, but without notable success. John Miles, for one, wrote entertainingly and instructively about his efforts to come to grips with the Lotus 63, pointing out that even when the torque split was reduced to the point where only 15% of the drive was going to the front, the car would still eventually understeer violently. The answer seems to lie in my analysis of the total-understeer rally 'moment': it is the *inability* to control the line of a four-wheel-drive car with power alone, the way so many of us instinctively do with two-wheel-driven cars, which eventually leads to trouble with one incautious steering movement.

Four-wheel drive has quite rightly been rejected by the Formula 1 brigade on the grounds of weight and complication. Finding the space for a propeller shaft, a front final-drive unit and two extra drive shafts would be a daunting undertaking. But the final argument, I am sure, is that in practice, rear-drive is the only arrangement that gives racing drivers the chance to retain control.

Chapter eleven

Suspension at work

I suppose one of the drawbacks of working as – among other things – an engineering road-tester is that people assume it is all such fun. In a sense it is, although from time to time, passengers who have volunteered to ride through handling tests with me have called a halt to the fun and elected to watch from outside. The critical difference between the young man having fun on his favourite stretch of twisting road, and the professional test driver is that the tester has to ask himself a series of questions. What exactly is happening in each carefully set-up situation? Why is it happening? And assuming he can work out why it is happening, what could be done to improve the car's behaviour?

It should, I hope, be evident that the ability to drive extremely fast round a circuit does not in itself make a good test driver. There are some extremely quick racing drivers who, as despairing engineers and team managers will tell you, almost completely lack the ability to analyze the car's behaviour and suggest to the pit team what might be done to ease particular problems so that they can go faster still. The few fortunate men who combine ultimate car control with this analytical ability are almost bound in the end to rise to the very top of motor racing: Jack Brabham, Jackie Stewart and, of the current generation, Alain Prost, are obvious examples.

Especially if you are involved with a wide range of vehicles, the only way to work in an organized way is to have benchmarks – built-in standards of what is acceptable, good and

excellent. Even then you have to take care that your judgment is not clouded by other features within the car. It is remarkably easy, for instance, to blame a car for twitchy handling when the real culprit is an unprogressive throttle linkage – the power goes on, or worse still comes off, unevenly and the received impression is of a car with an awkward kink somewhere in its handling curve. It is still more dangerous to apply subjective standards without allowing for one's position within the car: if you sit high, as in the Range Rover, the cornering force and all rolling moments are magnified. If you sit low, as in so many super-cars, the impression of speed is greater than the reality. For all these reasons, test drivers like to have the reassurance of objective measurements – readouts from accelerometers, strain gauges and other equipment. But they still need their personal benchmarks.

Through my own test-driving career there have been benchmark cars which have caused me to think even harder, and reposition my standards of what makes a good car. This resetting of standards has to be part of one's background. If I still judged all the cars I test by the standards of my first Morris Minor then I would think them all absolutely splendid except, perhaps, in the matter of steering feel. What, then, have been the significant cars in my testing life?

Volkswagen Beetle

In a sense, I am cheating here because the Beetle first saw the light of day before I did.

Yet such was its longevity that it was still extremely current after I became professionally involved with cars rather than aeroplanes, and I tested several different versions.

The Beetle, of course, had all-independent suspension via an odd system of twin trailing arms at the front, and swing axles behind, at a time when almost every British car still had a live axle and cart springs at the rear; some of them were still recovering from the shock of switching to independent front suspension. As a result, the Beetle's ride quality seemed almost miraculous, though I suspect it won even more British friends by virtue of its build quality and features like an effective heater.

Even by the early 1960s, the Beetle's drawbacks were becoming better known, but it was still a shock for the young test driver to discover how much the thing wandered in crosswinds if it was going at all quickly. The effect was aerodynamic, and there was nothing the chassis engineer could have done about it except to install the engine at the other end, but the behaviour was a lesson in itself. The Beetle's steering feel and its *initial* feeling of stability, on the other hand, were very good – thanks largely, I am sure, to those very large, narrow tyres (5.60-15in crossplies!).

The next most obvious thing to my mind was not the handling, but the braking performance. It was very easy, especially on a wet road and/or a downhill slope, to lock the front brakes even at low speed and slither helplessly onward. The reason, as I suggested earlier, was that you could lock the lightly loaded front wheels *before* the deceleration had time to rock the body forward and transfer the necessary weight to load them. As I later discovered, it was – and is – a common tendency among rear and mid-engined cars (I recall the Lancia Monte Carlo as another bad example) and sometimes difficult to eradicate without degrading overall braking efficiency.

As for the Beetle's celebrated handling, I have to admit that I had no trouble until I went looking for it. My natural driving technique seems always to have been slow-in, fast-out: I would far rather accelerate round a corner, knowing I can then modify the line with power without encountering handling problems, than risk entering too fast and find myself having to sort out a situation on a trailing throttle. With the Beetle, the technique works well because the initial throttle application practically ensures the tail is tucked well down so that the rear suspension geometry is as far as it can be from causing trouble.

11:1. Volkswagen Beetle: excellent ride compared with the competition in its earlier years. Handling could be tricky, though critics often exaggerated the problem. Progressive development greatly improved the later examples.

11:2. Ford Cortina Mk1: MacPherson strut front suspension, as pioneered for mass production by Ford, was combined with recirculating-ball steering, light to the point of vagueness in the straight-ahead position.

To get into Beetle trouble, it was necessary to lift right off the accelerator so that the back end lifted, angling the swing-axles downwards, and then snap the power back on while it was still reared up. Then the combination of positive camber and power killed virtually all grip at the back and the poor Beetle would spin. All I can say in the car's defence is that I had to screw myself up to do it deliberately on the test track, and it never happened to me in ordinary road driving; though it certainly happened to plenty of other people with, I presume, a different approach to entering corners. Eventually, the danger was pushed to a much higher threshold, first with the adoption of radial-ply tyres, which better tolerated rear wheel camber changes, and finally a switch from swing-axle to semi-trailing arm rear suspension. By that time, however, people had other reasons for not buying the Beetle.

Ford Cortina

A fairly early Ford has to appear somewhere in this list because the Dagenham Fords, starting with the Zephyr/Zodiac range in the early 1950s, were the first models to use the MacPherson strut front suspension in large-scale production. I arrived on the scene too late to take in those earliest models, and while a

100E features early on my list of cars owned, one tries I think *not* to test one's own cars in that sense. I am sure the various Mark 1 Cortinas were the first cars I really tested with the MacPherson strut front end.

The first impression of any early Cortina was of extremely light steering. Around the straight-ahead it was so light as to give a feeling of actual vagueness, which became notably worse if you had a heavy load in the back. This was my first serious meeting not only with MacPherson struts, but also with recirculating-ball steering, the answer to a designer's prayer when it came to keeping steering effort low, but at a price. As for the effect of the heavy load in the back, this was a good illustration of how a rearward shift of centre of gravity can affect overall stability, compounded in the Cortina's case by limited wheel travel, but relatively soft springs. A hefty rear load made the back end much stiffer in roll and therefore encouraged oversteer.

One final thought before I leave the Cortina: if Volkswagen fitted the Beetle with 5.60-15in tyres, what was the Ford doing on 5.20-13s? Was Volkswagen over-tyring in search of some residual grip at the back in adverse circumstances, or was Ford cheapskating? Actually, I suspect, a bit of both.

11:3. Citroen DS: years ahead of its time in terms of both styling and engineering. Michelin X radial-ply tyres, newly developed for this car, made an important contibution to the roadholding, though the idiosyncratic ride and handling remained a matter of taste.

Citroen DS

In terms of the year of its introduction, the big Citroen ought to come earlier, but when it was announced in 1955 it was generally acknowledged as years ahead of its time.

The DS handled tolerably, but that was due more to balance than intrinsic merit of suspension geometry. All four wheels were constrained to lean at the body roll angle and, without doubt, the DS's roadholding would have been abominable had it not been for the camber-tolerance of the newfangled Michelin X radial-ply tyres which were indeed specifically developed for the DS as their first major application.

The greatest attributes of the DS were, of course, its ride comfort and its straight-line stability. I have to admit I admired the latter more than the former. Through the driving of many a DS, SM, GS, CX and BX, I have become used to the Citroen philosophy of near-constant ride frequency made possible by hydropneumatic suspension. But is it only me, I wonder, who finds Citroen's chosen frequencies (they quote the CX as 0.7 Hertz at the front, 0.86 Hertz at the rear, even when fully laden) simply too low for comfort? I would willingly sacrifice the ability to bowl unhindered over *pâvé* and rubble-surfaced tracks for the

sake of a firmer feel. A higher spring rate would also imply a higher damper rate and this is another area where I have always found the 'hydro' Citroens lacking: not in the matching of damper and spring rates which, as you might expect, is superb, but in roll damping. Until the advent of the BX, which is certainly much better, the Citroens always seemed to flop over to their roll angle first, very quickly, and only start turning afterwards.

Still, it *was* an education to discover you could turn smartly off the test track onto the ploughed field alongside and hardly feel any difference in the ride – and the ability to adjust the ride height was an eternal fascination, and sometimes even useful. I might even have forgiven the DS, with its odd leading-arm suspension mounting (but parallel double-wishbone geometry) the frightening lesson it taught me, that front-driven cars, too, can suffer something which feels terribly like axletramp!

Peugeot 404

The big old Peugeot has to come into the reckoning in any such list not for its handling qualities, which were strictly average, nor for its ride comfort, though since it *was* a Peugeot, that was certainly good, but rather for its

11:4. Peugeot 404: average handling, good ride comfort, but brilliant supression of road noise achieved with apparently conventional suspension — double wishbones in front and a worm-drive live axle at the rear — by means not easy to identify.

11:5. Mini: an all-time trend-setter with brilliantly agile handling in the hands of a capable driver, it totally changed popularly-held beliefs about the nature of front-wheel-drive cars. The ride, though, is better forgotten. . .

144

noise insulation. Its significance was quite simply that somehow, possibly even by accident (Peugeot's engineering team has never been the most forthcoming, and certainly was not in those days), it stumbled on an effectively compliant suspension arrangement which reduced road noise transmission into the body to such an extent that, for years, the 404 was the yardstick against which other cars were measured for this quality.

How did they do it? One has trouble pointing to any particular feature, which only makes things worse. The 404 had an apparently conventional double-wishbone front suspension and a live rear axle with an odd worm-gear final drive, located by radius arms and Panhard rod – an arrangement which later, except for the worm-drive, become common enough. Whatever the secret of the 404, it was not repeated to the same degree in its 504 replacement, which switched to MacPherson struts at the front and semi-trailing-arm independent rear suspension. The 504 was quiet by most standards, but not magically quiet like the 404.

Mini

The Mini has to come in here somewhere. It was launched while I was reading engineering at university, and I recall thinking it an odd if interesting little beast, but not much more. At that stage, I am sure nobody gave it the credit for being one of the all-time trend-setters.

By the time I was seriously driving Minis, or navigating the hotter ones in club rallies, its reputation had been established. It was, and is, a reputation firmly based on handling. That is actually very significant, because until then, the front-driven car had mostly been regarded – quite rightly – as a fundamentally understeering beast with splendid stability and a roomy cabin, but not as brilliantly agile.

How did the Mini manage to overcome that image? Quite simply by showing that it was wrong. It could out-corner some of the most ambitious rear-driven machinery of its day, and regularly did, even in average hands. 'You have just been Mini-ed', as the window stickers of the early 1960s said, and drivers of cars like the MG Magnette and Riley 1.5 could only glower.

The Mini did understeer and often to excess; it also snapped back at the driver if he lifted off in mid-corner, even more if he braked. As a rally navigator I sat through two big Mini accidents caused exactly by that effect. But in familiar circumstances it could be leaned hard against its understeer with huge confidence (and a tremendous rate of front tyre wear) and the more able drivers soon learned how to allow it to assume huge sideways angles by lifting off, and still pin it down with re-applied power and the aid of its ultra-quick steering (2.3 turns between locks, lest we forget, and the turning circle wasn't bad either). Also, the mid-engined brigade, with its chant of low polar moment, might take a short break to examine the polar moment of a two-up Mini; it was no accident that the car built its reputation as much on nimbleness – crisp turn-in, in the jargon of three decades later – as on actual steady-state cornering power.

Renault 16

Most authorities now look back at the Renault 16 and think at once of the car that really started the hatchback movement rolling. Yet in truth it was also one of the pioneer 'second generation' front-drive cars. It deployed double-wishbone front suspension and trailing arms at the back, with torsion bar springing all round, together with a notably long wheelbase.

One imagines Renault was at least partly motivated to go halfway to meet Citroen with the 16. It had the soft springing and long wheel travel to achieve a low ride frequency, though in my opinion it was a better chosen frequency than Citroen's; it was enough to cause considerable body roll, but that seemed not to matter. Two doses of oversteer were fed into the strongly understeering design, first by inclining the roll axis down to the rear (wishbones front, trailing arms rear, just like the Mini but with that longer wheelbase to slow the reaction!) plus the rear tyre camber change with roll.

The success of the 16 was that it showed how acceptable handling and comfortable ride could be combined in a front-driven car without going to Citroen-type lengths. Certainly it rolled more than we would consider acceptable today, but its track was narrow by current standards, like that of so many of its contem-

11:6. Renault 16: pioneer 'second generation' front-drive car, with long-travel torsion bar suspension giving an excellent ride/handling compromise, strongly biased towards understeer.

poraries. Modern designers have found no magic formulae to make cars stiffer in roll than they used to be – they just build them wider, and take care to exploit all that width for spring mounting to create the biggest possible base.

In its day, the Renault 16 was an excellent ride/handling compromise, even if it achieved that result through some sacrifice of ultimate roadholding.

Lotus Elan

No list of postwar benchmark cars in the area of chassis engineering would be complete without the Elan. Here was one of the ultimately nimble cars, another which gainsaid in advance much of what has been claimed for the mid-engined layout. Colin Chapman certainly appreciated the advantages of low polar moment but he was realist enough, where a road car of that era was concerned, to know that if you kept down the overall weight, so you would keep down the polar moment, whatever the chosen layout. In any event, to reiterate a point I have made before, if you actually start calculating on the basis of a front engine set well back in the chassis, and two occupants just about on the static centre of gravity, your polar moment emerges very little different from that of the mid-engined equivalent. This is even more the case when you

add Chapman's inspired X-frame chassis to the equation.

Then again, Colin Chapman knew all about balance and how to preserve it. He deliberately eschewed an inclined roll axis, he avoided anti-roll bars, and obtained his balance from the original static weight distribution plus careful control of camber angles. The Elan's front double wishbones are of carefully calculated geometry; its rear Mac-Pherson struts and wide-based lower wishbones equally control the camber angle very closely. Doubtless Colin would have had an answer for the effect of roll centre migration (front up, rear down to give an increasingly oversteer-inclining roll axis) had I had the wit to ask him when I had the chance.

Whatever the mechanical details, the proof of the Elan was in its driving. It was the first car in which I had to admit to myself that I was not good enough, or perhaps not brave enough, to find and exploit its limits, except very briefly on a test track with plenty of spare room; but those limits were very high. Aided by low weight and a low centre of gravity, it was able to exploit the potential grip of its modest tyres almost to the full, just as Chapman intended it to. Also, due to its low unsprung weight (one reason why the wheels and tyres were apparently modest) it rode much better than the traditional sports car – at least, until it ran out of wheel travel...

11:7. Lotus Elan: very high limits of roadholding on modest tyres. Chapman's design, a marvel of balance, endowed this front-engined car with such good handling that many of the advantages subsequently claimed for the mid-engined brigade seemed difficult to substantiate.

Jaguar XJ6

I am cheating here. There are two Jaguar XJ6s, the 1968-86 one and the new one. I drove the original XJ6, as it happened, the day after returning from France where I had driven the equally new Peugeot 504. If the 504 was a slight disappointment for reasons I have outlined above, then the Jaguar was surely the reverse.

The reason was of course that the Jaguar was a huge contrast with the previous 'mid range' models which had become rather bulky and wallowy. What the engineers had done was to take the basic chassis arrangement of the E-type and adapt it for the saloon's use. Since this implied proper double-wishbone geometry all round, the effect on handling and roadholding was inevitably dramatic – and

was further assisted by a usefully lower centre of gravity and a switch to radial-ply tyres.

There was no doubt that by the standards of big saloons in 1968 the XJ6 set new standards of handling and grip, yet its most outstanding feature was its noise insulation. It was as though Peugeot had laid down the 404's mantle for Jaguar to pick up. Bob Knight's team had, by virtue of a strong commitment to noise insulation by every means they could devise, come up with the right (though complex) answer at very little cost in terms of chassis accuracy under load.

Almost, but perhaps not quite. As I drove examples of the old XJ6 over the years, I always had the feeling that somewhere, some-time, I might just have a very big accident in one without being sure why it had happened.

147

11:8. Jaguar XJ6: the basic chassis arrangement of the E-type applied to Jaguar's big saloon to set new standards of handling, grip and noise suppression for its class. Very hard to improve upon, though Jaguar have subsequently done just that.

11:9. BMW 1800: an early example of the formula of MacPherson strut front suspension and semi-trailing rear which has become almost an industry norm, a system with many advantages and also some drawbacks, the latter relating to rear-wheel camber angle changes during cornering.

It never did, even when I pounded the car round the MIRA handling circuit and various other tracks. Yet Jim Randle, now Jaguar's Engineering Director, knew exactly what I meant when I mentioned it at the launch of the new, the current XJ6. 'Yes', he said 'the old car did have a slight tendency for the back end to steer if you lifted off in mid-corner' – the classic, though subtle, transient roll-steer effect. Needless to say, Jim is confident that the new, much-modified rear suspension doesn't do it, even though it has been cunningly engineered to provide even more compliance.

BMW 1800

The original BMW 1500 appeared before I became seriously involved with test driving, which just goes to show how long the BMW formula of MacPherson strut front suspension and semi-trailing rear arms has been around. By the time I was responsible for a *Motoring Which?* BMW report in 1966, the car had already grown into the 1800. I am rather relieved to re-read what I wrote over 20 years ago: 'The steering was very light, and it could be driven very fast round any sort of corner with ease and precision. But the BMW needed watching on a wet road. The back wheels could lose their grip quite early and without much warning...' Those words have been echoed by many others through the years.

That BMW showed both the advantages and drawbacks of a system which has nevertheless become almost an industry norm: count today's models with a similar (on paper) layout. The switch to all-independent suspension reduced unsprung weight and improved both ride quality and, in many circumstances, roadholding. Given some degree of offset (positive in those days) and little in the way of kingpin inclination (today's BMWs

have a good deal more), the steering could indeed be light. But that semi-trailing suspension always has some degree of camber-change lurking, and when grip is at a premium anyway, as in the wet, it takes much less of a change to cross the summit of the much lower cornering force curve. Nor would that BMW 1800 have been helped by the fitting of cross-ply tyres (6.00-14in Goodyear Nylon, says the report). Camber-tolerant radials, steadily reducing trail angles and other developments have held the ultimate reckoning at bay – but the new 7-series BMW uses an additional separate link to control camber properly!

Fiat 128

The little 128 was a masterpiece in many ways. It signalled Fiat's embracing of front-drive for small-medium cars. It had a brilliant new overhead-camshaft engine. And from the chassis point of view it had the interesting feature of MacPherson struts all round. It may indeed have been the first car ever to do so;

11:10. Fiat 128: a masterpiece in many ways. MacPherson strut suspension both front and rear was cleverly developed to give extremely secure handling and a notably good ride, complementing the verve of the overhead-camshaft engine.

certainly it predated those other two notable users, the Datsun 240Z and the Honda Civic. At the time of the Fiat's introduction, Honda's staple car product was the N360/600 microcar, which used struts at the front, but a dead axle at the rear.

The Fiat 128 handled extremely securely, despite a tendency to lift its inside rear wheel when it was cornering really hard. This happened despite the fact that there was an anti-roll bar at the front end only, giving an additional understeer effect. This suggests there was also some transfer of the lateral weight shift from front to rear as might be achieved through a nose-up roll axis. Actually, the fundamental difference between the two ends of the car was that while the front struts wore conventional concentric coil springs, the rear struts worked with either end of a transverse leaf spring, which would have given an anti-roll effect and, given Fiat's cunning, a progressive-rate spring effect into the bargain. The wheel-lift may also have had something to do with the downward migration of both roll centres so that the actual act of rolling further increased the body's roll moment. The most important thing in the Fiat chassis engineer's eyes would have been to ensure that it was the inside rear wheel, rather than the driven front one, which lifted first.

Unlike some of its rivals, the Fiat 128 rode notably well for no immediately obvious reason: it felt as though the springing was soft by class standards, though ultra-soft springs and all-MacPherson-strut suspension are not normally easy bedfellows. This again suggests the 128 had its wheel travel limited by bump stops – and, of course, the progressive-rate springing at the rear would have given the impression of a soft ride as long as too much wheel travel was not invoked.

The 128 certainly showed that with a little ingenuity, the all-MacPherson suspension could be made to work very well (and its lesson was surely learned some thousands of miles away). The subsequent small Fiats, however, embraced the torsion-beam rear suspension system like almost everyone else...

VW Golf/Scirocco

The Golf was the car which opened everyone's eyes to the subtlety of the torsion-beam rear

suspension – eventually. At first it was simply – if such a word could be appropriate – the effective Beetle-replacement; as such it set the ultimate seal on the front-drive, transverse-engine layout as the only choice for a small family hatchback.

At the front, the Golf used MacPherson struts rather than wishbones, a choice certainly dictated in part by Volkswagen's ferocious weight-saving programme, which resulted in the Golf emerging extremely light compared with many direct competitors. At the back, there was this (then) peculiar-looking arrangement with flimsy-looking trailing arms joined by a transverse beam.

What Volkswagen's engineers had achieved, we quickly discovered, was another aid to structural efficiency which also did the the handling no harm at all. In line with the tradition already established by many light front-driven cars, the trailing arms forced a rear camber change to degrade the back end cornering force and counter the basic understeer. The torsion beam itself worked both for and against: by raising the roll centre (though it is difficult to work out exactly where the roll centre of a torsion beam is; certainly not at ground level though, as with simple trailing arms) it slopes the roll axis more nearly nose-down and pro-understeer, while by acting as a rear anti-roll bar it is anti-understeer.

Raising the rear roll centre actually does no harm at all because it then enables you, all other things being equal, to adjust the front-end geometry to raise the front roll centre also, reducing the overall body rolling moment – and the Golf has always appeared to be quite stiff in roll without sacrificing too much to over-stiff spring rate. Less roll also means less migration of the front roll centre. What the layout also means is that the rear weight transfer is quite high in total, and the Golf – especially in its more powerful versions – seems inclined to lift its inside rear wheel, even though the body is not at a very marked roll angle. The more important thing for the driver is that the inside front wheel stays firmly enough on the ground to ensure continued positive traction...

Renault 5GT Turbo

The little Renault brings me firmly up to date:

11:11. VW Golf: the Beetle was a very hard act to follow, but Volkswagen's answer to the problem set the seal on the front-drive transverse-engine layout as the only choice for the class. The torsion-beam rear suspension was gradually recognized for the very effective solution it is.

11:12. Renault 5GT Turbo: exploits the grip of its massive tyres while retaining a reasonable ride, adequate steering feel and freedom from torque steer. The engineers have learnt a lot about harnessing turbocharged power to front-wheel drive.

as I write, the memory of a recent long-term test is still fresh in my mind. For six months I had the pleasure of discovering with what contempt it treated most of my favourite corners.

The 5GT is turbocharged, and therefore its torque output is prodigious. There was a turbocharged version of the 'Mark 1' Renault 5 and that was an evil little car, all determined understeer, instant oversteer on lift-off, and torque steer whenever you changed the power setting, or so it seemed. The current 5GT shows just how fast engineers can learn from initial errors.

Since it is front-driven and nose-heavy, the 5GT cannot help but be a basic understeerer. Its suspension is MacPherson struts at the front, while the rear uses Renault's 'four-bar' arrangement – a Gallic variation on the torsion beam concept in which four transverse torsion bars act as two pairs, each pair together to provide spring effect and in opposition to oppose roll. Thus very neatly, Renault has arrived at a layout which even goes a stage further than the torsion beam, incorporating the full spring effect as well.

As with the torsion beam, it is difficult to say exactly where the roll centre of such an arrangement is – it depends on the extent to which you allow for the arms being trailing (roll centre at ground level) and for the bars and associated structure to act as a dead axle (roll centre at axle height). Certainly, though, the centre must be higher than ground level, for the 5GT shows every sign of suffering only limited body rolling moment. What the arrangement does mean is that, as with any other trailing-arm rear suspension, the rear tyres are forced to sacrifice grip to camber change as the body rolls.

There is a front anti-roll bar, too, and quite a stiff one at 23.5mm diameter (all but an inch). The other thing the Renault engineers have done is to stiffen the front springs far more than those at the rear. Both these moves favour additional understeer, but they also help cut the body roll to very small angles. This, together with the camber control of the MacPherson struts, means the car is well able to exploit the potential grip of its front 195/55R13 tyres.

The 5GT Turbo is a fairly light car – Renault claims a kerb weight of 1,885lb – and if we think back many chapters to our investigation of Ford Escort required cornering power, which was easily met by the 175/70R13 tyre, it is clear that the 5GT tyres must have a lot in hand at 0.75g. Even if the car understeers in a fairly determined manner, it has sufficient grip to take it to lateral acceleration rates which would alarm most people. And in practice the impression of understeer is not great, because the other advantage of those 55-series tyres is that they generate a lot of cornering force at relatively small slip angles.

There is even more to the Renault 5GT Turbo, as apt a car as I could imagine to provoke thought about where the limits of chassis engineering might be. Setting it up to exploit the grip of its massive tyres is an exercise in itself – but the Renault team has managed it while retaining at least a reasonable ride, adequate steering feel and freedom from torque steer. When you have learned to do that, maybe you begin to qualify as a chassis engineer *par excellence*.

Chapter twelve

Looking to the future

When I wrote the equivalent of this chapter in 1988, I discussed a range of technologies which seemed likely to play a major part in chassis design in the coming decade. My crystal ball must have been seriously clouded because for the most part they didn't! Before I try to do better this time, we ought to look at what went wrong with those earlier predictions.

Actually, my opening shot was not too bad. I pointed out that no significant new suspension linkage has been invented since the torsion beam first appeared in the VW Golf/Scirocco in 1974, and that is still more or less the case. The only exception is the appearance of the genuinely multi-link rear suspensions now found in a number of cars – suspensions in which each link has a particular computer-assigned task to perform, without interfering (except in benign and intended ways) with the action of any other link. Engineers have always appreciated, of course, that in theory (and neglecting the complication of steering), each wheel needed to have four of its degrees of freedom removed while being allowed to retain the other two – rotation around its spindle, and vertical movement in translation. But it is really only since the advent of computer power that the solution of the three-dimensional equations governing the movement of four or five inter-hinged links to achieve this aim with high precision became possible. The task is still not entirely simple: you define the wheel position and a couple of 'master'

suspension link attachment points, and the computer gives you a range of position-and-angle options for attaching the remaining links. You still have to engineer those attachments, and that involves making choices and arriving at compromises with the needs of other systems. We are still some way from being able to press a button and have the computer design a complete suspension for us, but at least we may be able to say that the multi-link arrangement is one of the main-choice suspension layouts of the future – along with our three old favourites, the MacPherson strut, the double-wishbone and the torsion beam.

I concluded my previous opening section with the remark that most engineers now accept that the way forward is through the refinement of basic components and the application of electronic control to achieve variations which simply cannot be mechanically achieved without vast complication. The previous paragraph already gives the lie to that. Not only does the geometry of the multi-link layout come close to perfection: the 'tweaks' which have been applied to the MacPherson strut and, especially, the double-wishbone have made them very nearly as good. It is rare in any modern car equipped with double wishbones to find that the axes of the two arms are actually parallel: by shifting one relative to the other you can reduce camber angle and track change almost to nothing throughout the whole range of wheel travel, and compliant suspension bushing or, if

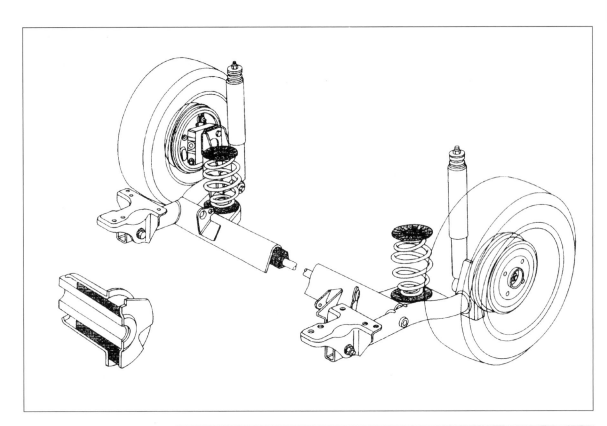

12:1. For many years, Renault equipped its smaller cars with variations on a single theme so far as the rear suspension was concerned: trailing arms with two or four transverse torsion bar springs, which doubled as anti-roll bars. But in the 1998 Clio II, a car engineered with a particularly ruthless eye to cost control, even Renault has accepted that the torsion-beam rear suspension layout gives a high payback for a modest cost in terms of handling, stability, structural efficiency and operating refinement.

necessary, ball-joints will take care of any resulting 'fight'. Even where perfectly accurate movement cannot be achieved, chassis engineers have learned not to fight it: instead, they make it work in their favour, most obviously in 'passive rear-steer' arrangements where the small residual movements of the suspension and its mounting bushes during cornering are used to create a self-stabilizing effect in which the rear wheels point a fraction of a degree into the corner.

The appeal of the torsion beam as a rear suspension was recently (as I wrote) borne out by the appearance of the Renault Clio II with this arrangement. Renault, the arch-developer of the trailing-arm layout into ever more sophisticated forms, with no fewer than four transverse torsion bars working in careful combination in its most recent applications, had made the switch at

last – and they quoted all the usual reasons for its adoption. They mentioned accurate tracking performance, lightness, easy to incorporate the most effective spring, damper and noise insulation arrangement . . . all they did not say (few spokesmen ever do) is that it is remarkably cheap in relation to its efficiency, and easy to install on the production line.

New materials: disappointment

In 1988 I predicted great things for new materials, and especially for high-strength plastic composites to replace steel in springs. Despite the apparent advantages, it hasn't happened – at least, not yet. One of the problems, certainly, has been the concern over end-of-life recycling: this is not something to which these composites readily lend themselves. Thus we are still, for the most part, looking at steel coil

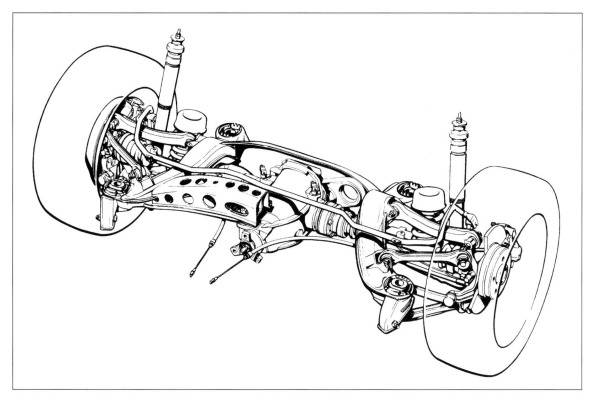

12:2. The designers of large and expensive cars are increasingly turning to true multi-link independent suspensions, especially for the rear wheels. Although often superficially resembling double-wishbone layouts, these new suspensions use four or five optimized links mounted at carefully calculated points and angles, each link being responsible for controlling a particular aspect of wheel movement so as to minimize camber and alignment change without restricting vertical movement. The Mercedes E-class rear suspension, seen here, shows how complex such arrangements can become – but there is no question that they are highly effective.

springs as the main suspension medium, and this is likely to continue for some time to come. As for other forms of spring, there have been few takers for air springs, and none at all for Citroen's compressed-gas springs, even though Citroen itself continues to use them with success and reliability in the XM and Xantia.

Elastomers have made steady progress, though their influence on suspension design as a whole has been limited. Very few customers ever realize that the quietness of recent car interiors, and the comfort of the ride, are both in large measure achieved with lumps of rubber or plastic – providing insulation where suspension arms are attached to the body, and acting as secondary springs when installed, like elongated bump-stops, inside steel coil springs.

Another technology which has seen less progress than anticipated is that of special viscous fluids. Ten years ago there were suggestions that such fluids might be used in dampers of much improved performance. Again, it hasn't happened. Even more advanced fluids in which the viscosity is controlled by an electric field are still being experimented with – but it could be a long time before they find their way into chassis design applications.

'Run-flat' tyres: here at last?

One idea I failed even to mention in the first edition is the issue of the 'run-flat' tyre. In one respect it is a side-issue to the main business of chassis engineering, except that if such tyres do become available, chassis designers will need to take them into account. Even in 1988 the run-flat idea was far from new; the Dunlop Denovo had already come and (pretty well) gone. Through the early 1990s, interest in the concept was confined to very special, and expensive, products for security purposes: for cars and other vehicles which needed to keep going regardless of whether their tyres were inflated. The average motorist seemed less than impressed by efforts to sell four run-flat wheels and tyres instead of five ordinary ones. However rarely it is used, that spare in the boot is a strong psychological crutch.

Then a market arose in the USA, where people in some parts of the country began, with whatever justification, to worry that stopping to change a wheel would make them ready targets for criminals. The tyre manufacturers decided quick action was needed. Michelin produced a modified version of a standard tyre, the MXV4 ZP (zero pressure) with heavily reinforced sidewalls which could carry the weight of one corner of the car for 50 miles at 55mph – still the most widespread US speed limit – following deflation, without damage or loss of vehicle control.

In 1997, Michelin followed up with its *pneu accrochée verticale*, or vertically anchored tyre concept (PAX) which, when fitted with an internal reinforcing ring to be offered as an optional extra, is capable of extending the deflated driving range well beyond 100 miles (though the 55mph speed restriction remains). Several other advantages are claimed for the PAX in normal, as opposed to deflated, running including improved wet grip, steering response and ride comfort.

The snag is that PAX is indeed a completely new concept and requires a wheel rim whose design is completely different from the one which is now internationally standardized for car use. It is a situation reminiscent of Michelin's launch during the 1970s of the TRX tyre, which likewise offered major dynamic advantages (though not run-flat ability) but required a non-standard rim. The TRX limped on for several years, but eventually vanished from the market; its advantages were not sufficient to persuade the car manufacturers (and their customers) to abandon the standard rim and the guarantee of universal interchangeability which came with it.

As with so many developments in chassis engineering, it is not a question of being better, but of being so much better that your product overcomes any problems from which it suffers. Where tyres are concerned, the TRX failed to do that; but in 1998 it looks as though Michelin sees better performance in normal use plus 'extended

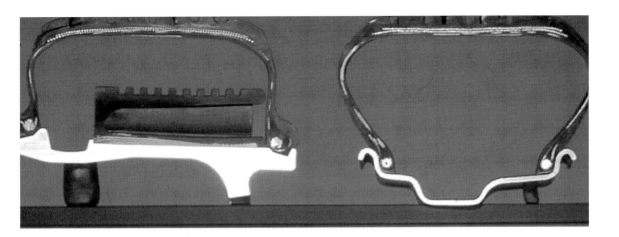

12:3. In 1997, Michelin proposed its new PAX wheel-and-tyre concept in which the inner section of the conventional tyre sidewall is deleted, leaving a much shallower section retained on a wider rim. Michelin has demonstrated the superior wet grip and transient response of the PAX while also arguing that the concept has valuable 'run-flat' characteristics when equipped with a suitable internal 'support ring'. The big question remains: are vehicle manufacturers (and their customers) prepared to abandon the existing standard rim, effectively a worldwide standard, for anything which is not interchangeable?

mobility' (run-flat) as giving the PAX a healthier chance of success, with the USA as its key early market. If that happens, Michelin's great rivals will not allow themselves to be left far behind – and the chassis engineer will be faced with the extra challenge of how much allowance needs to be made for the handling behaviour of a car with one flat tyre. More fundamentally, the European specialist at least will have to balance whether to offer the PAX with its run-flat reinforcing rings and accept the adverse effect of their considerable weight on ride comfort and roadholding, or simply to present it as a superior tyre. One worry at least has been overcome already, because Michelin stresses that the PAX will be sold together with a deflation warning system, to avoid the possibility of an extremely unaware driver continuing without realizing that any deflation has occurred.

Active ride control

The rapid rise of interest in active ride control (ARC) during the 1980s was, as it turned out, followed by a levelling-off of that interest in the 1990s, and perhaps even a decline. The basic objection was a simple one: leaving aside their cost and their complication, ARC systems consumed too much power. The problem is that ARC as it has been proposed and demonstrated over many years has always depended on a high-pressure hydraulic supply to move the suspension unit in response to the profile of the road surface, sensed in the form of a vertical load on the wheel. That hydraulic supply came from an engine-driven pump, and for consistent performance it needed to be a fairly large one. That in turn created a significant penalty in terms of fuel consumption, which was something no manufacturer was prepared to contemplate, it seemed. There were alternative suggestions for systems in which the movement of a suspension unit would itself 'pump up' a hydraulic accumulator, whose pressure could then be used to improve the ride quality without draining power from the engine, but most vehicle manufacturers seem now to have decided that an acceptable ride can be achieved with

conventional passive spring-and-damper systems, which have been continuously refined (the accuracy of damper settings in particular has been significantly improved in the last decade).

There has been more enthusiasm for automatic variable-rate damping, which is now offered on many of the larger and more expensive cars. Such systems do indeed offer improved ride comfort on a variety of road surfaces, but there are limits to the extent to which the damper rate can be varied. As explained in earlier chapters, the damper rate should in theory be closely matched to the spring rate – and nobody (except Citroen) has seriously suggested varying the spring rate, hence the limitation on the possible range of damper settings. Hence, in turn, the reaction of some road-testers that it is difficult to discern any difference in ride quality, no matter how the dampers are set, when demonstrations are run with displays to monitor system performance.

Citroen was the only company to do anything different – but it had the best starting point in the form of its existing high-pressure hydropneumatic suspension system. The company moved in two stages, first introducing its Hydractive system on the XM and later the Xantia, and following up with the Activa anti-roll system which first appeared on the Xantia. Hydractive switches between two spring-and-damper settings, achieved by providing an extra gas-spring sphere at each end of the car, to which the adjacent wheel units can be connected by opening a pair of valves; the connecting passages contain damper orifices, which is how Citroen matches the damper rate to the reduced spring rate. The valves open and close under computer control, shutting the valves to switch to the stiffer setting when, for instance, the electronic system senses that the driver is turning the steering wheel to enter a corner.

Hydractive works very well, but the impression created by the Activa system is more immediate. This system requires two extra hydraulic jacks between the body and the suspension, at diagonally opposite corners of the car. The high-pressure system

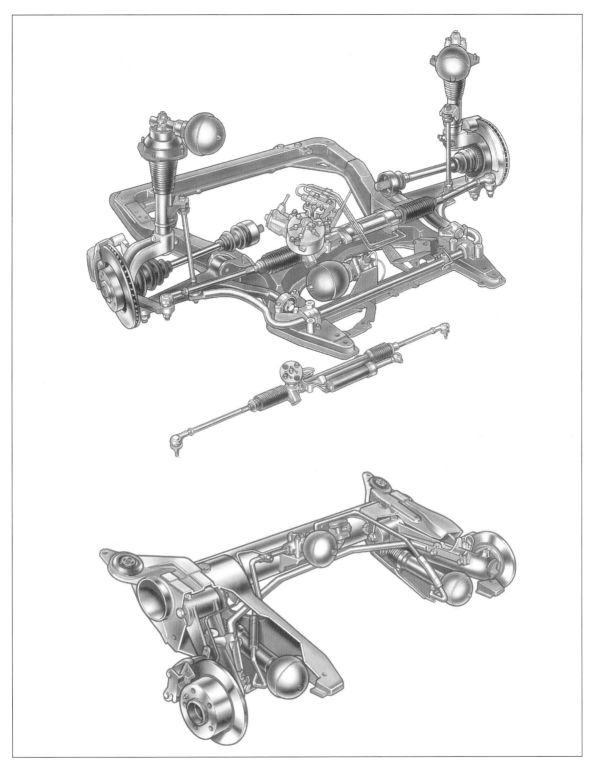

12:4. Citroen remains the only company mass-producing a truly active ride control system in which spring rate as well as damper rate is varied according to need. The Hydractive suspension, first seen in the XM (here) and later the Xantia, adapts the company's familiar high-pressure hydropneumatic suspension (which dates from 1954) by adding central spring-spheres which can be connected to or isolated from the rest of the suspension.

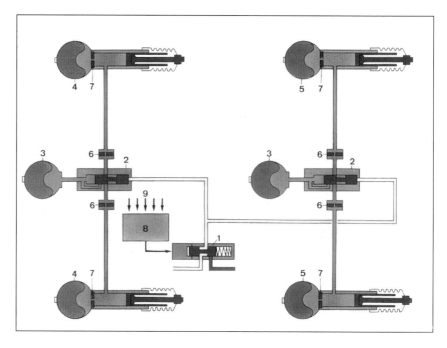

12:5. Schematic plan of the Hydractive system. Connecting the additional spring-spheres into the rest of the suspension softens the spring rate. The ability to transmit suspension movements to a remote springing medium and to provide damping by valves integrated in the circuit are inherent advantages of Citroen's hydropneumatic system. 1: solenoid valve. 2: regulator valve. 3: additional sphere. 4: front sphere. 5: rear sphere. 6: supplementary damper. 7: damper. 8: computer. 9: sensor input.

operates these jacks to limit body roll to half a degree, which from a driver's point of view means no perceptible roll at all. The half-degree allowance is enough to prevent the system perpetually 'hunting' – and wasting energy – every time the driver makes a small course correction, while ensuring that the body (and therefore the wheels) stays almost perfectly upright when cornering. Because the wheels and the tyres remain upright, cornering behaviour and grip are much improved.

It is still worth remembering, with this or any other effective system which appears in the future, that the car's roadholding still ultimately depends on the grip of perhaps 80 square inches of tyre tread rolling through the four contact patches. No advanced suspension system can rewrite the laws of physics, and the limits will always be there. That may be another reason (apart from their lack of a well-proven high-pressure hydraulic suspension system as a starting point) why no other company has followed Citroen into genuine active ride control. The results now being achieved with the best of conventional systems – not least by Citroen's sister company Peugeot in cars like the 406 – are good enough to keep most customers happy,

providing them with handling and roadholding limits which are well beyond their normal requirements or abilities, so why go to the expense and complication of breaking new technical ground? And unless he has a chance to drive the Xantia Activa, the average customer will never know what he is missing . . .

Electronic stability control

One development I failed to foresee in 1988 was that of electronic stability control. I went into some detail about the way in which active ride control might also be used to modify a car's handling at will, by altering the ratio of front to rear roll stiffness, under computer control or by driver command. Because ARC itself has not come to pass, that has not happened. Instead, we have electronic stability control (ESC), now quite widely fitted to large and powerful cars with rear-wheel drive, and in one case – which I shall discuss next – to a small front-driven car.

ESC is yet another spin-off from anti-lock braking (ABS). In a sense, it is a further step along the road from traction control, which (at low speeds) prevents a driven wheel from spinning by automatically applying a quick 'dab' of brake, allowing the

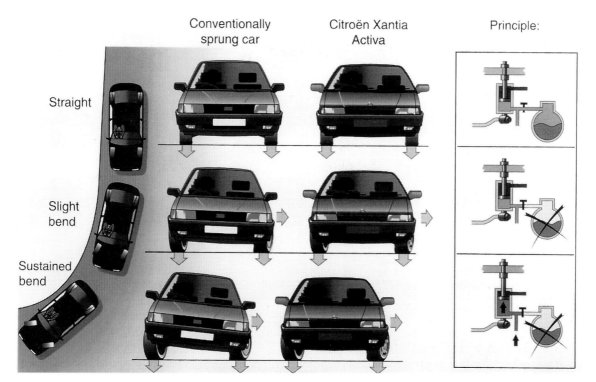

Straight

Slight
bend

Sustained
bend

12:6. In 1994, Citroen added its Activa roll-control system, in which two auxiliary jacks limit body roll to a maximum half-degree – in practice, barely perceptible. By keeping the wheels upright at all times, so that the tyres always run close to zero camber, Activa also improves roadholding.

opposite wheel to transmit extra torque. The system not only uses the ABS wheel speed sensor to detect when the wheel is starting to spin, but also takes the brake pulse from the ABS pressure accumulator and valve block. In fact, basic traction control can be added to almost any ABS system simply by writing some extra software for the control computer, although further complications arise because real-life TCS usually also controls engine torque output in one way or another, and this involves adding extra hardware and electrical connections.

However, ESC takes the principle a stage further. Suppose, for the sake of argument, the driver of a powerful rear-driven car on an icy road uses a fraction too much power in mid-corner. The rear wheels will immediately begin to slide outwards, and control may quickly be lost. But if, as soon as the rear wheels begin to slide, a dab of brake is applied to the front wheel on the outside of the corner, then the effect will

tend to yaw the car in the opposite sense – nose out of the corner rather than into it. At the same time, the car will be slowed down, gently and (hopefully) safely. Again, if the driver enters a corner too abruptly and the front wheels begin to run wide, a dab of the nearside rear brake will pull the car back towards its proper cornering line. This is the working principle behind ESC: if the car begins to get out of shape or off-line, small, rapid applications of brake on a single wheel at one corner of the car will restore the condition the driver is trying to maintain. Motor sport enthusiasts may (rightly) see some similarity here with the individual 'fiddle' handbrakes used in specialist trials cars. In fundamental terms, ESC uses individual wheel braking to modify a car's handling.

The key trick in achieving successful ESC is to determine what the driver is actually trying to do, comparing it with what the car is actually doing, and reducing the difference to zero. This calls for excellent

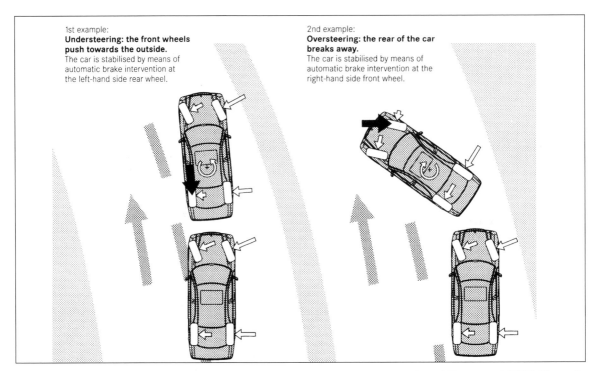

Understeering: the front wheels push towards the outside.
The car is stabilised by means of automatic brake intervention at the left-hand side rear wheel.

2nd example:
Oversteering: the rear of the car breaks away.
The car is stabilised by means of automatic brake intervention at the right-hand side front wheel.

12:7. Handling in low-grip conditions can be greatly improved by adding electronic stability control (ESC). The car's motion is computed using information from various sensors, and compared with the driver's intentions, deduced mainly from steering wheel movements. The control computer then works via the ABS valve block to apply momentary braking at one corner of the car – the outer front corner to reduce oversteer, the inner rear to reduce understeer. ESC, in combination with traction control, has proved especially valuable in powerful rear-driven cars in which control is easily lost in slippery conditions through premature power application in mid-corner.

sensing of the driver's control movements, and especially of steering wheel movement, and some rather more clever sensing of the car's movement. This latter calls for aerospace-type movement sensors – at the very least a lateral accelerometer, better still some form of solid-state yaw rate sensor. All the signals have then to be processed through the ESC sensor, a task not as easy as it may sound since, for example, the driver's basic intention may need to be determined through a mass of signals produced by him sawing away desperately at the steering wheel. When all the calculation is over, however, the final output is simple enough: a series of brake pulses to one wheel, possibly accompanied by an automatic reduction in power, until the car is back on course.

Among other things, ESC has proved to be a further nail in the coffin of four-wheel drive for road use. Just as traction control overcame the basic problem of wheelspin on slippery surfaces in a car with two driven wheels, so ESC has achieved with less weight and cost the other main advantage of 4WD, namely ease of control up to the natural limit of roadholding. This has been very good news for the remaining manufacturers of powerful rear-driven cars, since it had become clear that they were becoming very difficult to control on low-grip surfaces, and especially on snow and ice. Even the most diehard rear-drive enthusiast would have to admit, after driving a front-drive and a rear-drive car in back-to-back testing on a handling circuit on one of Sweden's frozen lakes, that without any kind of artificial aid the rear-drive car is far more difficult to control – more precisely, to recover from an out-of-line situation – while demanding far more concentration from the driver and creating far more mental stress. For a few laps that may actually make the rear-drive car seem more fun; but you soon become tired of seeing your front-drive rival pass you through and out of every corner. Traction control helps, but it is by no means a complete answer, because excess power will still induce a spin. But with an effective ESC system – and they are now highly effective – the mental stress vanishes and the cornering performance is consistently improved. Thus, as I said in my introduction, companies like BMW and Mercedes have discovered that by spending a few hundred dollars on ESC, they can make their cars as easy to drive on snow and ice as an Audi A6, a Saab 900 or a Volvo S70. Of course, they could achieve the same result by switching to front-drive, but we have been through all that.

The case of the Mercedes A-class

Lest we thought that vehicle stability and handling were now fully understood and adjustable at will, the story of the Mercedes A-class in late 1997 suggested otherwise. The A-class broke new ground for Mercedes: a small (C-segment) front-driven car from a company which had always specialized in large rear-driven models. But Mercedes is renowned for the thoroughness of its engineering, and when the A-class was first shown to the press in 1997 it was generally admired. However, in October 1997, a fully laden Mercedes A-class toppled on its side while negotiating a 'moose test' – a tight double lane-change manoeuvre entered at 60km/hour (37mph) and intended to reproduce the evasive action necessary should one of these very large animals emerge from the forest onto the road, as they sometimes do in Scandinavia. When the news broke, Mercedes initially responded by questioning the validity of the test, but had quickly to acknowledge that this approach was merely fanning the flames of criticism. The company then stopped production and sales, and undertook a major re-engineering exercise with the object of enabling the A-class to navigate the moose-test at least as fast as any of its class rivals without any untoward behaviour.

To achieve its objective, the company worked in two ways. One was to modify the chassis by various conventional means in order to make it more difficult to topple the car; these changes provide a good illustration of how the mind of the chassis engineer works when faced with a problem. The other was to exploit the potential of the most sophisticated electronic stability control system developed by Mercedes and Bosch, called ESP, to provide further insurance against misbehaviour, even in the clumsiest of driving hands.

The basic chassis changes were exactly what one might expect to emerge from a short-term programme of this kind. The springs and dampers were uprated, to increase roll stiffness but also, crucially, to increase the natural rolling frequency of the body. The undoing of the original A-class was that this frequency nearly enough coincided with that of the four yaw-reversals involved in the moose-test, so that each change of direction added still further to the toppling force – a mechanism remarkably similar to that of a child sliding back and forth in the bath, creating a bigger and bigger 'wave' until the water overflows – until it became sufficient to tip the car beyond the fulcrum of its outer tyre contact patches. Stiffening the suspension in roll meant it was virtually impossible for a driver to switch from one lock to the other fast enough to get into phase with the side-to-side rocking of the body.

Other changes were included in the package. The rear track was widened, so that a greater sideways force is needed before the car will topple. The front anti-roll bar was stiffened, leading to a moderate increase in understeer, in turn making the tail less likely to swing wide in a lane-change manoeuvre, while also causing the car to slow down more quickly by increasing front tyre slip angles and hence rolling resistance (the moose test is conducted without touching the brakes, which was why Mercedes accused it of being unrepresentative: in a real-life and unanticipated 'moose' situation, most drivers tend to brake and indeed, many of them do not even try to steer, but merely brake as hard as they can). For good measure, the chassis engineers also standardized the fitting of 195/50-15 tyres, whose rolling radius is 10mm less than

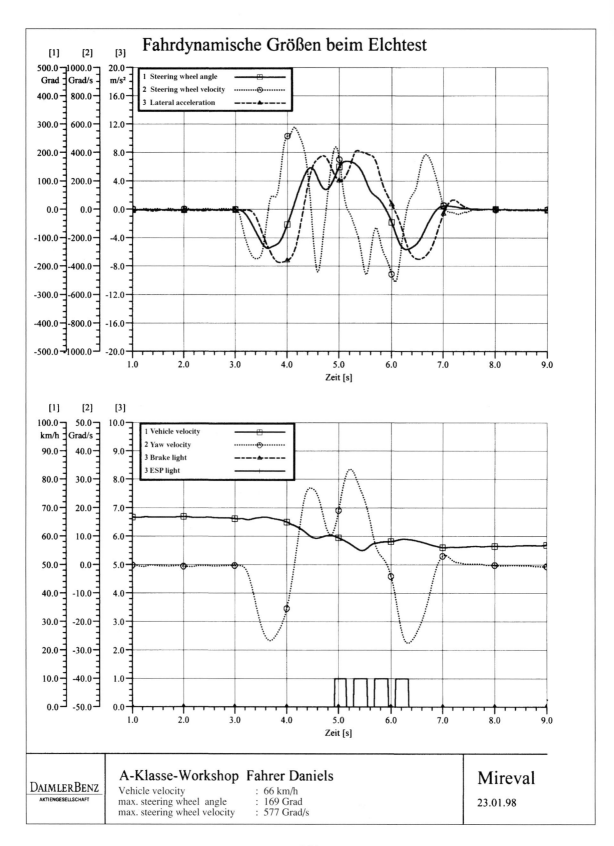

Fahrdynamische Größen beim Elchtest

Upper chart axes:
[1] 500.0 Grad [2] 1000.0 Grad/s [3] 20.0 m/s²

Legend:
1 Steering wheel angle
2 Steering wheel velocity
3 Lateral acceleration

Zeit [s]

Lower chart axes:
[1] 100.0 km/h [2] 50.0 Grad/s [3] 10.0

Legend:
1 Vehicle velocity
2 Yaw velocity
3 Brake light
3 ESP light

Zeit [s]

DAIMLERBENZ
AKTIENGESELLSCHAFT

A-Klasse-Workshop Fahrer Daniels
Vehicle velocity   : 66 km/h
max. steering wheel angle   : 169 Grad
max. steering wheel velocity   : 577 Grad/s

Mireval

23.01.98

164

those of the original 175/65-15 size. This lowers both the roll-centre and the centre of gravity, but in doing so it reduces the ratio of CG to roll-centre height, and thus further increases the 'critical' overturning moment.

When Mercedes invited European journalists to Goodyear's Mireval test facility near Montpellier to subject the A-class to a series of tests which, of course, included a carefully reproduced 'moose test', the results were convincing. I drove through the test without problem at 66km/h (41mph), and some journalists managed to approach 80km/h (50mph) without the vehicle appearing to lift a wheel, much less tip over.

The Mercedes printout of instrument readings from 'my' A-class is shown in *fig 12.8*. The upper chart shows the steering wheel angle, speed of steering wheel movement, and lateral acceleration when driving through the test: the lower one shows the car's speed, the yaw rate, and a series of 'blips' on the bottom line triggered by operation of the ESP. Bear in mind that the trace is the result of a violent left-right swerve, very quickly followed by another in the opposite direction, to regain the original side of the road. Among the points of interest, the traces show that the peak cornering force in both directions was around 8 metres/sec², or 0.81g. Also, the trace shows the effect of basic technique. I tried, rather untidily, to straighten up between the two closely spaced chicanes, and had to make the quick double-adjustment seen in the steering wheel angle and speed traces. Those who drove through the test fastest (and without knocking over any marker cones) simply drove the middle part in one smooth curve to the right, with no attempt to straighten the centre section. There is a lesson there for anyone interested in driving: the fewer the number of actual changes of direction you make, that is from one side of the straight-ahead to the other,

the smoother and quicker your progress will be. Note also the remarkably 'dead-beat' way the A-class regains its stable straight line after leaving the test, which may have something to do with me, but probably has a lot more to do with the car.

The changes made to the A-class by Mercedes in a 'crash' engineering programme were logical, with the element of overkill which one might expect of the company. One may speculate that in the longer term, more subtle measures (such as, for example, adjustment of the roll-centres independently of the CG position) may be introduced, if only to allow the ride comfort – which the stiffer springs and dampers, and the lower-profile tyres have made almost spectacularly harsh when travelling along poorly surfaced French back-roads – to be improved. Some further salvation may be found in improving the steering feel, since the poor feedback through the current system must make it more difficult for some drivers to appreciate whether they are approaching a limiting situation.

Four-wheel steering

One of my more serious mistakes in the first edition of this book was to suggest that four-wheel steering was a coming thing. At that time it had been introduced on production cars by Honda and Mazda, and virtually every major car manufacturer had a 4WS demonstrator and research vehicle. I vividly remember driving a Renault on the company's test track while the engineer beside me hit keys on his laptop computer to change its behaviour from '*Systeme Honda*' to '*Systeme Mazda*' and a couple of other variations on the theme. In the end, though, despite its apparent promise, 4WS never took off, though it is still offered on some models in the Japanese domestic market, where easy slotting into very tight parking spaces is a major sales point. Otherwise, it was yet another case of the advantages

Opposite: 12:8. The behaviour of any car (and of its driver) can now be tracked accurately with good instrumentation and real-time telemetry. This printout shows how several parameters, including steerng wheel angle, steering wheel rate of turn, vehicle yaw rate and lateral acceleration, varied while the author drove a Mercedes A-class through the now celebrated 'moose test' at 66km/hour (compared with the 60km/hour at which one tester overturned an A-class before it was modified). Note especially the series of 'blips' indicating that the electronic stability control system applied the brakes during the second of the two chicanes in the test sequence.

never managing to outweigh the weight, cost and complication.

There may be more mileage in some of the systems now being developed by the Japanese manufacturers (and probably others, but the Japanese always seem more eager to demonstrate them). In 1997, I drove a Honda demonstrator which, through careful gearing and graduated power-assistance, managed with just one turn of the steering wheel between locks, yet suffered none of the kart-like twitchiness of other cars with very high-geared steering (such as the Citroen SM, remembered with very mixed affections) but felt immediately 'natural'. From this clever but fundamentally conventional system – evolution rather than revolution – the next potential step is into 'steer-by-wire'.

'Drive-by-wire' and 'steer-by-wire'

There are already plenty of cars around with 'drive-by-wire' – with electrical connections replacing the mechanical cable link between accelerator pedal and throttle valve (or, sometimes, simply the engine management unit). The advantages of drive-by-wire are considerable. It allows the actual throttle movement to be calibrated to avoid the problems sometimes caused by clumsy driver technique, smoothing over the effect of a sudden slamming of the accelerator to avoid any 'blip' of hesitation (and any accompanying spurt of exhaust emission). It allows other systems, such as TCS and ESC, to intervene directly to reduce engine output without the need for an auxiliary throttle valve. And of course it overcomes the headache of having to find a nice smooth, maximum-radius run for a long mechanical cable through the increasingly crowded under-bonnet space.

All these advantages are magnified when you look at 'steer-by-wire', replacing the mechanical steering column with an electrical signal to a computer-controlled power steering pump. Clumsy and inexpert use of the accelerator can be wasteful and uncomfortable, but clumsy operation of the steering can be lethal. Rather in the way that ESC already does, but far more positively, a steer-by-wire computer could deduce that the driver actually wanted to change course very quickly, and not actually to lose control of the car, and would smooth and limit its own outputs accordingly. It would be very easy for other future technical developments, such as automatic traffic lane tracking, to feed signals directly into the steering computer. Inside the car, substituting some form of central 'joystick' for a steering wheel would mean an end to the huge headache – with so many safety implications – of finding room for a mechanical steering column. It would mean, for example, standardizing airbag installations on both sides of the car, and far fewer worries about changing from left to right-hand drive.

I have driven one steer-by-wire car, a Saab 900, with a central joystick control. It was much easier than I had anticipated, though it became more difficult when the engineer in the passenger seat (again!) demonstrated the way in which he could switch the control software to change the 900's handling from gentle and consistent understeer to sudden and vicious oversteer – or at least, something which gave exactly that impression. Far from being a mere trick, it underlined the potential of steer-by-wire for allowing the driver to select both steering response and handling characteristics by flicking a switch. Do we want the sports car or the limousine today?

The one thing which prevents the early adoption of steer-by-wire is the question of safety. We all have inherent trust in that mechanical link to the front wheels, and its failure rate is indeed very low (though not zero). But what happens if the electrics of a steer-by-wire system suffer a short circuit or a power failure? What happens if the computer begins producing erroneous output signals? The systems engineers think they have the answers, in the form of duplicated and independent paths and continuous automatic checking, but it will be a brave car manufacturer who ventures first into the field; and the one who does will probably install an emergency mechanical backup, in any case. But the potential advantages of steer-by-wire are so great that, in the end, they will become

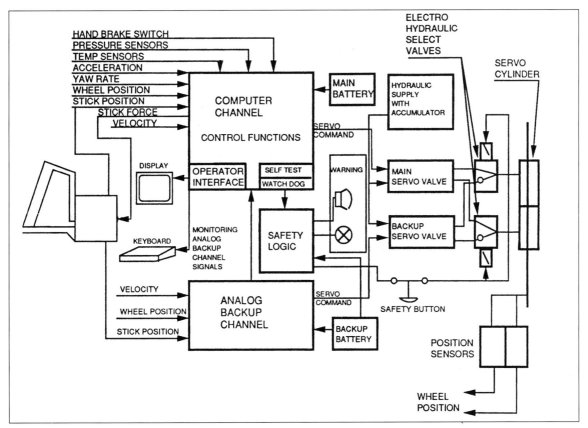

12:9. If steer-by-wire overcomes some fundamental safety worries and is adopted for production, the way is open for completely new approaches to steering, created by the ability to translate electrical signals into steering movements while filtering them electronically to ensure they do not exceed the limits of control. Saab has already demonstrated this system in which the steering input was provided by a 'joystick' on the centre console, enabling either driver to steer the car – and potentially overcoming many of the problems of converting between left-hand and right-hand drive!

impossible to ignore. The chances are, though, that the way will be prepared by the earlier adoption of brake-by-wire, with which the safety implications, while still severe, are not quite of the order created with steer-by-wire.

Active transmission

One of the concepts I mentioned in the first edition is still under active discussion by vehicle manufacturers, although it has yet to see a full production application. As pointed out when discussing 4WD, the ultimate in cornering force and traction ought to be achieved with a transmission system in which the distribution of drive torque was split in a positively controlled way, not only front to rear, but also from side to side and thus in effect between all four wheels, to

take account of weight transfer effects when simultaneously cornering and accelerating. Japanese concept cars with transmissions working on this basis have been turning up at motor shows for several years: they usually employ differential units with 'wet' multi-plate clutches which positively control the torque split – as opposed to conventional limited-slip units which simply react to wheelspin. To begin with, the emphasis was on achieving the best possible traction, but the interest has recently shifted to controlling the cornering path – in other words, to do the same job as ESC, but by shifting the balance of drive torque towards one side of the car, rather than by applying the brakes.

You do not need 4WD to achieve this objective. As long ago as 1996, Honda

12:10. Electronics can be combined with chassis engineering features to provide yet more methods of making the vehicle follow the driver's intended path (which is not, of course, quite the same thing as pointing it in the intended direction, at least when cornering). Mitsubishi's Active Yaw Control system is one of several concepts in which the left-right split of torque is varied to achieve subtle control of the cornering path. Such systems may complement or replace braking-based electronic stabilty control. Even more complex systems of this type can be used with 4WD, controlling the torque split to all four corners; varying the front-to-rear split will alter the amount of understeer. Such active control systems should not be confused with 'passive' limited-slip devices, which serve a different purpose.

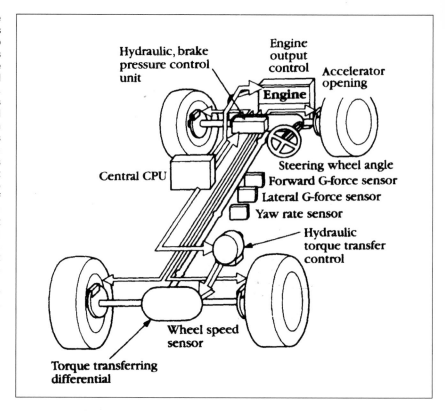

introduced such a system for front-drive cars and installed it on some of its most powerful medium-sized models in the Japanese domestic market. At first, the system was called Direct Yaw Control, but it was later redesignated Automatic Torque Transfer System (ATTS), apparently because too few people appreciated what was implied by yaw control! As in ESC, a control computer looks at the driver's actions and the car's speed and deduces the intended cornering line; it then alters the left/right torque split to keep the car as close to that line as possible. The system then continuously monitors the car's behaviour, taking signals from a yaw sensor mounted aft of the centre of gravity, and alters the initial settings if necessary.

If yaw control is the objective, it can be achieved in a 4WD car simply by controlling the left/right torque split at one axle. The rear axle is the obvious choice because there are then no worries about interfering with the steering. Honda has developed a suitable ATTS rear final-drive unit but, as I write, has yet to use it in a production

model, while at the 1997 Tokyo Motor Show, Mitsubishi showed a very similar-looking system which it called AYC (Active Yaw Control) on its Tetra concept vehicle.

If there is a question about all these systems, it is the extent to which they are really needed – or at least cost-effective. Adding something like ATTS/AYC to a car which already handles extremely well is going to do nothing for the average driver who will never exceed the car's limits anyway, except in emergency. A case can be made for traction control and brake-based ESC because, to a large extent, they use existing ABS sensors and other components, and consequently the extra system cost is moderate in relation to what it achieves. This, as much as any other consideration, is one that will weigh with the chassis engineer in the next few years. As I said in conclusion the last time round, whatever add-on electronic systems are developed in the coming decade, there will still be no substitute for a soundly engineered basic chassis to provide them with a decent platform.